Horseback Riding

FOR

DUMMIES®

by Audrey Pavia with Shannon Sand

BICENTENNIAL
1807
WILEY
2007
BICENTENNIAL

Wiley Publishing, Inc.

Horseback Riding For Dummies®

Published by
Wiley Publishing, Inc.
111 River St.
Hoboken, NJ 07030-5774
www.wiley.com

About the Authors

Audrey Pavia is the former editor of *Horse Illustrated* magazine and an award-winning freelance writer specializing in equine subjects. She has authored articles on various equine topics in a number of horse publications, including *Western Horseman, Horses USA, Stable Management, John Lyons' Perfect Horse, Young Rider, Appaloosa Journal, Paint Horse Journal, Equine Practice,* and *USDF Connection* magazines. She has written five horse books besides *Horseback Riding For Dummies,* including *Horses For Dummies* and *Trail Riding: A Complete Guide.*

In addition to her experience as an equine writer, she is also a former managing editor of *Dog Fancy* magazine and a former senior editor of the *American Kennel Club Gazette.* She has authored more than 500 articles on the subject of animals and has written several books on various kinds of pets.

Audrey has been involved with horses since age 9. She has owned and cared for horses throughout her life and has trained in both Western and English disciplines. She currently resides in Norco, California.

Shannon Sand has been riding horses since she was 3 years old. She competed in Western pleasure and bareback equitation at a young age and eventually showed in dressage, hunt seat, and three-day eventing. Shannon also showed jumpers on the A-circuit for many years and worked as an assistant trainer to Hap Hansen, a U.S. Olympic equestrian team member.

Shannon owns Sand Bar Stables in Wildomar, California, where she specializes in hunter/jumpers and in building confidence in horses and riders of all disciplines.

Dedication

Audrey: To my husband, Randy Mastronicola, for his constant love and support and for understanding my equine obsession.

Authors' Acknowledgments

Audrey: Thank you to editors Georgette Beatty, Tracy Boggier, and Danielle Voirol; technical editor Tara Wohlenhaus; Lesley Ward and Sarah Coleman of *Young Rider* magazine; my dear friend Kelly Mount; brilliant writer and friend Gina Spadafori; and my sister, Heidi Pavia, DVM. Heartfelt gratitude goes out to Sharon Fibelkorn and Pam Tanzey for their hard work on this book.

I would also like to thank our kind and patient equine models: Bailey, Milagro, Jitterbug, Evita, Pat, Hannah, Daisy, Buddy, Rocky, Remy, Tennessee, and Sophie.

Shannon: Thanks to my wonderful husband, Mike, for all his support; my parents, Bill and Valerie Sparrow, for dealing with my horsy addiction; Dawn Torres of Dream Gait Ranch; Sylvia Sanchez; Kim and Mike Stirratt; Taryn Woodward; and my little dog Katelynn, for bringing my spirits up when they were down.

Publisher's Acknowledgments

We're proud of this book; please send us your comments through our Dummies online registration form located at www.dummies.com/register/.

Some of the people who helped bring this book to market include the following:

Acquisitions, Editorial, and Media Development

Project Editor: Georgette Beatty

Acquisitions Editor: Tracy Boggier

Copy Editor: Danielle Voirol

Technical Editor: Tara Wohlenhaus

Editorial Manager: Michelle Hacker

Editorial Assistants: Erin Calligan Mooney, Joe Niesen, Leeann Harney

Cover Photo: © Sharon P. Fibelkorn

Cartoons: Rich Tennant (www.the5thwave.com)

Composition Services

Project Coordinator: Erin Smith

Layout and Graphics: Joyce Haughey, Barbara Moore, Alicia B. South, Erin Zeltner

Special Art: Sharon P. Fibelkorn (photos), Pamela Tanzey (illustrations)

Anniversary Logo Design: Richard Pacifico

Proofreaders: Dwight Ramsey, Nancy L. Reinhardt

Indexer: Aptara

Publishing and Editorial for Consumer Dummies

Diane Graves Steele, Vice President and Publisher, Consumer Dummies

Joyce Pepple, Acquisitions Director, Consumer Dummies

Kristin A. Cocks, Product Development Director, Consumer Dummies

Michael Spring, Vice President and Publisher, Travel

Kelly Regan, Editorial Director, Travel

Publishing for Technology Dummies

Andy Cummings, Vice President and Publisher, Dummies Technology/General User

Composition Services

Gerry Fahey, Vice President of Production Services

Debbie Stailey, Director of Composition Services

Contents at a Glance

Table of Contents

Introduction

. . . .

Welcome to *Horseback Riding For Dummies!* This book can be your tour guide as you navigate the exciting hobby of horseback riding.

Riding a horse is fun and relaxing, challenging and demanding, exhilarating and rewarding. As with any sport, horseback riding calls for training before you can participate safely and effectively. You probably have a sense of this already, which is why you're reading this book.

Horses are my greatest passion in life. I hope you catch horse fever, as I once did, and make horseback riding a regular part of your life. You'll find your life is never dull after you open your heart to these incredible creatures.

About This Book

Horseback Riding For Dummies is designed to supplement your riding lessons and to help you understand what horseback riding is all about. You discover how to find the right instructor to teach you how to ride, what kind of gear and apparel you need, and how to get on and off the horse. You also discover the details of actually riding a horse and find out ways to expand beyond the basics when you're ready to take the next step.

This book is set up as a reference for novices in this hobby. As with all *For Dummies* books, you can read sections of this book individually, or you can read it from cover to cover. Either way, I hope you find the text enlightening.

My coauthor and I have worked hard to provide you with guidance through the sometimes complicated world of horses and horseback riding. Although you may feel overwhelmed at times as you try to negotiate the lingo, protocol, and details surrounding the horse world, I hope you refer back to this book to help you find your way.

Conventions Used in This Book

In this book, I refer to horses with both male pronouns (*he, his,* and *him*) and female pronouns (*she, hers,* and *her*). I do so in alternating chapters to give both genders equal air time, with male pronouns in odd-numbered chapters and female pronouns in even-numbered chapters.

The following conventions may also be helpful in steering you through this book:

- *Italics* point out definitions and emphasize certain words.
- **Boldfaced** text indicates key words in bulleted lists and actions to take in numbered lists.
- `Monofont` highlights Web addresses.

During the printing of this book, some Web addresses may have broken across two lines of text. If you come across a Web address spread over two lines, rest assured that I haven't put in any extra characters (such as hyphens) to indicate the break. Just type in exactly what you see.

One last thing: Although you see two names on the cover of this book, you see the word *I* throughout the text in reference to your humble author. That's because the voice you hear in the text belongs to Audrey. Shannon provided her incredible expertise to this book, but it was Audrey who labored at the keyboard while Shannon had fun being outside and riding her many horses.

What You're Not to Read

Throughout this book, I tell you stuff that may be interesting to know but isn't crucial to your understanding of the topic. In such cases, I place the text in a sidebar, which appears as a shaded gray box. Don't feel like you have to read these sidebars — unless you're dying to sound like a better conversationalist at all those equestrian cocktail parties you go to!

Foolish Assumptions

In this book, I assume you can recognize a horse when you see one. That's really about all I take for granted. Well, I do assume that you're a beginning horseback rider who wants to learn how to ride in a particular discipline (either Western or English). You're looking to get the most out of your riding lessons and instructor, and you ride a lesson horse from the stable. Or perhaps you're a more seasoned horseback rider who's looking to brush up on your riding skills and boost your confidence. You may even own a horse!

One last thing I assume is that you're no fool. I think you're pretty smart; after all, you bought this book, didn't you? And it can help guide you throughout the process of learning to ride.

How This Book Is Organized

Horseback Riding For Dummies is made up of six parts. The following sections look at each of these parts and what they cover.

Part I: Beginning with Horseback Riding Basics

In Part I, I give you some background on the mind and mechanics of a horse and explain how to find a great riding instructor. I also show you how to get into shape and stay safe for riding.

Part II: Getting Set with the Right Riding Style and Gear

Before you can start riding, you need to decide what style of riding — or *discipline* — you want to pursue. After you've figured that out, you have to understand all the equipment associated with that discipline.

In Part II, you get to explore the basic disciplines and discover all the gear you need to know about so you can ride in your style of choice. I help you make heads or tails out of different types of riding equipment and even get into the apparel you need to look the part.

Part III: Settling into the Saddle and Easing into Riding

You're probably anxious to get into the saddle, but first you need to know how to handle a horse from the ground. You also need to know how to get in and out of the saddle, too. After all, you don't want to find yourself all ready to ride with no clue how to get on the horse — and then find out after your ride that you don't know how to get off!

Part III gives you the basics on handling horses before you mount, actual mounting and dismounting, riding the three main gaits, and ultimately, jumping. You discover pointers on how to sit in the saddle and hold the reins. You also find out how to move with the horse and cue the animal so he or she does what you want.

Part IV: Riding into Advanced Pastures

If you've done all your homework, taken lessons, and made the commitment to really figure out how to ride, you eventually leave the beginner category and move into the intermediate and ultimately advanced phases. Wonderful things happen when you move from beginning to experienced rider. You may want to get your own horse. Before you do that, however, you need to know how to take care of your new companion.

Part IV provides details on how to move to the next level of horsemanship. I get into whether to buy (or lease) a horse, how to house and feed a horse, how to groom, and basic preventive care. Even if you don't want to buy a horse of your own, you can still advance your skills by finding a new instructor or trying out a new discipline and growing stronger with additional conditioning; I explain what to do in this part.

Part V: Having Fun with Other Styles and Activities

You've mastered the basics of Western, hunt seat, or dressage riding, and you think you want to explore some other riding styles and activities. Go for it!

In Part V, I cover some uniquely skilled breeds of horses (called gaited horses) and different ways to ride your horse, with or without a saddle. I also delve into my favorite sport, trail riding, and discuss ways you can compete on trail. I explore the exciting world of horse shows in depth, with information on how to prepare your horse for his or her first show. And finally, I give you a taste of the sports, activities, and alternative riding disciplines you can enjoy with your mount.

Part VI: The Part of Tens

In the Part of Tens, I tackle two very different subjects: the rules of riding etiquette and horseback games. In the riding etiquette chapter, I outline some basic rules that every equestrian should know. In the games chapter, I give you a number of riding games you can take to your riding instructor in the hopes that he or she will implement a play day for you and the other students where you ride.

Icons Used in This Book

As with all the other books in the *For Dummies* series, this book uses icons in the margins to highlight specific types of information. Here's an explanation of what each icon means:

This icon appears next to information that's very important — don't miss it! Make sure you take this info with you as you head out to the barn.

This image alerts you to helpful hints regarding horseback riding. Tips can save time and help you avoid frustration.

This icon indicates something serious to watch out for. It indicates anything that can harm you, your horse, or your riding if you don't pay attention.

Procedures in the horse world may not seem to make much sense at times, yet they're practically written in stone and people always follow them. This icon indicates these types of procedures.

Where to Go from Here

You can start at Chapter 1 and read all the way through the Appendix if you want. Or you can skip here and there. Before you start jumping from place to place, though, I recommend taking a few moments to read Chapter 1, which gives you an overview of everything you need to know to get involved in horseback riding.

If you're brand new to riding and have never done it before, take a look at Chapter 3, where you get the lowdown on how to choose a good riding instructor. You may also want to read through Chapters 6 and 7 to get an idea of which discipline may suit you best.

If you want to go right to the basics on how to ride each of the covered disciplines (English, which includes hunt seat and dressage, and Western), check out Chapters 13 through 15. Of course, if you want to skip to the fun and games, you can flip to Part V.

Now go ahead and hit the trail!

Part I
Beginning with Horseback Riding Basics

The 5th Wave   By Rich Tennant

"This breed comes from a long line of horses dating back to the ancient Greeks."

In this part . . .

In the chapters of Part I, you find the basic information you need to know about horses and how to start riding them. I show you how to identify the parts, colors, and markings of horses. I also explain how the equine mind works and give you pointers on how to communicate effectively with these friendly beasts. You discover what's involved in finding a riding instructor and getting yourself ready to ride. And don't forget — safety first! I explain what you need to know to stay secure both in and out of the saddle.

Chapter 1

Giddy Up! Welcome to Horseback Riding

The act of riding horses has been going on for thousands of years. In the old days, people did it because they had to — it was the only way to efficiently travel from one place to another. Today, we ride horses because we want to.

Why do some people love riding horses so much? Is it a way to connect with nature in our highly technical world? Or is it a product of genetic memory? Are we drawn to horses because it's in our DNA?

Whatever the reason, horseback riding is an activity that millions of people enjoy the world over. If you've ever done it, you know why it's so popular; if you haven't but want to, you can imagine how much fun it is. And you're right. When it comes to horses and riding, you'll never find yourself at a loss for things to do. For those who love these friendly beasts, horses make the world go round. Start riding, and you'll see why!

In this chapter, I introduce you to the world of horseback riding. It's a world where human and horse become one and where you can leave the cares and pressures of your daily life behind in the dust.

Discovering the Horse's Mind and Body

I've heard people say that horses are dumb, but that idea couldn't be further from the truth. Horses are brilliant in many ways, which is why they've been around for so many millions of years. You can't be stupid and manage to stay alive for that long!

Likewise, the horse's body is an amazing machine, designed for speed, agility, and survival. Horses can run incredibly fast, turn their 1,000-pound bulk on a dime, and react physically with lightning speed to even the slightest sound. If you want to ride horses, you need to understand all these abilities in depth.

As a rider, you want to understand and communicate with your mount. Horses don't see the world the way we do. Cellphones, computers, and fax machines are not their world; hay, dirt, and other horses make up the bulk of their existence. Seeing the world from the horse's perspective can make you a better rider and provide you with more enjoyment when you're around these really neat animals.

The equine mind and body are at your fingertips if you just know how to use them. In Chapter 2 of this book, you get a primer on equine psychology and discover the language that horse people use to describe their favorite animal and her various body parts. Each part of the horse has a corresponding name that horse people toss around like so much confetti. If you want to fit in with the crowd and know what people at the barn at talking about, make sure you take a good look at the diagram in Chapter 2.

Taking Riding Lessons

Getting up on a horse's back can be an exciting experience, but it can also be frustrating and even scary if you don't know what you're doing. Learning to ride in a formal setting, with an instructor or trainer who knows how to properly teach riding basics, is imperative.

Even though horses have minds and can think and see where they're going (unlike cars, which need direction every inch of the way), don't fall victim to the notion that you just need to sit up there and let the horse do his thing. This approach only lets you discover that you and the horse may not have the same ideas about what to do next. Instead, figure out how to ride before you start doing it on your own, just like you'd take skiing lessons with an instructor before heading down the slope.

Riding lessons are a lot of fun, but they're also hard work. You find yourself using muscles you never knew you had and are challenged to coordinate different parts of your body in ways you've never done before. If you enjoy learning and challenging yourself, you'll likely enjoy horseback riding lessons. You'll also discover the wonderful feeling that comes when you communicate with a horse while on his back.

In Chapter 3, I give you advice on how to get started with riding lessons. Here are some examples of what you can find there:

- **Finding a stable.** A friendly atmosphere, a clean environment, healthy equine tenants, and a professional demeanor from the staff are all things you should seek out when picking the stable where you'll learn to ride.

- **Choosing your instructor.** The person you pick to be your instructor should have a teaching style that you like, be experienced in the discipline you've chosen (English or Western), and be familiar with training adult beginners.

- **Being a good student.** It's not all up to the teacher! The best students (and the ones who get the most from their training) are the folks who show up on time, pay attention, speak up when they need to, and do their homework.

Getting into Riding Shape

Horseback riding is hard work! It may not look all that difficult when you're watching an experienced rider, but the truth is that a whole slew of muscles, along with balance and stamina, come into play as you're riding.

To prepare your body for the rigors of riding a horse, do some or all of the following:

- Lose weight
- Build strength
- Cross-train
- Improve endurance
- Increase flexibility with stretching exercises

Mental challenges also come along with this sport. In order to get the most from your riding lessons and your time in the saddle, deal with any fear issues you have about riding and understand your role as the leader of your team of two (that is, you and the horse). To find out how to prepare your body and mind for riding, take a look at Chapter 4.

Keeping Yourself Safe around Horses

Horses are large animals, and handling them takes some know-how. You can perfect this skill with training and experience. In order to get the most from the time you spend with horses, you need the right kind of instruction from a qualified expert. When you have some knowledge under your belt, you can safely handle a horse in a variety of situations.

To keep yourself safe around horses, you have to follow some basic rules that those who've come before you have set up. These concepts were created out of experience, so take them seriously.

First, you need to make sure you're wearing the right clothing. Boots designed for riding are necessary because they have a special heel that helps keep one of your legs from getting caught in the stirrup should you fall from the saddle — getting dragged is the danger here. A safety helmet is also a must if you want to protect that valuable gray matter. And your legs can get chafed if you ride in shorts or in the wrong kind of pants, so riding pants are preferable. And *before* you ride, you handle the horse from the ground, so wear heavy boots for safety in case a clumsy equine steps on your foot. (I've had it happen — not fun.)

Understanding how horses move their bodies is also a necessity for safety, as are knowing when to enter a stall (when you know the horse sees you) and dealing with stupid horse maneuvers, such as pulling back when tied. Of course, you likewise need to know the various rules that apply to riding, both alone and with others, either in the arena or on the trail. Concepts such as what to do when another rider falls off and when you need to pass another rider are part of rider safety. All this and more await you in Chapter 5.

Selecting the Right Riding Style and Gear

Before you can start riding, you need to determine which discipline you want to pursue. Here are your options:

✔ Western riding, the most popular discipline in the U.S., is often the style of choice for beginning riders because Western saddles provide the most security. Western riding is popular with casual trail riders, as well as those working with cattle. I discuss Western riding in Chapter 6.

✔ English style riding is made up of some subtypes, including hunt seat and dressage (see Chapter 7 for details).

    • People who'd like to jump their horses opt for hunt seat, although plenty of hunt seat riders don't jump — they simply enjoy this style of riding. Hunt seat riders sit in a small saddle and wear their stirrups shorter than Western riders do. Many hunt seat riders enjoy "hacking" (riding) out on the trail.

    • Dressage, the ballet of horseback riding, involves precise movements and stringent training of both horse and rider.

You may soon discover, after you start riding, that horses come with lots of stuff. Here are some items every horse needs:

- ✔ Saddle and pad
- ✔ Bridle (including a bit)
- ✔ Halter and lead rope

You need some equipment for yourself as well:

- ✔ Riding boots or shoes
- ✔ Riding pants
- ✔ A proper shirt
- ✔ A helmet (if you're smart)

For more details on these and other items for both you and the horse, see Chapters 8, 9, and 10.

Riding High from the Start

Okay, it's almost time to get on! You still have a few more things to figure out before you get in the saddle, including how to put on the saddle and bridle and how to climb aboard. Before you actually find yourself up there, you also need to know how to get off.

Preparing on the ground

You have to do some work on the ground before you can actually ride. First, you need to know how to catch a horse, whether in a pasture or stall. Approach horses in pastures quietly and confidently to encourage them to allow themselves to be caught (don't think for a moment that you can catch a horse if he doesn't want to be!). If the horse is in a stall, safety dictates that you wait until the horse is facing you before you go up to him.

Putting on a halter is another task you need to master. The halter is the horse equivalent to a collar and leash. When you place a halter on a horse's head, you're taking control of that horse's movement on the ground.

In Chapter 11, you discover how to catch a horse and how to put on a halter. You also get details on how to put on an English saddle, a Western saddle, and a bridle — a necessity before you can ride.

Mounting and dismounting

Horse people have been mounting and dismounting for centuries, and they've pretty much figured out the safest and most effective way to get on and off a horse.

Protocol dictates that you always mount from the left side. (This rule began out of necessity with the military, because mounted soldiers wore their swords on their left hips.) You should also consider using a mounting block or high ground, which makes getting up into the saddle easier and reduces the amount of pressure on the horse because you end up pulling less on the saddle.

Just as you mount from the left, you also dismount to this side. Again, protocol dictates as such, and the vast majority of horses have been trained in this way. For details on mounting and dismounting, see Chapter 12.

Getting a grip on gaits

As a new rider, you get to master three of the four gaits of the horse: the walk, the jog or trot, and the lope or canter (the fourth gait is the gallop, which you get to after you have more experience in the saddle):

✔ The walk, which is the slowest gait, comes first; it's the one you use the most, especially if you plan to trail ride.

✔ The jog, as Western riders call it, and the trot, as English riders say, is the bouncy gait and the one most beginning riders have trouble with at first. After you master this one, you know you're well on your way to becoming an experienced rider.

✔ Called the lope by Western riders and the canter by English riders, this gait is the fastest of the three you use as a beginning rider. The lope or canter is faster than the walk or trot, and it's probably the most fun of the three. This gait has a rocking-horse feel to it that many riders really enjoy.

Mastering each of the gaits takes time and practice. A good instructor observes your riding and helps you train your mind and body to cue the horse exactly as you need to in order to get what you want from your four-footed friend. For the basics on how to ride the walk, trot or jog, and canter or lope, see Chapters 13, 14, and 15, respectively.

Jumping

Many hunt seat riders have the goal of jumping on horseback. If you're not sure why riders enjoy jumping, it's because it's a whole lot of fun! Many riders get hooked on this activity.

Jumping can take place in an arena or out in the field. Arena jumping consists of a series of jumps arranged in a course that the horse-and-rider team has to negotiate. Some of these jumps include oxers (two sets of jump standards — vertical poles — and two sets of horizontal poles) and crossrails (two jump standards with two rails placed between them in an X position).

Jumping out in the field is called cross-country jumping, and it's a test of courage and endurance. A series of obstacles are laid out on a designated course, which covers 2 to 4 miles in length. Obstacles can include telephone poles, low shrubs, and water jumps (in which the horse has to jump over something into a shallow pond). To find out what it takes to jump a horse, flip to Chapter 16.

Adjusting to Advanced Riding

After you become addicted to horseback riding (and I know you will), you'll start thinking about moving to the next level. You may just want to find a new instructor or switch disciplines, but in many cases, the next step means adding a horse to your family. I introduce some important points in the following sections.

Stepping up your current riding routine

As you become more proficient in your riding, you may want to switch to a different instructor to help you find your greatest potential in the saddle. After all, some instructors specialize in teaching only beginners. Should that day come, you want to seek out the most qualified teacher you can afford. You may also want to consider switching disciplines or at least trying a different one to see whether you like it. This step means searching for a new instructor who's qualified to teach the discipline you want to try.

Moving to the next level of riding also means becoming even more physically fit. You may want to start cross-training to help your body prepare for the more-rigorous riding in store. Jogging, swimming, and aerobics are just some ways you can improve your endurance and muscle tone. For details on how to move to the next level or riding, take a look at Chapter 17.

Buying your own horse

It's inevitable: After you start riding, it isn't long before you start longing for a horse of your own. Horse ownership is a big responsibility in time and money, and it isn't one to be taken lightly. Find out what's involved in owning a horse before you take this big step. One way to find out what horse ownership is all about is to lease a horse first. With leasing, you can get an idea of the time commitment involved in horse ownership. You can also get a good sense of what owning one of these amazing creatures is like before you take a plunge.

Should you decide to buy, getting the right horse is vital. Just as with human relationships, you have to find a good match. As a beginning rider, you need a horse who's quiet, well-trained, and easygoing. A horse like this can help you develop your skills.

When you're ready to go horse shopping, enlist the help of a horse expert. This person can be your riding instructor, a local trainer you trust, or even an equine vet or farrier (who works with shoes and hooves) if no instructors or trainers are available in your area. Start searching for horses for sale on tack-store bulletin boards, through trainers and breeders, and in local horse publications. For more details on buying a horse, see Chapter 18.

Looking after your horse

If you love horses, chances are you'll also love caring for one. Horse care isn't hard after you discover what you need to do to keep your horse happy and healthy.

If you live on property zoned for horses, make sure you have adequate facilities for your charges. A stall, paddock, or pasture is necessary. If you don't have your own horse property, you need to board your horse, most likely at a commercial boarding facility. Choosing the right facility is important, both for your horse's well-being and for your own enjoyment. You want a place that's well-maintained, provides good care for the horses, and has arenas and trail access for riding.

Feeding your horse is a significant part of horse care. Horses were designed to eat roughage for many hours a day, so hay is an important part of their diet. Several kinds of hay are available, depending on which part of the country you live in.

To keep your horse looking clean and pretty, groom him on a regular basis. You need tools for this task, including brushes, combs, and a hoof pick to keep his feet clean. Baths are a part of keeping your horse clean, too, and they're best performed on warm days with horse shampoo.

Preventive care is the most important kind of care for horses. Have your horse vaccinated regularly against diseases such as equine influenza and encephalitis. Horses also require regular deworming to help control intestinal parasites. Regular visits from the vet to check the horse's teeth and file them down if they develop points (something that happens when the molars rub together over time) are also important. For these details and more on how to keep your horse healthy, see Chapter 19.

Enjoying Fun and Games on Horseback

The best part about riding horses is all the cool stuff you can do with them. So many equine activities abound in the horse world that it's hard to name them all.

The most popular horseback pastime in the United States is trail riding. Both relaxing and fun, trail riding takes you and your horse into the countryside if you live in a rural area or along "urban trails" if you're in a suburban or even urban environment. Chapter 21 has the full scoop on hitting the trails.

Horse shows are another popular horse activity. In Chapter 22, you discover the different kinds of horse shows out there and may get some ideas of what kind of showing you'd like to do. All kinds of horse shows exist for all kinds of horses and riders, including

- Schooling shows
- Rated shows
- Open shows
- Breed shows
- Specialty shows

Horse shows and leisurely trail riding aren't the only ways to enjoy being on horseback. A whole slew of other options are available:

- Bareback riding
- Competitive trail rides
- Drill teams
- Endurance rides
- Historical reenactments
- Parades
- Polo

  ✔ Saddle seat riding

  ✔ Sidesaddle riding

  ✔ Vaulting (gymnastics)

As if all this weren't enough, you can also take your horse on vacation with you. Or if you don't have your own horse, you can go on a horseback vacation to places where horses are provided. For details on these equine activities, see Chapter 23.

Chapter 2

Head to Hoof: The Mind and Mechanics of a Horse

*B*efore you get on the back of a 1,000-pound animal, understanding how that creature thinks is a pretty good idea. Contrary to what some people believe, horses are intelligent animals who learn quickly. They're also creatures of instinct, and they have a unique way of looking at the world.

It's also a good idea to become familiar with the physical aspects of a horse. This step means memorizing the different parts of the horse's body so you know what your riding instructor means with phrases such as *above the withers* and *near the fetlocks*. Finding out all about the amazing breeds of riding horses is important, too. When you understand the breeds and how they differ, you have a more complete picture of the horse world — something every rider needs.

In this chapter, I describe the psyche and physical traits of a horse, and I walk you through the differences among some of the most popular horse breeds.

Understanding How Horses Think

To truly comprehend what goes on in the equine mind, imagine yourself as a horse. You're big yet fragile (as evidenced by the injuries suffered by racehorses). You evolved over the eons as a prey animal, which means a host of scary critters have thought of you as a dinner entree for a very long time. You're also very sociable, thriving on the company of others.

All these factors add up to create a powerful, delicate, and wary yet friendly beast. In the following sections, I describe the behavior and communication of these very special animals, and I provide guidance on getting along with them.

Getting a grip on equine society

One of the biggest factors in equine behavior is the fact that horses are herd animals (safety in numbers, right?). Much of what they do stems from this trait. Horses are capable of recognizing and participating in a complex social hierarchy that places them at the top, the bottom, or somewhere in the middle of the pecking order. They also like to be with other horses — a lot — just like most people enjoy being with other humans.

In terms of horse behavior, the biggest question for many people (at least those who like to ponder such things) is "Why do horses allow us to ride them?" The opinion of most experts is that the horse's very social nature allows her to accept a rider on her back. Horses — at least tame ones — recognize humans as dominant members of their herd and act accordingly when asked to do something, no matter how little sense it makes to them.

Another important factor in equine behavior is the horse's status as a prey animal. You can't spend millions of years being eaten by saber-toothed tigers and hunted by wolf packs without getting a bit paranoid. This less-than-pleasant experience is the reason horses *spook* (react dramatically) when startled, are nervous in unfamiliar surroundings, and usually run first and ask questions later when something scares them. If you ride horses, you encounter these behaviors sooner or later.

Interpreting equine expressions

Because horses are such social creatures, they've developed very distinct methods of communicating with each other. They use these same techniques to communicate with humans. If you understand the horse's language, you're well on your way to being able to "talk" — or whisper — to your horse.

Horses are great at expressing themselves through body language, and it's up to us humans to know how to interpret their signals. Horses express a variety of attitudes and emotions in their faces. Make sense of these expressions, and you can read the mood of just about any horse you approach (Figure 2-1 shows the various facial expressions of horses):

- **Relaxed:** Horses who are calm and content have a relaxed expression. They're comfortable in their environment, with the person handling them, and with what they're being asked to do. This expression is the one you want to see on a horse you're about to ride.

- **Afraid:** Horses are easily frightened. If a horse throws her head up in the air and shows the whites of her eyes, she's scared. You may have approached too fast, or perhaps something else is frightening her.

Reassure the horse by talking softly to her and stroking her until she calms down before you proceed. (See "Getting along with horses," later in this chapter, for tips on handling horses effectively.)

✔ **Threatening:** Some horses exhibit nasty behavior for various reasons. They may be in pain, or they may hate being ridden and handled. One horse I met was nasty because he was underfed and felt hungry all the time. After he was put on a proper diet, his threatening expression disappeared.

Warning: If a horse you're handling is pinning her ears back and showing you what looks like an angry expression (teeth bared, nostrils flared), back off and get help from someone more experienced. Horses sometimes follow these expressions with a bite or a kick.

✔ **Alert:** Horses are always watching for predators, real or imagined. A horse with an alert expression — head up high, eyes wide, ears pointed forward — is checking out something that's in the distance or may be approaching. An alert expression can turn into a fearful one or may be replaced by a relaxed expression after the horse determines that all is safe. Some horses, such as those who are leading a group on a trail, maintain an alert expression the entire ride. Such behavior is normal, because horses expect the leader of the group to be the lookout.

Figure 2-1:
Horses communicate with four basic expressions.

Relaxed

Afraid

Threatening

Alert

Getting along with horses

The key to a harmonious existence with horses lies in understanding the herd and prey factors that are so much of a part of the horse's mindset (see "Getting a grip on equine society," earlier in this chapter). If you put yourself in the animal's horseshoes and think about life with humans from the equine perspective, you'll likely find yourself able to get along with just about any horse. The following sections contain some key points to keep in mind when you're dealing with horses.

A horse is a horse: Recognizing your horse for what she is

Remember that horses and humans are alike in some ways (we both feel pain and experience fear) and vastly different in others (they see the world differently). Whenever you handle a horse, keep her perspective in mind and judge her as a horse, not as a fellow human. Remembering these ideas can help you treat your horse appropriately:

- **Fairness:** One of the saddest mistakes people make when handling horses is lack of fairness. They often expect a horse to know exactly what they want and when they want it, and they don't give the horse the chance to learn or adjust to a new idea. Horses can read your emotions but not your thoughts. Remember to be fair to your horse in every situation so she can come to trust you.

- **Patience:** Horses are like 1,000-pound toddlers. Some horses may test you to see what they can get away with, while others may just irritate you with annoying behaviors and habits. And although most horses are quick to learn, some people aren't so good at teaching. Whenever dealing with a horse, be as patient as possible.

- **Consistency:** When dealing with any animal, consistency is key. If you want your horse to stand still when you get on, make sure you require this behavior each and every time you mount. Letting her walk off some of the time teaches her that you don't really mean what you say, and you may find yourself with a horse who does whatever she feels like. Know what you want from your horse and insist on it each and every time.

Sending the right signals

Horses are astute readers of body language, so you can best interact with a horse if you're attuned to your own emotions and behavior. Here are some key tips for keeping a horse at ease:

- **Show confidence.** Horses can quickly discern if you're apprehensive and fearful or confident and at ease. Because you want the horse to see you as a leader and trust your judgment in all things, you want to exude confidence. Otherwise, the horse may feel compelled to take over the leadership role and start bossing you around.

✔ **Move slowly.** Horses are generally alarmed by quick movements, especially waving arms. When dealing with a horse, move slowly but deliberately. Talk to the horse in a soft voice, too, especially if you're approaching from behind.

✔ **Keep the volume down.** Shouting and screaming are two good ways to scare a horse or at least make her uneasy. Reserve a louder voice for corrections. When a horse does something you don't want her to do, a loud "Quit!" or "Hey!" can get her attention. Otherwise, be quiet when you work around horses or talk to them in a gentle, soothing voice.

✔ **Don't handle your horse or ride when you're angry.** The worst thing you can do when you're having a bad day is be around a horse. True, spending time with horses can make stress melt away; on the other hand, they can really push your buttons and make you want to explode. If you find yourself in an angry mood, skip taking your horse out that day. The last thing you want to do is take your anger out on the horse.

✔ **Stay positive.** Some people think horses are psychic because they have an uncanny ability to read our minds (if you're afraid your horse will spook, she probably will, as though you literally gave her the idea). Whether horses can read minds or are just adept at picking up on very subtle human cues, it's important to think positively and visualize your horse doing what you want her to do, not what you *don't* want her to do.

Examining the Equine Body

Horses are very corporeal creatures. One of the reasons we love them so much is because of their great physical beauty. The horse's grace, elegance, and power can be breathtaking when you appreciate this amazing animal.

When riding horses, being familiar with the equine body is important not only on an aesthetic level but also on a technical one. Horse people frequently refer to parts of a horse's body, how a horse is put together, the way horses move, and a horse's color and markings. If you want to converse with horse people and know what they're talking about, understanding this special equine lingo, which I cover in the following sections, is vital.

The parts of a horse

The best way to figure out the parts of a horse is to memorize them. When I was a horse-crazy child, my parents enrolled me in a military-based riding group. As part of my training, I received a diagram much like the one in Figure 2-2 and was told to learn the various parts of the horse. Failure to pass the subsequent test would've meant not moving up in rank. The assignment wasn't really a problem because I was horse-obsessed and couldn't think about anything else!

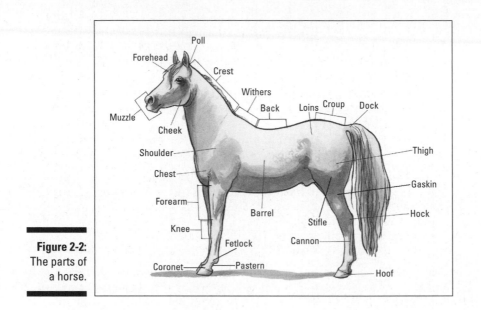

Figure 2-2:
The parts of
a horse.

Hopefully, you're more well-rounded than that and have other things going on in your life besides knowing where the cannon and gaskin are located. Memorizing the various parts, however, is still a good idea. This knowledge is mandatory for anyone who plans to be a serious rider or even spend time around horses. In particular, make sure you can identify the following parts:

- Muzzle
- Poll
- Shoulder
- Withers
- Hock
- Pastern

The height of a horse

A horse's size is significant if you plan to ride, because some horses may be too small or too tall for your liking. The average horse weighs from 1,000 to 1,200 pounds; however, weight is the least-favorite way to refer to the size of a horse. Horse people prefer to describe a horse's height in terms of hands, which is a uniquely equine measurement.

In horse lingo, one *hand* equals 4 inches, which was historically considered the width of the average man's palm. Horses are measured from the top of the *withers* (the area between the base of the neck and the back) to the ground. A horse standing 60 inches from her withers to the ground is 15 hands high. If the horse stands 63 inches from her withers to the ground, she's 15.3 hands in height. (Note that the dot is not a decimal point; it simply separates the number of full hands from the number of additional inches.) Because a hand is a 4-inch increment, a horse 64 inches from her withers to the ground is 16 hands high rather than 15.4 hands. Height in hands is sometimes written as *h.h.*, which is short for *hands high*.

In practical terms, an average-sized woman can comfortably ride a horse that is anywhere from 14.2 hands to 16.1 hands. A man of average height probably prefers a horse on the taller side of that range.

People have different reasons for liking larger versus smaller horses, although preference is mostly aesthetics. If you're a tall person, you'll look better on a taller horse. Of course, you may have other reasons for choosing one size over another. For instance, if you're above average in weight, a larger horse can carry you more comfortably. Height may also be a consideration if you plan to show your horse or perform particular events with her (see Chapter 22 for info on horse shows). Bigger horses make for a grand appearance, but smaller ones are less painful to fall from. Your trainer or instructor can help you figure out your preferences (Chapter 3 can fill you in on instructors and riding lessons).

The buildup: Horse conformation

Conformation is horse lingo for the way a horse is put together. Conformation is important not only because it affects the way a horse looks but also because build affects the horse's ability to move and remain *sound* (free from lameness) throughout her life.

Some horses are born with good conformation, others with poor conformation. Generally speaking, if the parents have good conformation, then their offspring will, too. A horse's genes have the greatest impact on body structure, though in rare cases, poor diet in the growing years and improperly healed injuries can cause problems.

Learning the difference between good and poor conformation takes time, experience, and practice. The best way to develop this skill is to look at a lot of different horses with a critical eye. Horses with good conformation are visually pleasing. When you see a good-looking horse, take note of her overall appearance and make mental notes of her body structure. If the horse is well-balanced, meaning her parts are all in proper proportion to each other, she likely has good conformation. Talking to expert horse people and asking their opinions of certain horses is also is a great way to build your skills.

Horses with good conformation also have correct angles:

- ✔ Their legs are straight when viewed from the front and back.
- ✔ Their shoulders and *croups* (rump, or the area that lies between the hip and the base of the tail) are nicely sloped.
- ✔ Their heads are pleasing to the eye and well-shaped.

If you're really interested in conformation, you may want to check out the excellent book *Horse Conformation: Structure, Soundness, and Performance,* by Equine Research (Lyons Press).

Stepping out: The gaits of a horse

Oh, the possibilities! Four-footed animals have quite a few options when they decide to move — how many feet should be touching the ground, which legs to lift at the same time, the length of the stride, and so on. If you plan to ride a horse (and you probably do, because you're reading this book), then you'll get to experience the horse's gaits up close and personal. The gait of the horse affects the speed you're going as well as the whole feeling of your ride.

Most horses have three natural gaits that people use often in riding: the walk, the trot or jog, and the canter or lope. The walk is the slowest gait, the trot or jog is the medium-speed gait, and the canter or lope is the next-fastest speed. The gallop, the fastest gait, is only for special occasions and more-advanced riding; this book focuses on the other three main gaits.

Speed isn't the only difference among the gaits; the way the horse positions her legs also determines the method of motion. Take a look at the difference in foot patterns for each gait (see Figure 2-3):

- ✔ **Walk:** At the walk, the horse puts each foot down one at a time, creating a four-beat rhythm. Most horses walk at about 3 to 4 miles per hour.
- ✔ **Trot (jog):** In the trot or jog, one front foot and its opposite hind foot come down at the same time, making a two-beat rhythm. Horses generally trot at 7 to 10 miles per hour.
- ✔ **Canter (lope):** In the canter or lope, one hind leg strikes the ground first, then the other hind leg and the opposite foreleg come down together, and then the other foreleg comes down. This movement creates a three-beat rhythm. Horses usually canter at 10 to 17 miles per hour.

  Note: A gallop is similar to the canter, only faster and with an extra foot-fall. This fastest gait creates a four-beat rhythm that can have the horse traveling at 30 to 40 miles per hour.

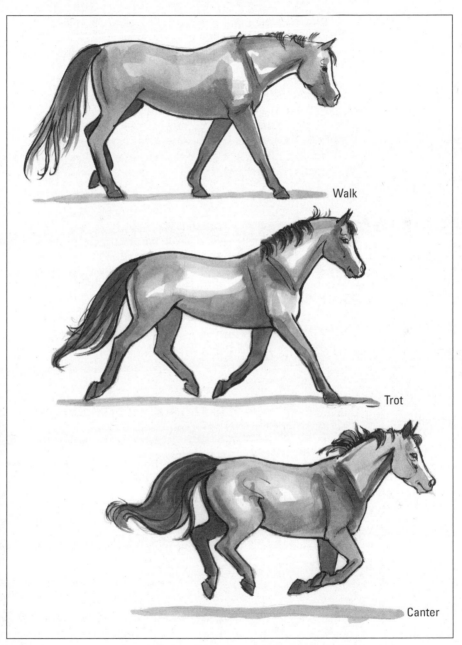

Walk

Trot

Canter

Figure 2-3:
The three
most
common
riding gaits
of a horse,
from
slowest to
fastest, are
the walk,
trot or jog,
and canter
or lope.

Keep in mind the discipline you're riding in when talking about gaits. English riders say *canter,* but Western riders say *lope.* English riders say *trot,* but Western riders say *jog.* Fortunately, both disciplines say *walk!*

Riding lets you feel each of the rhythms of the walk, trot or jog, and canter or lope, and you can discern which one you're experiencing. Check out Chapters 13, 14, and 15 for more information about riding each of these gaits.

Here's something to throw a small monkey wrench into things: Some horses have more than the gaits I describe here. These talented equines are called *gaited horses,* and they possess one or more gaits in addition to or instead of one or more of the basic gaits. Chapter 20 contains details on the breeds of gaited horses, their unusual gaits, and how to ride them.

Colors and markings

Horses come in a vast array of colors and patterns, with a host of different markings. Familiarize yourself with the names of the following colors, patterns, and markings, because appearance is an important way to identify horses. In other words, if your instructor tells you to go "saddle up the bay pinto," knowing what color *bay* is and what *pinto* means can really help you know what she's talking about.

A horse of a different color

Horses don't quite come in all the colors of the rainbow, but you may notice quite a bit of variation. Here's a list of the most common horse colors:

- **Chestnut:** Chestnut is a distinct reddish color covering the entire body. The mane and tail are usually the same color, although some chestnuts have what's called a *flaxen* (blond) mane and tail. Chestnuts come in different shades, from very light (sorrel) to very dark (liver).

- **Bay:** Bay is a rich brown color on the body with a black mane, tail, and legs. Bays can be dark tan to reddish brown in hue.

- **Brown:** In the horse world, brown describes a horse who has a very dark brown coloration to her body with a lighter brown around the muzzle and flank and inside upper legs. The mane and tail of brown horses are black.

- **Black:** For a horse to be correctly described as black, she must be jet black with no light areas anywhere on the body, including the mane and tail.

- **Gray:** A horse described as grey can be nearly white to dark gray and everything in between. Gray horses often have *dapples* (circular, indistinct spots), and these horses are referred to as *dapple grays.* Most gray horses are born dark and gradually develop their gray color.

✔ **Dun:** A dun horse has a gold, reddish, or tan body color and a black or brown mane and tail. All duns have a dark stripe down their backs. Within the family of duns, you can also see roans (see the next section) as well as *grullas,* which are a mousy grey dun.

✔ **Buckskin:** A buckskin looks very much like a dun but without the dorsal stripe. The color can be anything from light to dark tan, always with black leg points and a black mane and tail.

✔ **Palomino:** A golden yellow body with a white mane and tail is characteristic of the palomino coloration.

Patterns galore

Horses come in different patterns, depending on their breed (I cover breeds later in this chapter):

✔ **Roan:** The term *roan* describes a horse who has a dark base color that's intermixed with white hairs. The head and lower legs of the roan are usually darker than the rest of the body. Roans come in different colorations, most often red (white hairs mixed with chestnut or red hairs) and blue (white hairs mixed with black hairs). You can see this pattern in a number of different breeds, especially the Quarter Horse.

✔ **Pinto:** A pinto horse is marked with irregularly shaped patches of dark color against white or white irregularly shaped patches against a darker base color. The dark patches can be just about any color, including palomino, bay, chestnut, black, and buckskin (see the preceding section on color). You can see pinto markings in the Paint breed, in Saddlebreds, and in certain Arabian crossbreeds.

✔ **Spotted:** Spotted horses feature one of several different coat patterns that often consist of oval, egg-shaped spots. These spots can be distributed throughout the body or blanketed over the horse's rump and hips. Spotted patterns are among the characteristics of the Appaloosa and Pony of the America breeds.

All that chrome: White markings

In addition to color and body patterns, horses are known by their facial and leg markings. Horse people use a handful of common terms to describe white markings, or *chrome.* Some horses have a combination of these markings.

Here are some types of facial chrome (see Figure 2-4):

✔ **Star:** A white spot on the horse's forehead

✔ **Snip:** A white spot on the muzzle, on or just below the area between the nostrils

✔ **Stripe:** A narrow white strip that runs down the center of the horse's face, from the forehead down the bridge of the nose

✔ **Blaze:** A wide white area that starts at the horse's forehead and runs down along the bridge of the horse's nose

✔ **Bald:** A large amount of white on the face that starts above the forehead, runs along the front of the face to the muzzle, and extends beyond the bridge of the nose to the sides of the face

Star

Snip

Blaze

Bald

Stripe

Figure 2-4:
White facial markings can help you identify horses.

Types of chrome on the legs include the following (see Figure 2-5):

✔ **Coronet band:** A small white band just above the hoof

✔ **Half pastern:** A white marking that starts at the edge of the hoof and extends halfway up the pastern (which goes from the hoof to the fetlock joint)

✔ **Sock:** A white marking that starts at the edge of the hoof and extends a third of the way up the leg

✔ **Stocking:** A white marking that extends from the hoof to the knee (front legs) or hock (back legs)

✔ **Half cannon:** A white marking that starts at the edge of the hoof and extends halfway up the middle of the leg

Figure 2-5:
Horses display a variety of white leg markings.

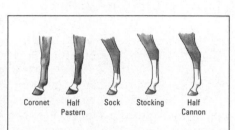

Coronet   Half Pastern   Sock   Stocking   Half Cannon

Sifting through Breed Differences

Everyone knows that dogs come in hundreds of different breeds, but did you know horses come in nearly as many? As with dogs, horses have been bred to do different jobs over the centuries. These jobs have determined the overall conformation (body structure) and even temperament of these breeds. Today, most of these breeds retain much of their original tendencies.

In the following sections, I explain why the breed of the horse you ride can be important and describe some of the most popular breeds around.

Realizing that breed may matter

The breed of horse you ride may or may not make a difference, depending on what you plan to do in the saddle. If you just want to poke along on the trail a couple days a week, what breed of horse you ride really doesn't matter as long as the horse is a nice, easy trail horse. However, if you plan to jump competitively or work your way into to the upper levels of *dressage* (a competition where the horse is judged on intricate movements), breed becomes much more of an issue. (See Chapter 22 for details about horse competitions.)

For this reason, breed does matter if you plan to do certain types of riding—especially if you want to go on to compete. If you aren't planning to go into competition, you may still discover that you have a breed preference. People fall in love with certain breeds for reasons that can be hard to explain. Sometimes it's just love at first sight.

Each horse is an individual, so no one breed of horse is best for beginning riders. Do some research, read through the following sections, and talk to other horse people to see what breed may be a good match.

Picking through popular breeds

Some horse breeds are more popular than others, and they're the ones you see most of the time when you're at a riding stable or out on the trail. The following breeds are the most popular horses in the U.S. and are the ones you're most likely to encounter when you're taking riding lessons, shopping for a riding horse, or just watching TV or the movies. You can find out more about these breeds by contacting the breed associations that I list in the Appendix. You can also read about gaited breeds in Chapter 20.

Go to "The height of a horse," earlier in this chapter, if you need more information on hands and horse size. The earlier section "Colors and markings" can give you additional info on appearance.

Appaloosa

The Appaloosa horse is synonymous with the Nez Percé Indians of northern Idaho, who kept the breed in the 1700s and 1800s. When the Nez Percé were forced onto reservations, the Appaloosa breed nearly died out. In the 1930s, a concerned group of horsemen gathered to start the Appaloosa Horse Club in an effort to save the breed. Since that time, the breed became very well-known.

The Appaloosa horse is known for its spotted coat, which comes in a number of different patterns, including *leopard* (white with dark spots over the body) and *blanket with spots* (dark body color with white over the rump, which is covered with dark spots). The breed's other distinguishing physical traits include white *sclera* (the tissue that surrounds the pupil), striped hooves, and mottled skin. Appaloosas measure from 14.3 to 16 hands in height.

Appaloosas tend to have quiet temperaments and are seen often in Western riding events as well as in jumping. They also make popular trail mounts.

Arabian

The Arabian is one of the oldest and purest breeds of horse still in existence. This horse was developed in the Middle East several hundred years ago and has been used to improve the quality of other breeds throughout the centuries.

Arabian horses are known for their elegance and stamina. The breed has an easy-to-recognize head, with a concave, or *dished,* profile. The Arabian's ears are small and curve inward, and its neck is long and arched. Most Arabian horses have only five spinal vertebrae rather than six, the number typical in most other breeds. This difference makes the Arabian's back shorter and stronger.

Most Arabians measure 15 hands or less. You can find them in gray, chestnut, bay, and black. Arabians are friendly and often high spirited, and they're known for their prowess in endurance competitions. They also make good show horses (see Chapter 22 for info on shows).

Morgan

The Morgan is an American breed developed in Vermont during the 1700s. Started from one horse, a stallion named Justin Morgan, the breed was created by breeding a variety of mares to this stallion.

Morgans today are small but strong horses, rarely reaching more than 15.2 hands in height. They come most often in bay, black, and chestnut. They're known for their willing attitudes and endurance. Morgans make great trail horses and are also shown in saddle seat, Western, and hunt seat classes.

Paint

In the early 1960s, a group of horse lovers formed an organization called the American Paint Horse Association to preserve horses with pinto markings that were born of Quarter Horse matings (see the next section for info on the Quarter Horse). Previously considered an anomaly, the Paint horse was not eligible for registration with the American Quarter Horse Association and was basically unwanted. Today, the Paint is one of the most popular breeds in the United States.

The Paint horse comes in specific patterns — including the *tobiano, overo,* and *tovero* — that involve white or dark patches on a contrasting dark or white base (visit www.apha.com/breed/index.html for links to some images and detailed descriptions). Aside from its coloring, the Paint horse is identical to the Quarter Horse, and it stands 15 to 16 hands in height. The Paint is known for being quiet and easygoing. Paints are popular trail horses and appear most often in Western shows.

Quarter Horse

The Quarter Horse is the result of American colonists' crossing horses kept by the Chickasaw nation to horses they had imported from England in the 1600s. Later developed to work cattle, the breed became a mainstay in the

American West. The breed was used to herd cattle and carry cowboys across rangeland in the 1800s. The breed's name comes from its ability to run a quarter-mile distance faster than any other breed.

The Quarter Horse is a rugged horse with a small head and muscular neck. The breed's hindquarters are powerful, and the legs are straight and solid. Quarter Horses can be sorrel, chestnut, bay, black, dun, grulla, palomino, roan, or gray, and they stand anywhere from 14.3 to 16 hands tall.

Quarter Horses are well known for their quiet temperament, which is steady and easygoing. The Quarter Horse makes a good mount for beginning riders, who need a quiet and forgiving horse to help them learn.

In the show ring, Quarter Horses prevail in Western events; you see this breed most often in cattle-working competitions, Western pleasure classes, and *gymkhana* events (timed speed events). The Quarter Horse is the most popular breed of horse in the world; it numbers in the millions.

Saddlebred

The Saddlebred was developed in Kentucky in the 1700s, using Morgans, Canadian horses, Narragansett Pacers (now extinct), and horses of Spanish breeding. Breeders hoped to develop a horse who could comfortably carry riders over long distances.

The Saddlebred is a *gaited* horse, capable of performing the *stepping pace* and a four-beat gait called a *rack* in addition to an animated walk, trot, and canter. (See Chapter 20 for details on gaited horses.)

Saddlebreds have a distinctive look that features a long, arched neck and a fine head carried high. The breed's body is lithe and lean, and it ranges in height from 15 to 17 hands high. The most common colors for this breed are bay, black, brown, chestnut, sorrel, and gray.

Saddlebreds make excellent show horses because of their flashy appearance. They're also good trail mounts and are very comfortable to ride because of their smooth gaits.

Standardbred

Standardbred horses were originally created for use as harness racers, but many are being retrained as saddle horses. The breed originated during the early part of U.S. history and was created to race under harness at either the trot or the pace. The breed is still used for this purpose today.

Standardbreds are able to move at great speeds without galloping. Some individuals are natural trotters, and they can trot at nearly 30 miles per hour. Others are born *pacers* (where the legs on one side move in unison) and are just as fast as trotters. The early training of Standardbred race horses fine-tunes these skills while discouraging the urge to gallop. Standardbreds *are* physically capable of galloping, however, and so can be trained for riding.

Standardbreds have large heads and powerful legs, and these horses measure anywhere from 15 to 16 hands high. They come mostly in bay and chestnut, but in some cases you may see them in brown, gray, or black. The Standardbred's disposition is gentle and trainable.

Tennessee Walking Horse

The Tennessee Walking Horse was developed in the early part of the 18th century by Southern plantation owners who needed a horse that could cover ground comfortably. This breed is a *gaited* horse (see Chapter 20), and it can perform a four-beat running walk for which it is famous. This gait is so smooth that it gives the rider the sensation of floating on air. Tennessee Walkers can also trot and canter.

The breed has a distinct look featuring a straight head with large ears. The neck is gracefully arched, and the withers are prominent. The breed appears in chestnut, bay, palomino, black, grey, and just about every other horse color. These horses range from 15 to 16 hands high and are known for their easygoing personality.

The Tennessee Walking Horse makes a great trail horse. It's also popular in breed shows that emphasize the breed's gaited aspects.

Thoroughbred

The Thoroughbred is the breed you see most often on the racetrack. Famous horses such as Man O' War and Secretariat were Thoroughbreds. The breed was developed in England in the 1700s for the purpose of racing and was later imported to the colonies in the New World.

Thoroughbreds typically have straight profiles, high withers, and long, fine legs. They stand from 15 to 17 hands high and have a lean, lanky appearance. They come in bay, chestnut, black, and grey.

Thoroughbreds are the fastest horses in the world, and they can reach speeds of 40 miles per hour when they gallop. They're also talented jumpers and dressage horses.

Chapter 3

School's in Session: Taking Riding Lessons

*I*f you want to enjoy horseback riding, you have to learn how to do it properly. And *that* is probably the best piece of advice you can get from a book.

I imagine you sense the need to find out more about this hobby before you begin. Not everyone takes this approach. Some people just get on a horse for the first time and seem to expect to know what to do — after all, they've seen people ride horses in movies hundreds of times! The idea of taking riding lessons beforehand never occurs to them. They wouldn't dream of going downhill skiing or sailing without some instruction, but they'll climb aboard a 1,000-pound animal without the slightest idea of how to control the creature.

Maybe people think they don't need training because horses are living beings with their own brains. These untrained riders figure that the horse knows what to do. However, the fact that the horse has a mind of his own is precisely why you need lessons first. Convincing the horse to do what *your* brain is telling him to do — not *his* — takes some skill.

In this chapter, I provide advice on how to find the best riding stable and the most suitable instructor. I also give you tips on being a good student and getting the most from your time in the saddle.

Finding the Best Stable for Your Needs

The first step in figuring out how to ride is finding a good place to take lessons. The environment where you discover the nuances of riding makes a big difference in your enjoyment of this pastime. In the following sections, I explain how to find and evaluate stables in your area.

The initial search: Identifying stables in your area

You can search for stables in a variety of ways. Here are some good resources:

- **Word of mouth:** Getting recommendations is the best way to find a riding stable. Talk to people who ride and ask them which stables (or *barns,* as horsy people often call them) they like. Or visit a local tack store and talk to the staff — and even other customers — about what they recommend. Odds are they can refer you to a stable that has some of the best instructors.

- **The Internet:** You can try looking for stables in your area online. By putting "riding lessons" and the name of your county or city in a search engine, you can come up with a list of riding stables in your area.

- **Telephone directory:** The old-fashioned method of looking in the phone books still works. Look under "Horses" or "Stables" and see what comes up.

Some people prefer to find the instructor first and then look for the stable. For additional ideas, see the upcoming section entitled "When you strike out with stables: Seeking out a different teacher."

Your major: Finding a school that offers your discipline

Which stable you choose depends on the riding discipline you're interested in. Some stables have riding instructors who teach more than one discipline; other stables specialize in only one. Knowing what you want to get out of horseback riding can help you narrow down your search. Take a look at the disciplines (Chapters 6 and 7 explain Western and English riding in detail):

- **Western:** Because the Western discipline provides more comfort and security and requires less stamina than English styles, Western riding is popular with beginners. Western is the discipline of choice for pleasure and trail riders; you can also work with cattle or participate in shows that feature the horse's speed, obedience, and athletic ability (as well as your own riding skills).

- **English:** Here are the basic English styles:
  - **Hunt seat:** Hunt seat is ideal if you're interested in jumping fences.
  - **Dressage:** Dressage is a chance to show off a horse's training. This "horse ballet" features graceful and disciplined movements.

If you aren't sure which discipline you'd like, find a stable that offers lessons in both and discuss your options with the riding instructors at that stable. You may want to take a lesson in both English and Western to see which you prefer.

Campus visit: Evaluating stables with a sharp eye

After you find a stable in your area that teaches the discipline you want, pay a visit to the barn. You want to determine whether this stable is the kind of place you want to spend your time in. Look for the following qualities to make sure you find a stable where you can easily develop your skills:

✔ **Friendly atmosphere:** Approach people you see at the stable, either individuals caring for their own horses or employees of the facility. You can ask around for directions to the office (every good stable has one, even if it's located in the feed room) and see whether the stable manager is available to give you a tour. Ask the manager about the instructors at the barn and find out what services they offer. People should be courteous and welcoming. If everyone's in a bad mood, you probably don't want to do your riding there.

✔ **Clean premises:** Even though riding stables are loaded with dust and dirt, the facilities should still be relatively clean and tidy. The horse stalls should be free of excessive piles of manure (a few are okay, but more than that indicates the stalls aren't cleaned often enough); the barn aisles should be free of clutter and mess. Look for a facility that's in good overall repair and has a neat appearance. Flies are always present where you find horses, but the pesky insects shouldn't be crawling all over you.

✔ **Safe environment:** Make sure the stable has enclosed riding arenas with gates that shut. This feature is important for all riders' safety, especially beginners. Avoid stables that have a lot of animals such as dogs, goats, or chickens running loose as well — these critters can pose a safety hazard to horses and riders.

✔ **Healthy and happy horses:** Take a look at the horses at the stable. You want to make sure they're well cared for before you give this place your business. A healthy horse has bright eyes, a rounded body (no bony hips or ribs sticking out), and a shiny coat. (Keep in mind that very old horses can sometimes look a little worse for wear.)

Come up to the lesson horses' stalls and talk to the animals; the horses should approach you. Their sociability indicates that they're happy and not overused. Overusing lesson horses is a form of mistreatment, and these animals usually aren't pleasant to ride.

✔ **Good policies:** Find out what the stable's policies are regarding riding lessons. Are helmets required? Such safety gear is important, especially for children. Also, ask what happens if the weather takes a turn for the worse or if you have to cancel a lesson. Will you get credit for the lesson?

Don't worry if you're asked to sign a liability waiver stating that you hold the stable harmless if you're injured while riding. This waiver is typical; many insurance companies that cover riding stables require it.

✔ **Cost:** Cost per lesson varies from one stable to another, so make sure you can afford the lessons before you sign up for them. Keep in mind that in most cases, you get what you pay for. Choose the best lessons you can afford.

When making your final decision about stables, keep all these points in mind. Look for a stable that's conveniently located and maybe even offers special features, such as a covered riding arena if weather is an issue where you live. Remember, though, that a good instructor is just as important as a good stable — possibly more so (see the following section). Try to combine the best stable and instructor that you can.

Choosing an Instructor or Trainer

After you find a stable where you'd like to ride (see the earlier section titled "Finding the Best Stable for Your Needs"), you're ready to sleuth out an instructor or trainer from among the professionals working at that stable. As with any activity, you can find both good and bad teachers. Your task is to find a good teacher who understands your goals, has a teaching style you like, and thoroughly understands riding. The person you pick is the one who will teach you how to ride and the one whose lesson horses you'll ride.

In the following sections, I explain how to decide between an instructor and a trainer and tell you what to look for in either one. And if you can't find someone at a stable you like, don't worry — I give you tips on finding other teachers in your area.

Deciding between a riding instructor and a horse trainer

Most large riding stables have both riding instructors and horse trainers. Before you start interviewing prospective teachers, be sure you understand the difference between these two types of professionals:

✔ **Instructors:** Riding instructors focus on teaching people how to ride. They don't generally ride other people's horses for a living but instead own lesson horses they use for their students.

✔ **Trainers:** Horse trainers are people who provide instruction to both the rider and the horse. Horse trainers are most valuable to people who own their own horse and who need someone to teach them to ride as well as school the horse on how to behave under saddle.

If you don't plan on buying a horse right away (and you shouldn't until you've spent considerable time riding), a riding instructor is your best bet. This person can let you ride his or her lesson horses and teach you the basics of controlling this very large beast.

In some rural areas, you may find only horse trainers and no riding instructors. If you're in that situation, go with a horse trainer for riding lessons, but be clear that you're a beginner and need a very quiet horse. Some trainers make arrangements with their horse-owning clients to borrow their horses for riding lessons with non-horse-owning clients.

Understanding what to look for in an instructor or trainer

If you've found a convenient stable that you like, choose an instructor or trainer from the group of professionals who work at this facility. Interview at least two people, and ask them the following questions:

✔ **What's your background?** Look for an instructor who's been teaching riding lessons to adults for at least two years. Find out whether this person has shown horses or done anything else that indicates knowledge about the horse industry.

✔ **Are you certified with any groups?** Because riding instructors aren't licensed in the U.S. (as they are in Britain and Canada), you can't ask for official credentials. However, you can ask whether an instructor is certified with one of the groups I list in the Appendix of this book (such as the Certified Horsemanship Association and the American Riding Instructors Association). Because the number of certified instructors is low compared to those who aren't certified, you may not be able to find a teacher with certification. However, if you're trying to choose between two instructors, all else being equal, go for the one who's certified.

✔ **Do you have lesson horses?** Because you probably don't own your own horse, you need an instructor who has horses you can ride. Try to go with an instructor who has more than one lesson horse. If one horse is sick or lame, you can still ride another one.

✔ **Do you work with adult beginners?** Make sure the person you choose regularly works with adults just learning how to ride. Some instructors focus on intermediate or upper-level riders and don't have the experience or patience for a beginner. Other instructors deal only with children. You want someone who knows how to teach adults the basics of riding.

✔ **What are your fees?** Find out how much the instructor charges per lesson. If you buy a package of lessons, the instructor should offer a discount. If the instructor offers both individual and group lessons, find out the difference in cost. (I cover the differences between individual and group lessons later in this chapter.)

✔ **When do you give lessons?** Be sure the instructors' lesson schedule is compatible with your leisure time. If the instructor works only from 10 to 6 on weekdays and you have a 9-to-5 job, you'll have a problem trying to coordinate your rides. (I discuss setting up a lesson schedule later on.)

✔ **May I observe one of your lessons?** Ask the instructor whether you can watch a lesson to get a sense of his or her teaching style. The instructor should be more than willing to have you observe. When you watch, look for patience, clear instructions, and praise and encouragement for the student.

If you're satisfied with the answers to these questions and like what you see when you watch the instructor give a lesson, your next step is to take a sample lesson. Be sure to take one lesson as a trial before you commit to a package of lessons. Make sure you're comfortable with this person as a teacher and that his or her style is compatible with your personality.

When you strike out with stables: Seeking out a different teacher

If you don't like what you see in terms of instructors and trainers at the stables you explore, consider looking for a teacher using the following methods:

✔ **Contact an organization that certifies riding instructors:** You can find a stable by first searching for a riding instructor and going with the stable where that person works. Organizations that certify riding instructors (see the Appendix) can provide you with the names of certified instructors in your area.

✔ **Attend local horse shows:** Look in your local newspaper or horse-related publication for listings of horse shows in your area. (Choose shows that include the discipline you hope to ride in.) Go to the shows and watch the classes. You may notice riding instructors and trainers working with their students on the sidelines. The instructor or trainer is the one functioning as a coach, giving both advice before the student enters the ring and constructive criticism after the class is over.

When the time is right (after the show, during a lunch break, or when the instructor or trainer doesn't seem busy), approach instructors or trainers and tell them that you're a new rider. Ask what stable they work from, request a card, and get basic information about their program to make sure they work with beginners in your chosen discipline. Instructors and trainers may not have time to talk to you at length at the show but should be happy to discuss their program with you over the phone at a later date. See Chapter 22 for details on horse shows.

✔ **Ask for referrals:** Talk to other people you know in the horse community (other horse owners, horse vets, tack store owners, and the like) and see whom they recommend as a teacher for a beginning rider in your discipline. Sometimes word of mouth is the best way to find a good instructor.

Getting the Most from Your Lessons

Perhaps you've found a good stable and instructor and are ready to start your lessons. To get the most from your training, you need to be a good student. Your education starts with this book, so you're partway there! In the following sections, I explain how to choose between individual and group lessons, establish a regular riding schedule, and work well with your teacher.

Deciding between individual and group lessons

Riding lessons come in two varieties: individual and group. See Table 3-1 for the benefits and disadvantages of each type.

Table 3-1	Comparing Individual and Group Lessons		
Lesson Type	**Description**	**Pros**	**Cons**
Individual	Also known as private lessons, individual lessons consist of you, the instructor, and the horse.	Lots of one-on-one attention; the instructor is focused on you and you only, and you don't have to share his or her attention with anyone else.	Individual lessons are more expensive. You also don't get the chance to meet and ride with others as you would in a group setting.
Group	When riding in a group lesson, one or more other riders are sharing the instructor's attention. Group lessons can be as small as two riders or as large as ten.	Group lessons are less expensive than individual lessons and are a great way to meet other beginning riders and learn to ride in a group setting.	You're sharing the teacher with other people and don't get as much instruction as you would in a private lesson.

You can take either type of lesson, depending on your personal preferences and your budget. Most people prefer individual lessons, and I've always favored them for myself because I like the one-on-one attention; however, group lessons do teach you how to maneuver your horse with other riders in the ring, which is a valuable skill.

Setting up your lesson schedule

Consistency is key. When you ride often and regularly, the concepts sink in more rapidly. And because horseback riding is a physical activity, your body can better develop strength and skill if you participate in it on a regular basis (for info on the physical requirements of horseback riding and how to prepare your body, check out Chapter 4). Of course, the time of day is also pretty significant when you work out your lesson schedule. In the following sections, I cover both lesson frequency and time of day.

Frequency

The amount of time you have and how much money you can afford to spend determine the number of lessons you take per month. Two lessons a week is ideal — you learn faster, and your body builds balance and muscle more quickly at this pace.

If you can't afford to ride twice a week or don't have the time, schedule at least one lesson a week. Once a week is really the minimum you should ride, because riding less often slows learning and doesn't properly condition your body.

Time of day

The time of day that you schedule your lessons probably depends on your work schedule. If you have a 9-to-5 job, you may be able to ride only on the weekends or after work. If you're self-employed or otherwise free during the day, you have more flexibility. Most lessons run 45 minutes to an hour.

Your instructor should be able to provide you with some advice about the best times to ride at his or her stable. If you want private lessons, during the day Monday through Friday is probably the quietest time at the barn. If you're hoping to meet other riders and make your lessons a social event, you may want to schedule them for the weekends or in the evenings.

Note the season when scheduling lessons; in warm weather, early mornings or late afternoon/early evening is best. Riding is a strenuous activity for both you and the horse, and you'll be pretty miserable if you ride in the heat of the day during the summer. During winter, the middle of day may be best for a lesson so you can keep warm.

Working with your instructor or trainer

A large part of getting the most from your riding lessons is how you work with your instructor. A good relationship with your teacher brings faster results. Also, you have more fun if you and your instructor get along, and that's what horseback riding is really all about. I explain how to foster a good relationship with your teacher in the following sections.

Engaging in good communication

Working with a riding instructor is all about communication. Your instructor puts you up on a horse and then tells you, mostly through words, how to control the animal. That's why signing up with an instructor who is patient, easy to understand, and experienced in teaching beginners is crucial.

Riding is a complicated activity that requires you to do more than one thing at a time. You have to do one thing with your hands, another with your legs, and yet another with your seat — all while staying in balance and moving in rhythm with the horse. Figuring out how to coordinate all these parts of your body at once can be tricky, and coaching a beginning rider at this task takes a talented teacher.

In order to make sure your instructor is communicating effectively with you, you need to be a good listener. Stay focused during your lessons and live in the moment. Don't bring family or other potential distractions with you when you ride. If you do, your mind may end up half on whatever is distracting you and half on the task at hand. When you're riding, remember you're just riding and nothing else.

If you find yourself confused about something your instructor has told you to do, or if you find that you can't physically or mentally perform the task he or she is asking of you, talk to your teacher. Let your instructor know that you don't understand or that you feel anxious. A good teacher rephrases the instruction or demonstrates a task for you so you know what he or she is looking for; a good instructor also helps you adjust to trying new things and goes more slowly if necessary.

If you're experiencing pain or discomfort while trying to hold your body in a certain way or maintain a particular position, let your instructor know. Remember, your body needs time to adjust to any new physical activity, and horseback riding is no exception. "No pain, no gain" can definitely apply to horseback riding, but you don't want to hurt yourself. Discuss any discomfort you're having with your instructor so you can find out whether what you're feeling is normal for a beginner or whether you're experiencing more pain than appropriate for the activity. (Chapter 4 has more details on getting into riding shape safely.)

Also speak up when your instructor asks you a question or wants you to count out loud. Some beginners are hesitant to ride and talk at the same time. Have no fears! It's okay to vocalize to your instructor while you're riding.

Teacher's pet: Acting like a model student

A good riding student is someone whom instructors enjoy teaching. A good student is also someone who learns and has fun doing it.

Becoming a good riding student is easy if you follow a few guidelines. These conventions can help both you and your instructor make the most of the experience:

- **Arrive on time:** Nothing messes up a riding instructor's schedule like a student who's chronically late for lessons. Most good instructors have a full plate and schedule lessons one after another. If you're late for your lesson, your instructor will have to take the next student later than scheduled or cut your lesson short. Either way, a loose understanding of punctuality can frustrate your instructor and give the impression that your lessons aren't a priority in your life. (Keep in mind that if you're expected to groom and saddle the horse before your lesson, you need to arrive early.)

- **Cancel early:** If you have to cancel your riding lesson, don't call an hour beforehand if you can help it. Give your instructor as much notice as possible so he or she knows which lesson horses are available for students, which slots are open for new students, and so on.

- **Take care of your horse:** A good instructor or trainer has you groom and tack up the horse you're going to ride before your lesson. (See Chapter 11 for details on how to *tack up,* or saddle and bridle, a horse.) This step isn't designed to save the instructor time; it's to teach you how to prepare a horse for riding and care for him after you're finished with your lesson. Don't be a prima donna (or primo don!) and expect your horse to be ready to ride when you arrive at the stable or plan to hand the horse off to some groom when you dismount. These luxuries are reserved for the rich, the famous, and characters in movies. Besides, interacting with the horse before and after the ride is half the fun of this sport.

- **Don't whine or argue:** Horseback riding lessons are hard work, but that doesn't mean you should complain incessantly to your instructor about what you're being asked to do. You're paying this person because you recognize his or her expertise in this area, so don't argue when the instructor tells you to do something. Respect your instructor as a professional and a human being, and you should get the same consideration in return.

✔ **Pay attention:** You expect your instructor to be fully engaged during your lessons, and that idea goes both ways. Don't engage in chitchat with people who are in the arena or hanging out on the fence rail, and stay focused. Your instructor will recognize you as a serious student.

✔ **Do your homework.** Some instructors may give you homework to do to help improve your riding. This work can be anything from exercises to strengthen your muscles to reading a book or article to help educate you on something you're working on. Do this extra work to help improve your riding ability and to keep your instructor invested in your learning.

✔ **Pay your bill:** Most riding instructors are kind enough to give you your lessons first and collect payment later. Don't make your instructor regret this policy by not paying when the money is due. Late payment breeds bad blood between you and your teacher and can seriously affect your relationship.

Expecting the right behavior from instructors and trainers

Just as riding students have rules to live by, so should trainers and instructors. Expect certain behavior from your instructor during your lessons and in your professional relationship. Instructors should be

✔ **Focused:** You're paying your instructor to teach you to ride a horse. If your teacher is chatting with his or her friends during your lesson, schooling a client's horse, or talking on a cellphone, he or she isn't focused on you and your riding. Although an occasional lapse in attention is not a big deal, chronic distractions are unacceptable.

✔ **Patient:** Being able to teach others is a special skill. Your instructor should be patient with you as you learn and should teach you with respect. Don't tolerate yelling or humiliation of any kind from a riding instructor. Anyone who uses this method shouldn't be in the business of teaching beginners to ride.

✔ **Courteous:** Just as you should give ample notice if you need to cancel, the same goes for your instructor. Sometimes last-minute cancellations are unavoidable, such as in the case of a lame or sick lesson horse or another type of emergency. But chronic cancellations, especially at the last minute, indicate a lack of respect for the student.

✔ **Consistent:** Riders of any level need consistency in their riding schedule in order to develop their skills and build up their muscles and balance. Expect your instructor to schedule regular lessons for you so you can get the most out of your lesson program.

If you find you aren't getting what you need from your riding instructor, discuss your problems with him or her. If you still aren't satisfied after the talk, consider finding another teacher.

Chapter 4

Mind and Body: Conditioning Yourself for Riding

In This Chapter

▶ Discovering the importance of fitness for riders

▶ Exercising to get in riding shape

▶ Readying your mind for riding

Many people think that in horseback riding, the horse does all the work. Although the horse may do the *majority* of the work, she certainly doesn't do all of it. You, the rider, have plenty to do up there on the horse's back, both physically and mentally. In this chapter, you find out how to prepare your body for the rigors of riding a horse. You also discover the mental challenges involved in this exciting sport.

Understanding Why You Need to Condition Yourself

Although a lot of riding is skill and finesse, much of it is muscle strength, balance, flexibility, and endurance.

When you're first figuring out how to ride, you work mostly at the walk (see Chapter 13 for details about the walk). This gait is the least physically challenging gait to ride. However, just sitting in the saddle does require some flexibility. You know this fact if you've ridden in the past and have been sore the next day even though you didn't go faster than a walk.

The faster gaits of the trot (or jog) and canter (or lope) require not only flexibility but also muscle strength and stamina. You need strength to hold yourself in position at both gaits, and you use strength and endurance to move up and down in the stirrups if you're riding English and *posting* (rising up and down in the saddle in rhythm with the horse's trot). At the canter, or lope, you need strength and stamina to move with the horse and hold yourself in position at this faster speed. (Check out Chapter 14 for more about the trot or jog and Chapter 15 for details on the canter or lope.)

Not only are rides more enjoyable if you're in good physical shape, but the experience is also easier on the horse. A fit rider can hold himself or herself in position and balance on the horse's back. An unfit rider feels like dead weight to a horse and is a burden to carry.

Getting into Riding Shape

Before you start riding, preparing your body for the task at hand is a good idea. This preparation means being at the right weight, developing muscle strength, and increasing your flexibility and stamina. I explain how to get your body in shape in the following sections.

Put yourself on a health and exercise regimen a few weeks before you begin your riding lessons. Your instructor will go easy on you at first, so you don't have to be completely fit when you start. Also, the riding itself can help your body develop some of the muscles you need for this activity. You do, however, want to make sure you don't get so sore that you can't walk for days after a lesson and that you're strong enough to perform some of the basic skills you need right from the beginning.

Before you begin any exercise regimen or change your diet, talk to your doctor to make sure you're in good enough health to tackle these changes.

Lightening the load: Shedding those extra pounds

Weight can be a touchy subject, and most people have struggled with it at some point in their lives. Although most people would rather not have to think about weight, it's an important issue when you're riding. Here's why:

- **Saddle comfort:** Your riding instructor probably has saddles that are made for people of standard weight. If you're a heavy rider, you need a saddle with a larger-than-normal seat. You won't feel comfortable or secure in a saddle that's too small for you.

- **Strain on the horse:** Many equine professionals believe that a horse shouldn't carry more than 20 percent of her body weight. More than that can cause soreness or even injury to the horse's back. Most horses weigh around 1,000 pounds, so if you weigh more than 200 pounds, you need a horse on the larger side. Your riding instructor may not have a horse that's big enough for you and so may put you on a horse who isn't comfortable carrying your weight. And although most lesson horses are troopers and will carry you anyway, that's really not fair to the horse.

✔ **Ease in getting on and off the horse:** If you've ever mounted a horse, you know that pulling yourself up into the saddle takes some upper body strength. The more weight you have to pull up, the harder it is. Very heavy riders often can't get on without having to stand on a mounting block or something that's very high. Using a mounting block is fine if you have one available, but if you can't get on without one, you may find yourself stranded off your horse. You may be especially prone to long walks home if you trail ride, because trail riders frequently need to get on and off the horse. (See Chapter 12 for details on mounting and dismounting; Chapter 21 discusses trail riding.)

✔ **Energy for riding:** Riding a horse requires physical strength and endurance. If you've ever carried excess weight on your body, you know how much harder it is to participate in strenuous activities without getting winded. When you're at a healthy weight, you have an easier time keeping up with your horse.

If you need to get down to as healthy a weight as possible before you start riding, the real question may be how to do it. Scores of diet books and fads can coach you through weight loss. I've found that eating plenty of protein and green vegetables, with a minimal amount of carbohydrates, does a great job of keeping my weight down while giving me the energy to ride. Cutting out sugar is also important if you're a rider, because excess sugar causes weight gain and makes your energy levels fluctuate.

A calorie is a calorie, no matter which food group it comes from, so you need to choose a diet you can stick to. The key to weight loss is using more calories than you consume in a day. You do this by eating less and moving more. So set some reasonable goals and take your time. Eat a balanced diet and start using some of the activities in the following sections in your exercise routine. If you're interested in finding out more about losing weight, check out *Dieting For Dummies,* 2nd Edition, by Jane Kirby, R.D., and the American Dietetic Association (Wiley).

Developing endurance with aerobic exercise

Although all riders need good stamina, endurance is particularly important if you plan to ride English (see Chapter 7) and/or take up trail riding (Chapter 21). English riders spend much of their time in the saddle *posting* (moving up and down in the saddle), which requires lots of stamina. Trail riders spend hours in the saddle and need endurance to hold themselves in the saddle for long periods of time.

Taking in the O$_2$

Knowing how to breathe properly is a handy skill in almost any air-filled environment — especially when you're participating in athletic activities — but it's particularly important in horseback riding. Not only does proper breathing give you the oxygen your body needs to perform the rigors of riding, but it also helps you relax and communicate effectively with the horse.

If you work with a good riding instructor, he or she will most likely remind you to breathe during your lessons. Riders tend to hold their breath when they're concentrating very hard or are nervous. When you remember to breathe, your muscles

relax and you're able to move more fluidly with the horse. You can also communicate confidence and relaxation to your mount. Horses are very sensitive to their riders' bodies, and they often take their cue from the rider's mood. If you feel tense because you aren't breathing, your horse may sense it and tense up, too.

Get into the habit of breathing — continuously — during all your workouts. Whether you're pumping iron, playing tennis, or just getting in a nice stretch, establishing good habits now can serve you well when you finally climb aboard your trusty steed.

To build up your endurance, consider walking, jogging, playing tennis, shooting baskets with your buddies, or doing some other type of aerobic exercise as often as you can. Start this new regimen at least a month before you start riding lessons.

After you start riding, continue to ride regularly to help your body maintain its aerobic conditioning. If you take lessons or ride at least twice a week — preferably more — you can build and keep your stamina.

Building strength

The muscles most necessary for riding are those in your arms, legs, and abdomen. The more strength you have in these areas, the better you can communicate to the horse with your movements and maintain your balance in the saddle. The following sections include suggestions for building muscles in these three crucial areas. For more help, check out *Fitness For Dummies,* 3rd Edition, by Suzanne Schlosberg and Liz Neporent, M.A. (Wiley).

Arms

Strong arms help you pull your body weight into the saddle. Arm strength is also valuable if you're riding in the English discipline, because you need to maintain contact with the horse's mouth through the reins (see Chapter 7 for the scoop on riding English). You don't need arm strength to pull on the horse's mouth (a major no-no), but you do need it to hold your arms in position for extended lengths of time while putting some tension on the reins.

The following exercises, which use free weights and the weight of your body, can help build arm strength. By using light weights and more repetitions, you can build lean muscle mass instead of bulking up. Men may want to use 15-pound weights and build up to 20 repetitions for each exercise; women may want to start with 5-pound weights and build to 20 repetitions. When you're ready to make the exercises more challenging, increase the weight or repetitions, do several sets of repetitions, or slow down your movements.

- ✔ **Arm curl:** This exercise helps build your biceps. Sit on a chair with your feet flat on the floor. Have a weight in each hand, and let your hands hang at your sides. Alternating arms, slowly bring the weight toward your shoulder while keeping your elbow at your side. After you lift each arm all the way up, hold the weight at the top, and then slowly lower it the starting position.

- ✔ **Triceps extension:** To work out the triceps, which lie on the back of your upper arms, lie down with a weight in one hand. Straighten your arm so it's standing straight up, perpendicular to your body; then bend at the elbow, lowering the weight toward your shoulder. Slowly extend the arm upward again. Switch to the other arm after you've finished your repetitions.

- ✔ **Shoulder press:** This move strengthens the muscles between your shoulders. Sit on a chair with a dumbbell in each hand. Hold the weights at shoulder height, with elbows bent and palms facing forward. Extend your hands upward above your head without completely straightening your elbow. Then lower your arms back to the starting position.

- ✔ **Push-ups:** This good, old-fashioned exercise helps build your upper body strength, particularly in your chest, shoulders, and triceps. Start with five and build up to ten or more. Don't cheat! Hold your back straight and keep the movements slow and smooth.

Legs

Leg strength is one of the most important physical attributes for a rider. When on the horse, you use pressure from your legs to impart instructions. You also use them to balance in the saddle. And of course, your legs need to be strong enough to help you launch yourself into the saddle when you mount.

The more you ride, the more strength you develop in your legs. To further this process along, try the following activities:

- ✔ **Knee bends:** This exercise helps strengthen your quadriceps, which run along the front of the thighs. Stand with your back against a wall and slide down slightly until your knees are bent at about a 135-degree angle. Let your arms dangle at your sides. Hold this position for 30 seconds, and do this exercise three times a day. After it becomes easy, you can deepen the bend, working up to a 90-degree angle.

- ✔ **Leg lifts:** This move can strengthen and stretch your adductors (at the inner thigh) and abductors (at the outer thigh). Lie on your side and support your head with your lower arm. Put your other hand on your hip, and lift your leg into the air as far as you can without pain. Hold it here for two seconds, and then slowly lower it to the ground. Start with ten repetitions on each side.

✔ **Hamstring curls:** This exercise strengthens your calf muscles and the backs of your thighs. Face the back of a chair and hold on for balance. Lift your leg and try to bring your heel all the way to your buttocks; then bring your foot back to the floor. Repeat 20 times for each leg.

Abdomen

Your abdominal muscles serve as the core of your balance when you're sitting in the saddle. Strong abs help you maintain the proper position when you're riding and keep you stable while the horse moves. Use the following exercises to tone your abdominals and keep them in shape for riding. Remember to keep breathing as you're working:

✔ **Crunches:** Lie on the floor on your back with your hands behind your head and knees bent, with feet flat on the ground. Keep your head straight and lift your shoulders off the floor. Push your ribs toward your hips and hold this position for two seconds. *Slowly* lower your shoulders back to the floor. Repeat 5 times to start and build up to 20.

✔ **Reverse curls:** Lie on the floor on your back with your knees bent toward your chest as far as they go comfortably. Contract your stomach muscles and lift your hips up off the floor, bringing your knees toward your chin. Hold for two seconds and then lower your hips. Repeat 5 times to start and build up to 20.

✔ **Diagonal (oblique) crunches:** Lie on the floor on your back with your knees bent and feet flat on the floor. Put your hands behind your head and raise your shoulders, turning your torso to touch your elbow to your opposite knee. Start with 5 repetitions on one side and then switch to the other elbow and knee. Build up to 20 reps.

Cross-training: Practicing yoga and Pilates for flexibility and strength

One way to get yourself in good shape for riding is to enroll in a yoga or Pilates class. These disciplines provide an excellent, low-impact body workout that stretches and strengthens the muscles you need for riding.

Yoga

The ancient activity of yoga increases the body's flexibility and helps with balance and muscle strength. Yoga also helps you figure out how to control your breathing and truly relax, something that can come in handy when riding.

Different types of yoga classes are available to the public, with Hatha yoga among the most popular. Any type of yoga can help you get fit for riding. Some yoga schools are even starting to offer yoga for equestrians, with exercises specifically designed to help riders with their work in the saddle. If you're lucky enough to live near a yoga school that offers this class, by all means, enroll. If not, consider ordering a videotape or DVD that offers yoga for equestrians. You can also check out *Yoga For Dummies* by Georg Feuerstein, Ph.D., Larry Payne, Ph.D., and Lilias Folan (Wiley).

Pilates

A type of strengthening exercise developed by Joseph H. Pilates, this type of workout is popular with riders. It strengthens and stretches the entire body, particularly the core muscles that you need for stability and balance. Designed to improve flexibility and strength without building bulk, Pilates also includes mental conditioning that can help with coordinating your brain and your body — something infinitely useful when riding. Pilates classes are available around the country, and you can also purchase tapes and DVDs at video stores and fitness centers and over the Internet. *Pilates For Dummies* by Ellie Herman (Wiley) is another resource to try.

Stretching yourself: Increasing flexibility just before you mount

Flexibility is important when you ride. If your muscles stretch easily, you can move more freely with the horse. You're also less likely to injure yourself during a vigorous lesson and a lot less likely to be sore afterwards.

The following exercises can help you stay flexible when riding. Leave yourself extra time before your lesson or ride (at least 5 to 10 minutes) so you have time to perform these stretches before you get on the horse. Be careful when you stretch, too. Use slow, smooth movements, and don't stretch beyond the point where you feel more than a slight pull and mild discomfort.

Quadriceps

To stretch your quadriceps, stand up with your back straight and bend your leg up behind you. Hold onto your ankle so your knee is bent and slowly pull your ankle so your knee points down and behind you. You should feel tension along the front of your thigh. Hold this stretch for ten seconds and then switch to the other leg. Repeat this move twice for each leg. See Figure 4-1.

Hamstrings

The hamstrings are a set of three muscles at the back of your upper leg. For this stretch, stand up in front of a fence; use your hand to brace yourself forward as you reach your leg up onto the fence, as high as you can go. Bend forward at the waist and hold this position for ten seconds. Do this stretch with the other leg, too, and then repeat. See Figure 4-2.

Figure 4-1:
To stretch your quads, hold your ankle rather than your toes — pulling on the toes stretches the shin instead.

Figure 4-2:
Bend forward while you hold your leg against a fence to stretch your hamstrings.

Inner thighs

To stretch out your inner thighs, sit on the ground with your knees bent out to the sides and the soles of your feet touching each other. Relax your hips and then push down gently on both knees with your hands. Do this exercise twice for ten seconds each time. See Figure 4-3.

Figure 4-3: Put your feet together and push on your knees to stretch your inner thighs.

Lower back

This stretch is particularly important if you have lower back issues that cause your muscles to tighten up when you ride. Lie on your back with your knees to your chest. Wrap your arms around your legs just below your knees and pull your knees toward you. Hold this position for a few seconds, and then relax. Repeat three to five times. See Figure 4-4.

Figure 4-4: To loosen your back, lie down and pull your knees toward you.

Neck

To prevent tension in your neck, stretch the muscles by tilting your head slowly first to the right (your ear toward your shoulder) and then to the left. You should feel a stretch in the muscles along the side of your neck. Then tuck your chin forward into your chest and then back up toward the sky. Next, turn your head as far to the right as you can while keeping your shoulders straight. Do the same to the left. Follow this routine several times, holding each stretch for at least five seconds. See Figure 4-5.

Figure 4-5:
Avoid tension in your neck by tilting your head in several directions.

Preparing Your Mind

Horseback riding is as much a mental activity as it is a physical one. Not only do you need your brain to coordinate your body so you can balance and send signals to the horse, but you also need to maintain a mental attitude that gives the horse confidence and helps her see you as the one in charge. In the following sections, I explain how to conquer fears you may have and project confidence around any horse.

Knowing your role as the horse's leader

If you think about it, the fact that horses allow people to ride them is pretty amazing. After all, they're a lot bigger than we are and could just buck us off and run away at any given time. But they don't, and there are good reasons for that.

Horses live in complex social hierarchies, with leaders and followers. Horses are therefore genetically programmed to accept the leadership of whoever seems to be in control. Because domestic horses are raised with humans and learn (or should learn) that people are the ones in control, they automatically defer to human leadership.

Although horses naturally view people as leaders, they're smart and quickly figure it out when someone doesn't really have the chops to be in charge. Some horses are bossy by nature (these are the ones who'd be the leaders in the wild) and may quickly decide that you aren't qualified to be the leader.

Be confident and consistent when you're dealing with horses, whether on their backs or on the ground. Be gentle but firm, and insist that the horse listen to you. Avoid the tendency to let the horse get away with stuff. For example, if you ask the horse to stand still while your instructor is talking to you, make sure your mount doesn't walk off until you cue her to do so. If you allow her to do whatever she feels like doing instead of listening to your commands, you'll soon be riding a horse who thinks she's the boss.

And what are the consequences of having a horse who thinks she's head honcho? The vast majority of horses would rather be in a stall or pasture eating or hanging out with their friends than working. You can't blame them for that. If they believe they're the ones in charge, you'll soon find yourself doing what the horse wants to do. And chances are it won't be what you had in mind.

Banishing your fear

If you rode as a child, you probably remember having no fear sitting on top of a large animal and trusting her with your well-being. But things change as you get older, and fear can begin to creep into your psyche.

I have childhood memories of galloping along the trail on my mare, sans saddle, and not having a care in the world. Now, when I gallop on the trail, a twinge of fear looms in my mind, telling me that something bad may happen. If you're like many adult riders, you want to ride but are also afraid of getting hurt. Maybe the change happens because as adults, people have others who depend on them to stay in one piece. Adults also have an acute awareness of what can happen to victims of riding accidents. The story of actor Christopher Reeve's paralysis comes to mind.

If you're about to start horseback riding (or have already started) and are feeling fearful, take heart. Being nervous is normal. However, that's not to say you should ignore the feeling. Fear can hold you back, affect your ability to enjoy what you're doing, and in some cases, also frighten your horse. (Some sensitive equines assume that if their rider is scared, they should be, too. See Chapter 2 if you want to find out more about how horses think.)

Work on getting rid of your fear in the following ways:

- **Take lessons.** If you're not already convinced that you should take riding lessons before you get on a horse, I'm going to take another stab at it. Lessons are invaluable in helping you build confidence in the saddle and in giving you the feeling that you're in control. When riders feel like they know what they're doing, they're much less fearful when they ride. Chapter 3 contains more information on taking lessons.

  Lessons can give you a good primer in safety, as well. Knowing what to watch out for and being confident that the equipment fits can put your mind at ease. For more information on safety, check out Chapter 5.

- **Go slowly.** If you feel your riding lessons are moving too fast, you aren't comfortable riding beyond a walk or trot, or are afraid to jump, it may be time to slow down. Communicate with your riding instructor about your worries. A good teacher will talk to you about your fears and help you overcome them by going slowly and taking more time to move to the next level of riding. At some point, you may need to face your fears if you want to really learn to ride. But do so only when you're physically ready to go to the next level.

- **Change horses.** Sometimes riders are anxious when riding one horse but have no fear when riding another. A close look at the situation often reveals that this fear is justified. A rider can be *over-mounted,* which means the horse is too much for the rider to handle. If you're afraid when you ride because you don't trust the horse you're on, try a quieter, gentler animal instead and see whether your nerves subside. If they do, you know that you and the first horse aren't a good match, at least not at this stage in your training.

- **Go to a therapist.** If you've tried taking lessons, moving more slowly, and changing horses yet are still uneasy when you ride, consider getting professional help in the form of psychotherapy. Your fear may be irrational, perhaps stemming from something else in your background. Or you may be scared because you once had a bad experience on a horse and can't seem to shake it, despite becoming a better rider and riding only safe horses. If you seek help from a psychotherapist for your fear, look for one who also rides (the best way to find out is to ask). A fellow equestrian will have a better understanding of the activity and is unlikely to have a fear of horses.

Chapter 5

Safety First: Protecting Yourself around Horses

In This Chapter
▶ Dressing safely
▶ Staying secure on the ground
▶ Employing safe riding practices

Most horses are gentle creatures who would never intentionally hurt anyone, let alone someone they like. However, they're big animals, and accidents happen.

Horse-related mishaps have been a fact of life for centuries, no doubt ever since the horse was domesticated. I remember hiking once in Yosemite National Park and coming across an old cemetery from the 1800s. One of the tombstones said that the occupant of the grave had been "killed by a horse." I realized that no matter how much experience you have with horses, bad stuff can happen.

People wise in the ways of horses have come up with general safety rules to follow when in the presence of these large animals. In this chapter, I detail the safety protocols you need to follow to keep yourself out of harm's way, both on the ground and in the saddle. And remember — I give you plenty of safety tips throughout the rest of this book.

Dressing the Part with Safe Clothing

The clothing you wear around horses affects your safety. This fact may not seem obvious at first, but your apparel can protect you from errant hooves, falls to the ground, and nasty chafing. Read the following sections to see why and to find out what to look for. Chapter 10 has additional information about discipline-specific riding attire.

Covering your head

A lot of riders don't wear protective headgear, but helmets are probably the most important part of your wardrobe if you plan to ride. In the event of a fall, a helmet is the only thing between your skull and the hard ground. Stories abound of riders who came off their horses without helmets and suffered serious brain injuries as a result.

If you still aren't convinced, consider this: A fall from a horse's back can take place at high speed. Imagine jumping out of your car, head first, at 30 miles per hour. That's how fast you may be going if you fall off a galloping horse. For the sake of your brain, always wear a helmet when you ride.

The style of riding you do can determine the type of helmet you wear. Or if you aren't showing and are just schooling or going on a trail ride, you can wear a regular trail helmet. Figure 5-1 shows the three different types of helmets available:

- ✔ Riders wear the English show helmet in hunt seat and lower-level dressage shows (riders at the upper level wear a non-protective top hat). English show helmets are almost always black, do not have vents, and are often velvet-covered.

- ✔ Trail riders and people who are just schooling wear the trail helmet. These helmets are lightweight, feature vents throughout, and come in a host of different colors. (See Chapter 21 for info on trail riding.)

- ✔ The Western trail helmet, shaped like a cowboy hat, isn't often worn — many people find them awkward-looking. Most Western riders who choose to wear a helmet opt for a trail helmet instead.

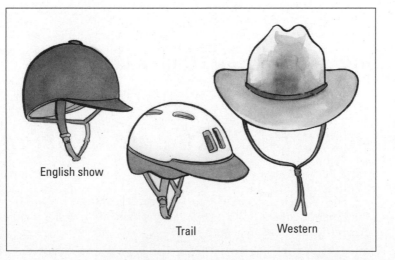

Figure 5-1:
The English show helmet, trail helmet, and Western trail helmet.

English show

Trail

Western

The danger of head injuries

According to the Centers for Disease Control and Prevention, the rate of serious injury for horseback riders is greater than that for motorcyclists and auto racers. State medical examiner records from 27 states over an 11-year period identified head injuries as the cause of 60 percent of horseback riding-related deaths.

For this reason, a number of riding organizations, such as the U.S. Pony Club and U.S. Equestrian Federation, require youngsters to wear helmets when riding in competition. Although adults are rarely required to wear helmets, they should do so for their own safety. Helmets have been proven to prevent or lessen the severity of brain injuries in riding accidents.

When you shop for a helmet, make sure you buy one for equestrians — bike helmets don't protect the part of the head most affected in a fall from a horse. In the U.S., the American Society for Testing and Materials (ASTM) sets standards for helmet construction. If a helmet meets these standards, it receives a seal of approval from the Safety Equipment Institute (SEI); buy only an SEI-approved helmet. And don't waste your money by not wearing your helmet properly. It shouldn't rock back and forth on your head but should rather be stable. The chin strap should be snug and not hanging loose.

Find out whether the riding instructor you'll be working with can provide you with a properly fitting helmet. If not, purchase one of your own at a tack store or through an equine catalog or Web site (see the Appendix for some catalog resources). Helmet prices vary by design, and you can pay anywhere from $30 to $200 for a helmet.

If you experience a fall and hit your head while wearing your helmet, buy a new one as soon as you can. An impact can compromise the helmet's effectiveness.

Slipping into the right shirt

When just hanging around the stable, you can wear just about any shirt you want. That said, keep the following points in mind when choosing what to wear above your waist when you ride:

- Long, baggy shirts that aren't tucked in can get caught on parts of the saddle, arena gates, and stall latches. You're safer in a well-fitted shirt that's tucked in. You look nicer, too!

- Riding is a physical activity, so you want to wear materials that breathe well and are absorbent. Cotton lets you stay cooler and drier.

- Long-sleeved shirts can protect your skin from the sun. I know quite a few equestrians who are dealing with skin cancer as a result of spending hours in the sun with exposed skin.

Protecting your legs

When the weather is hot, you may feel tempted to ride in shorts instead of donning a pair of riding tights or jeans. But keep in mind that if you're wearing shorts, your bare skin will rub against the leather of your saddle and give you some very unpleasant chafing.

Riding pants are designed not to rub on the rider and to protect the rider's legs from the leather of the saddle. They can also come in handy should you fall off, serving as a top layer of protection between your skin and the ground.

English riders can find breeches and riding tights at tack stores, in equine catalogs, or on the Internet (see the Appendix for some resources). Usually made of a cotton and nylon or Lycra blend, these pants are form-fitting and are very comfortable for riding in an English saddle.

Western riders typically wear denim jeans, made from cotton. These jeans have a boot cut to allow riding boots to fit under the lower pant leg.

These boots are made for riding: Donning the right footwear

Boots made of the right material and designed with the proper heel are your only choice if you plan to handle or ride a horse; you can buy them at tack stores, through equine catalogs, or on the Internet. Follow these rules to keep your feet — and the rest of your body — safe:

- ✔ **Wear heavy boots when working on the ground.** Heavy boots are mandatory if you plan to be on the ground and working around horses. Few things are as painful as having your foot stepped on by a 1,000-pound klutz wearing metal shoes. If you're wearing tennis shoes or sandals when this happens, you're at risk for a broken foot, broken toes, or at the very least, a lot of bruising and swelling. Wear heavy boots designed for equestrians for maximum safety.

- ✔ **Wear riding boots when you're in the saddle:** Never ride in a saddle with tennis shoes. You may see people doing it, but that doesn't mean the practice is safe. Riding boots made especially for equestrians are the best footwear for riding because they're equipped with a heel that keeps your foot from sliding through the stirrup and trapping your leg. This feature can be a lifesaver should you fall from your horse; you don't want to get dragged. The soles are also smoother for the same reason.

  Figure 5-2 shows riding boots with a proper heel. The heel is square and about an inch high. Riding boots come in a variety of different styles, but all good riding boots have this safety heel in common.

Figure 5-2:
Riding boots
with a
distinctive
heel are key
for safety.

Removing your jewelry

Most people don't imagine getting dressed up to go down to the barn, but some people actually do. Ditching your silver and gold may sound like a silly warning, but here it is anyway: Refrain from wearing jewelry when you're around horses.

Jewelry — especially big rings, hanging earrings, necklaces, and bangle bracelets — can catch on just about any part of the saddle or bridle. This stuff can also catch on the various items at riding stables, such as gate latches, *cross-tie rings* (apparatuses that tether the horse; see Chapter 11 for details on cross-ties), and saddle racks. Save the sparkle for a more appropriate and safer venue.

Keeping a Close Eye on Horses When You're on the Ground

Some people believe you're safer riding a horse than you are working with one on the ground. It's true that you're more vulnerable when you're standing next to the horse, because the horse can easily step on you, knock you down, or kick. When you're on the horse's back, all you have to worry about is not falling off or running into low-hanging branches.

If you're working around a kind, well-mannered horse, you have little to worry about in terms of intentional injuries. Horses who kick and bite humans are not the norm, and they certainly have no place in a beginning rider's lesson program. However, staying on the safe side and being prepared for anything when you're handling horses is always a good idea. Even the calmest horses react when startled.

Knowing what to expect from a horse when you're working around him and taking certain precautions can help ensure your safety at the stable. In the following sections, I explain how to stay safe in close quarters with a horse and around a tied horse. I also show you how to recognize some dangerous horse moves so you know to get out of the way.

Being in close confines with a horse

Horses are big animals who can easily step on you or crash into you without meaning to. Combine this reality with their tendency to spook (see Chapter 2 for details), and you can see why being alert and knowledgeable when in close confines with a horse is essential.

Horses who have learned they shouldn't encroach on a human's space are less likely to crowd you or step on you in close quarters, but accidents happen. And some horses just don't know they're supposed to keep some distance from you. If you discover that a horse doesn't know to move away when you ask him to, avoid getting in close quarters with that animal.

When in a barn with a horse, follow these rules to keep yourself safe:

- ✔ **Don't stand between a horse and an unmovable object.** Find a way to move the horse if you don't have enough room to gain access to that side of the horse. If a horse gets too close to you, push on the horse's body and cluck your tongue to get the horse to move over and give you some room. (Try this technique, but don't assume it'll work with all horses; unfortunately, some horses haven't learned this lesson.)

- ✔ **Keep things tidy.** Watch for objects that could pose a hazard to you and your horse. If you spot a rake, pitchfork, bucket, hose, halter, lead rope, or other object lying on the ground or leaning against a wall, put it where it belongs — even if you didn't leave it out. A horse can knock over or get tangled in these objects and may injure you or himself if he panics.

- ✔ **Don't enter a box stall with a strange horse without first determining the horse's attitude.** Nothing's more terrifying than finding yourself in a small space with a horse who doesn't want you there. Judge the horse's attitude by paying attention to his facial expressions, which I detail in Chapter 2. If you're unsure, ask the horse's owner or someone familiar with the horse.

- ✔ **Make a horse aware of your presence before you approach from behind.** Horses are easily startled, and kicking is one of their defenses. Before you walk behind a horse, make sure the horse is aware of your presence. If you need to pass closely behind a horse you don't know, talk to him and then wait for his reaction (he'll look at you and/or turn his ears to you in response). Pass *very* close to the horse's body, nearly touching him. That way, if the horse tries to kick, you'll make contact only with the point of the hock (the "elbow" of the back leg) and not receive the full force of his hoof.

Moving around a tied horse

Many horses feel vulnerable when they're tied to a post or cross-ties (see Chapter 11 for details on tying horses). To avoid accidents, follow these basic rules around tied horses:

- **When deciding where to tie your horse, choose an object unlikely to come out of the ground or break loose.** A horse running down the barn aisle with a stall door attached to his lead rope is not safe for anyone!

- **Tie short and high.** Tying a horse with too much slack in the lead rope and too low on the post is a recipe for disaster. The horse will inevitably get a foot hung up in the rope or end up with the rope over his neck. Always tie a horse with a short rope (12 inches of slack is a good length) at the horse's eye level so he can't get in trouble.

- **Use safety restraints.** When tying a horse to a hitching post or horse trailer, always use a safety knot (see Chapter 11 for instructions). A safety knot allows you to quickly release the lead rope of a panicking horse. If you're cross-tying your horse, use quick release snaps on cross-ties and light ropes that break easily if the horse pulls back.

- **Don't duck under.** Never duck underneath a horse's neck to get to the other side. Take the long way and walk around the horse's front or back. If you walk under the horse's neck and the horse panics and rears up, you could end up seriously injured.

- **Deal with pull-backs:** Horses can sometimes panic when tied. Something spooks them, and they throw all their weight on their hindquarters, exerting enough force to rip a hitching post out of the ground or at the very least, break the halter. Some horses do this act routinely just to get out of being tied, while others have to be very frightened before pulling this stunt.

To avoid prompting a horse to pull back, be slow and quiet when approaching from the front. If you need to move toward the horse with an object in your hand, watch the horse's body language carefully to determine whether the horse is scared. A horse who's ready to pull back has a frightened expression (see Chapter 2) and has moved his weight to the back of his body. To help ensure that the horse is okay with whatever you have in your hand, allow him to take a good look at it first and even sniff it before you raise your hand up near his head or neck.

Identifying dangerous horse moves

The way horses move can be dangerous for the humans in close proximity. Recognizing these moves can tell you where the horse is going so you can get out of the way:

- **Body swing:** When a horse's front end moves to the left, the back end concurrently moves to the right (and vice versa).

- **Head jerk:** If a horse wants to get his head away from something, he jerks his head upwards and sometimes to the side at the same time.

- **Sideways move:** When a horse is afraid of something on his right-hand side, he leaps to the left (and vice versa).

- **Forward move:** If something spooks a horse from behind, the horse moves forward rapidly.

- **Backward move:** If you approach a horse from the front holding something he wants to avoid (medication, a dewormer, or a frightening object, for example), he throws up his head, places all his weight on his haunches, and backs up at significant speed. If this happens, don't pull back on the lead rope, because doing so only excites the horse more and causes further backing up. Just relax, hold the object behind your back, talk softly to the horse, and give him a chance to settle down.

Staying Secure on a Horse

When you ride a horse, you challenge gravity by being up in the air. That said, you need to take certain steps to give yourself an advantage over the pull of the ground. Keeping your equipment in good working order, along with knowing how to behave on horseback, is a good start. I explain what you need to know about staying safe in the saddle in the following sections.

You should also avoid participating in equine activities that involve speed and precise rider skill, such as jumping or *gymkhana* (timed speed events), until your instructor says you're ready. See Chapter 16 for info on jumping.

Checking your tack before you saddle up

Having good riding equipment in decent condition helps you stay safe in the saddle. Just like working parts in your car's engine, tack can break when you least expect it if you don't keep it in good order.

Before you climb into the saddle, do a quick check of your tack to ensure everything makes the cut. Take a look at the following details:

- ✔ **The bridle:** Your instructor should give you a bridle that fits properly. Make sure all the buckles are tightly fastened and all pieces are securely attached. (See Chapter 9 for details about bridles.)

- ✔ **The girth:** On Western saddles, check the left latigo strap to be sure it's snugly tied to the saddle ring and that the offside billet is securely buckled to the cinch. On English saddles, inspect buckles on both sides to make sure they're securely fastened. (See Chapter 8 for diagrams showing the parts of the saddle.)

- ✔ **The stirrups:** For Western saddles, inspect the stirrup buckle to make sure it's not loose. On English saddles, make sure that the stirrup leathers are securely buckled and positioned on the stirrup bar. Later, after you dismount from your horse, push your stirrup irons up to the top of the leathers so the irons are flush with the saddle skirt. This step keeps your irons from catching on anything and banging around on your horse.

Riding with others

When you start getting into riding, you may find yourself riding on the trail with friends or sharing an arena with other riders. In situations where horses are kept at boarding stables and boarders share riding facilities, riding in groups isn't usually a choice — it's mandatory simply because everyone is forced to use the same arenas.

Follow these safety precautions when riding around others:

- ✔ **Go slowly:** Don't jump on your horse and take off like they do in the movies. When you first mount up, walk the horse slowly to the point of destination, whether it's a riding arena or a trailhead. Don't trot or canter through the aisles of the stable, and don't stress your horse by tearing off into a gallop from a standstill. These actions aren't good for the horse or your reputation with other riders.

- ✔ **Shut the gate:** Alert other riders when you're about to enter the arena and shut the gate behind you after you come in. A runaway horse — which can result from a bad spook or a falling rider — is often unable to exit the arena if the gate is closed.

- ✔ **Stay back:** When you're riding around the perimeter of an arena (or on a trail), keep your horse several feet away from the horse in front of you. (You should be able to see the hind feet of the horse in front of you between your horse's ears.) Most horses tolerate having another horse behind them, but some don't. If your horse starts crowding the one in front of him, both you and your horse may get kicked.

If you're riding a horse who kicks when other horses get too close, tie a red ribbon at the base of your horse's tail to warn other riders at horse shows, organized trail rides, or other events. Likewise, when you see a horse with a red ribbon in his tail, stay back.

✔ **Approaching from the rear:** If you're approaching a horse from behind while in the arena, pass using a wide berth (one horse's length from the side and the front of the horse you're passing) to the inside of the ring. Otherwise, if you're going faster than the other rider, the other rider's horse may spook, causing a serious accident.

✔ **Be quiet:** Yelling, hollering, and yee-hawing while on horseback is fine for actors in Westerns, but in real life, this kind of behavior can frighten your horse and those around you. The only exception to this rule is when you're riding in gymkhana or some other competitive speed event where such vocalizations are considered acceptable (see Chapter 22 for info on competitive events).

✔ **Dealing with two-way traffic:** When riding in an arena, you end up riding in one direction while one or more riders are traveling the opposite way. When passing one another face to face in a riding arena, riders use the left-shoulder-to-left-shoulder rule; their left shoulders pass when they ride by each other. To stick to the rule, you may need to stay close to the rail so the approaching rider passes you on your left. Or you may need to stay to the inside, away from the rail, so the approaching rider can pass you to the left.

Hitting the trail by yourself

Probably the only time you can really choose to ride by yourself is on the trail. Of course, you shouldn't go solo unless you're quite proficient in the saddle. Otherwise, look for some company.

If you decide to go out by yourself, follow these guidelines for safety (see Chapter 21 for more information about safety and etiquette specific to trail riding, whether you're alone or in a group):

✔ Let someone know where you're going and when you plan to return.

✔ Map out your route beforehand.

✔ Stay on the trail.

✔ Keep a cellphone and ID on your person, and have some kind of identification on your horse.

✔ Bring food, water, and sunscreen for yourself, as well as insect repellent for you and your horse.

Part II

Getting Set with the Right Riding Style and Gear

The 5th Wave   By Rich Tennant

"I'm just curious—where did you get your saddle?"

In this part . . .

Here, you discover the differences between the two main disciplines of horseback riding: Western and English. I also give you details on types of saddles and bridles and provide you with a primer on how to dress when you ride. You can be ready in no time!

Chapter 6

Off into the Sunset: Western Riding

A lmost all people, no matter how little they know about horses or horse-back riding, are aware of the Western discipline. Western riding is the stuff of cowboys, Hollywood westerns, and sprawling ranches in the West. It's hard to be alive today and not have seen a photo or film of someone riding Western.

In this chapter, I tell you about the discipline of Western riding and how it came to be. I also describe how riders around the world use this type of riding today. (Head to Chapter 7 if you're interested in finding out about English riding.)

Looking at the Nitty-Gritty of Western Riding

Western riding is as American as apple pie. A style of riding that developed in the 1800s, Western riding was initially used by cowhands on large ranches. Since then, this discipline, influenced by the Mexican *charro* (cowboy) tradition, has spread throughout not only the rest of the Americas but also the entire world. Europeans have embraced Western riding over the last 20 years.

In the following sections, I explain key elements of Western riding, including its tack, apparel, and horses. I also describe the uses of Western riding and cover the basics of Western riding mechanics.

Uses

Although Western riding developed as a working discipline for ranchers and cowhands dealing with livestock and the open range, the discipline has taken on new forms in today's modern world. Ranchers and livestock tenders still use Western as it was originally intended, but all kinds of other people ride Western, too.

In the U.S., Western riding is the most popular of all the disciplines, probably because of the comfort and security it lends to the rider — a factor that appeals to many beginners. It's the discipline of choice for many trail riders and casual pleasure riders. It's also a popular show discipline, and it appears in a variety of classes in the horse show ring. (I cover shows and other Western riding activities later in this chapter.)

Tack and apparel

Western riding encompasses use of a Western saddle, saddle pad, and Western-style bridle:

- **Saddle:** The Western saddle is the key to Western riding, and it's made up of a deep seat, a high *pommel* (the front of the saddle's seat) and *cantle* (the back of the seat), a horn, and large *fenders* (the flaps of leather that attach to the stirrups). This design is meant to help hold the rider securely in the saddle when the horse is making abrupt turns and stops. It's also supposed to provide a comfortable ride for long hours in the saddle. The horn was originally used as a place to tie the end of a rope, with the other end being attached to a cow. See Chapter 8 for a diagram of a Western saddle.

- **Saddle pad:** Western saddle pads are most often rectangular in shape, and they provide a leather support at the *withers* (where the horse's shoulders meet between the base of the neck and the back). See Chapter 8 for more information on Western saddle pads.

- **Bridle:** Western bridles feature a browband with a one-ear or two ear design. See Chapter 9 for more details on Western bridles.

Western apparel is more casual than English and reflects the working heritage of the Western discipline. Western riders typically wear blue jeans and boots as well as cowboy hats. Check out Figure 6-1 to get an idea of what Western riders look like. For more details on Western riding apparel, see Chapter 10.

Figure 6-1:
Western
riders wear
casual
apparel and
use deep
saddles.

The horses

Horses in separate disciplines receive different training. The Western horse is expected to carry her head and neck lower and to jog (see Chapter 14) and lope (Chapter 15) more slowly than an English horse trots and canters. Western horses are also trained to be ridden with the reins in one hand and so know how to steer with neck reining (see Chapter 13).

Horses for Western riding often have a certain body type. They tend to be smaller than English horses, a bit stockier and built *downhill,* which means the point of their withers (where the shoulders come together) is lower than the point of their hips.

Although you can ride any breed of horse in a Western saddle, certain breeds appear most often in the Western discipline. These breeds include the Quarter Horse, Paint, and Appaloosa. Other breeds, such as Arabians and Morgans, also show up in Western tack. Check out Chapter 2 for an introduction to different breeds and a diagram of a horse.

The ride

The Western discipline has a distinct look that people throughout the world recognize. Western riding involves a Western saddle (which I describe earlier in this chapter) and consists of a deep seat and balanced position. The saddle's deep seat provides security for the rider. Unlike English hunt seat riders, Western riders sit upright when they ride the faster gaits instead of leaning forward at the hips.

Western riding is about more than just the saddle. Unlike English riders, Western riders hold the reins with one hand. This method enables them to have a free hand (usually the right) for roping and other tasks performed on horseback.

See Chapters 13, 14, and 15 for more information on Western riding positions.

Checking Out Western Riding Activities

Western riding lends itself to a wide array of activities, and I describe a few of the most popular ones in the following sections. This comfortable and secure discipline is a popular choice for beginning riders, who tend to find it easier to pick up than English. This situation isn't surprising, because basic Western requires less physical stamina than English riding. After all, the Western discipline was designed to be easy on the rider.

Hitting the trail

Trail riding is probably the most popular use for the Western discipline. The design of the Western saddle and the ease of the Western riding style lend themselves to long hours on horseback through the wilderness. With longer stirrups that make the position easier on the knees and fenders that move freely with the rider's legs as the horse goes up and down hills, Western is a natural way of riding for those people who want to explore the countryside.

See Figure 6-2 for a photo of a rider enjoying the trail in a Western saddle. Western trail riders typically wear helmets, like the one on the rider in the photo, or cowboy hats. Chapter 21 has full details on trail riding.

Figure 6-2:
Trail riding
is the most
popular
form of
Western
riding.

Horsing around at shows

Shows are a popular activity among serious Western riders, who participate in a variety of events designed specifically for their discipline. The breeds you see most often in Western shows are the Quarter Horse, Paint, and Appaloosa, although many Western events are open to all breeds. Morgans, Arabians, and several other breeds have Western classes within their own single-breed shows.

Western classes at horse shows consist of events in which you can show off the Western horse at her best. Take a look:

- ✓ **Western pleasure classes:** These classes illustrate the slow, smooth gaits and short strides of the Western horse. (See Figure 6-3 for a photo of a Western pleasure horse and rider.) Horse-and-rider teams that participate in Western pleasure are judged on the horse's smooth way of going and head carriage.

- ✓ **Horsemanship classes:** Here, your Western horse illustrates her precision and obedience to nearly invisible cues from the rider.

- ✓ **Western equitation classes:** These classes emphasize the rider's abilities.

Figure 6-3:
A Western
pleasure
rider shows
off the
horse's
smooth
gaits.

You don't have to ride to show Western. Entrants in showmanship and halter classes handle their horses from the ground, showing them off to the judges:

- **Showmanship:** The handler is judged on how well he or she presents the horse to the judge. This presentation involves moving the horse at the judge's direction.

- **Halter classes:** In these classes, the horse is judged on how well she's physically put together. The horse is compared to a breed *standard,* which is essentially a blueprint of the ideal horse of that breed.

Even though you don't use a Western saddle in showmanship and halter classes because no one rides the horses, Western-style show halters adorn the heads of horses in these classes and handlers dress in Western apparel.

Some shows also reveal the speed and heart of the Western horse. *Gymkhana,* a general term for classes in which the horse is timed against a clock, consists of having horses race around poles or barrels.

Reining is another popular event with Western riders; it shows off the obedience and athletic ability of the Western horse. Reiners perform a pattern in a show arena at a lope, illustrating such complicated maneuvers as *sliding stops* (the horse keeps her back legs still as she slides to a stop), *lead changes* (the horse switches from leading with one front leg to another while loping), and *rollbacks* (the horse pivots on her hind end to change direction).

For more information on shows, see Chapter 22.

Working with cattle

Western riding was originally created for and by those who worked with cattle. The horn on the Western saddle serves several purposes, including serving as leverage for riders on horses who are separating cattle from the herd. So it's not surprising that this discipline is still considered the only way to ride when dealing with cattle.

Ranchers out in the American West still ride horses to move their livestock, and the cowhands who do this work ride Western. Moving cows to and from their spring and fall pastures is only one of their tasks. Cowhands also separate cattle from the herd, fix miles of fence that need mending, and rope cattle for branding — all from the back of a horse. Figure 6-4 shows a ranch hand working cattle in a Western saddle.

Figure 6-4: Ranchers ride Western when they handle cattle.

Likewise, people who compete in cow classes at competitive events employ the Western discipline. *Cow classes* consist of

- **Cutting:** Removing a cow from the herd
- **Roping:** Lassoing a cow at a gallop
- **Steer daubing:** Marking a designated cow with paint while on horseback
- **Reined cow horse competitions:** Working with a cow along a fence line

These events mirror the working aspect of ranch hands of both today and yesteryear.

Chapter 7

Not Just for the Brits: English Riding

In This Chapter

▶ Focusing on English riding fundamentals

▶ Recognizing English subdisciplines

*E*uropeans have been riding horses for centuries, both in battle and for sport. The English riding discipline, most prevalent in Europe during modern times, is closely associated with the elite. Prince Charles and Camilla ride this discipline, as do all the rich British people in Hollywood movies and riders who jump. This discipline is also featured in all the equestrian events at the Olympics.

In this chapter, I tell you about the sport of English riding and its main subdisciplines of hunt seat and dressage. I also describe how riders around the world use this type of riding today. (Check out Chapter 6 to read about Western riding.)

Examining the Basics of English Riding

English riding was the original cavalry style of riding in Europe (with some modifications). In the 1600s, this riding style morphed out of the military saddles and was adopted by the British elite. They rode this style to fox hunt, a favorite sport of wealthy English folk. Regular people also hunted foxes and used the English saddle.

In the 1650s, this style of riding came to the United States with British transplants. Today, it's a popular discipline with serious riders throughout the world. In the following sections, I describe English riding's uses, tack and apparel, and horses.

Uses

Besides the chance to indulge in fantasies of wealth and sophistication, what can English offer you? Well, English riders often compete in the show ring because this style of riding lends itself to competitive events (Chapter 22 can fill you in on shows). And if you want your horse to fly over fences, English is your best bet. Despite the focus on showing, many English riders also enjoy *hacking* (riding on the trail), as you can see in Figure 7-1.

Tack and apparel

You can do English riding in two types of saddles: hunt seat (also known as an *all-purpose saddle* or a *forward-seat saddle*) and dressage. These saddles are generally known as *flat saddles*, which distinguishes them from the deep Western saddles.

Each saddle designed for English style riding serves a unique purpose, and the one you choose depends on whether you want to jump or ride dressage. Protocol dictates that the horse wears a contoured pad underneath the hunt seat saddle and a light square pad under the dressage saddle. (See Chapter 8 for full details on saddles and saddle pads.)

Figure 7-1:
An English rider enjoys a hack on the trail.

The bridles that English riders use typically consist of a browband and noseband, with the option of adding accessories (which have nifty names like *flash* or *gag*). The reins that attach to English bridles are often braided.

English riders in the two subdisciplines I discuss here wear similar apparel when schooling, but they get dress differently for the show ring. The clothing riders wear in the subdisciplines reflects the traditions associated with each particular style of riding:

- **Hunt seat apparel:** This getup consists of breeches, tall boots, a "rat-catcher" shirt, and a tailored jacket. A helmet finishes off the ensemble.

- **Dressage apparel:** Lower level dressage riders typically wear the same apparel as hunt seat riders, but in the upper levels, they dress very differently. White breeches, tall boots, a white shirt, a dark jacket with tails, and a black derby are the formal apparel of the upper level dressage rider.

For more details on English riding apparel, see Chapter 10.

The horses

The type of horse that people use most often in English riding is taller and leaner than its Western counterpart. Ideally, English horses are built *uphill,* meaning that the horse's *withers* (where his shoulders come together) are higher than the point of his hip. (See Chapter 2 for a diagram showing the parts of the horse.) However, horses of all shapes and types, as well as all breeds, may sport English saddles. Generally speaking, the horses you see most often in English tack are Thoroughbreds and Warmbloods, although many Quarter Horses, Paints, Appaloosas are also ridden English.

The training for English horses involves teaching them to be collected and on the bit. *Collected* means that the horse is expected to hold himself a certain way and drive his forward movement from behind. *On the bit* refers to the horse's connection — the line of communication — to the rider's hands through the bridle.

Activities are specific to the subdisciplines. Riders often ask horses in hunt seat to jump, so their training includes this activity (see Chapter 16 for details on jumping). Horses in dressage are trained to perform dressage maneuvers, such as the *piaffe,* in which the horse essentially trots in place. The next section gives more information on these English subdisciplines.

Brushing Up on the Basic English Styles

The basic English styles of hunt seat and dressage have more elements in common than differences. Yet knowing these subtleties is important, and I describe them in the following sections. The English discipline you choose to ride determines the types of activities you perform on horseback.

Each of the English subdisciplines involves a slightly different position in the saddle, yet each requires that the rider be well-balanced. English riders also use two hands to hold the reins and have more contact with the horse's mouth through the reins than Western riders do. (See Chapters 13, 14, and 15 for more information on the mechanics of English riding.)

Jumping around in hunt seat and riding on the flat

Hunt seat gets its name from the tradition of fox hunting, from which it was born. Keeping up with the hounds and clearing obstacles were essential aspects of the fox hunt, so hunt seat saddles are designed primarily for jumping; hunt seat riders, with hardly an exception, participate in this activity.

Riders who use hunt seat sit in a slightly forward position, meaning they lean forward at the hips when they ride. This leaning puts them in a prime position for jumping, because putting weight over the horse's withers frees up the horse's hindquarters. Hunt seat riders also ride with their stirrups shorter than riders in dressage do, again to assist in jumping. (For more information about jumping, see Chapter 16.) Figure 7-2 shows a hunt seat rider in hunt seat apparel riding a horse in hunt seat tack.

A horse trained for jumping and for *the flat* (hunt-seat riding done without jumping) is taught to respond to his rider's cues to speed up and slow down at each gait. This training comes in especially handy between jumps, when the rider is responsible for helping the horse approach the jump in the best way possible.

Beginning riders who start with hunt seat often find riding a bit more difficult than Western riders do. Novice English riders must rely a lot on their balance to stay in the saddle because English saddles are flatter than Western saddles. On the plus side, riders who start out in English often develop their balance and riding muscles very quickly.

Figure 7-2:
A mounted
hunt seat
rider moves
among
fences
intended
for jumps.

Making moves in dressage

Dressage — the French word for *training* — is a very old discipline. This style of riding has its roots in ancient Greece, and it came into its own during the Renaissance. Stemming from European military maneuvers performed on horseback for centuries, dressage is sometimes called *horse ballet* because of its disciplined yet graceful movements.

Some of the maneuvers, or *movements,* in dressage include

- The *passage,* a slow-motion trot
- The *half-pass,* in which the horse travels on a diagonal line, keeping his body almost parallel with the arena fence while stepping forward and sideways with each stride
- The *pirouette,* a 360-degree turn without moving forward or backward

Accomplishing these movements with great precision takes years of training for both horse and rider.

Dressage riders have a more upright position in the saddle than hunt seat riders, sitting more deeply to "drive" the horse with their legs. They hold the reins with two hands, as do all English riders. Figure 7-3 shows a dressage rider in dressage apparel riding a horse in dressage tack.

Figure 7-3:
A horse and rider perform in dressage.

Dressage has seven levels that represent different stages of a horse's training. These levels are Novice, Training, 2nd, 3rd, 4th, Prix St. George, and Grand Prix. Novice level is for horses who are just learning dressage and are worked only at the walk and trot. As a horse improves, he progresses toward Grand Prix.

Novice riders who begin their training in dressage quickly develop their balance, timing, and feel of the horse. Dressage is an excellent way to start riding. It can be challenging for any rider, however, especially a beginner. This riding style is hard work!

Chapter 8

Dressing Up Horses with Saddles

· ·

In This Chapter

▶ Checking out the basic makeup of all saddles

▶ Understanding saddle differences

▶ Discovering details about saddle pads

▶ Finding out about fitting

· ·

*T*he saddle is probably the most important piece of equipment in horse-back riding, especially if you're a new rider. The saddle helps keep you on the horse's back, makes your ride more comfortable, and assists you in finding the right position when you ride. Saddles also help the horse. A saddle that fits properly distributes the rider's weight evenly over the horse's back, preventing injury.

When you're taking lessons, your instructor provides you with the saddle and pad you need for the horse you're riding. If you decide to buy your own horse someday, which I discuss in Chapter 18, you can find this equipment at a tack store.

In this chapter, I tell you about both Western and English saddles and the differences in their design. I also discuss saddle pads and the importance of fitting saddles correctly.

Going Over the Basic Makeup of a Saddle

Regardless of whether a saddle is for Western, hunt seat, or dressage riding, its basic construction is the same. Following is a description of the basic parts of a saddle that are common to all types:

✔ **Tree:** The tree of the saddle is essentially the saddle's skeleton. Everything on the saddle is built around the tree, which can be wood, fiberglass, or another synthetic material. The size and shape of the tree is different for each kind of saddle. (Treeless saddles are also available; see the nearby sidebar for details.)

Unframed: Treeless saddles

A recent invention in the world of saddles (I say *recent* because saddles have been around for centuries) is the *treeless* saddle. This type of saddle, which is available in both Western and English styles, doesn't have a wooden or fiberglass frame like other saddles do. In fact, it doesn't have a tree at all — hence the name!

The theory behind treeless saddles is that they move more easily with the horse than a treed saddle does. This flexibility allows unrestricted movement and reduces the likelihood that the horse's back will become sore. Unlike treed saddles, which must be fitted to a particular horse, treeless saddles are one-size-fits all; thus, these saddles are particularly useful for horses who are hard to fit.

From the outside, a treeless saddle looks just like a regular saddle. Although some riders say they feel a difference when they ride in a treeless saddle, others can't tell a thing. Regardless, treeless saddles are fine for beginners; the rider's level of experience makes no difference.

Debate rages throughout the horse community over whether treeless saddles are better for the horse. Some people believe these saddles don't provide enough support and can harm a horse's back, claiming they don't distribute the rider's weight properly. Opponents disagree, saying that the lack of a tree makes the saddle more comfortable for the horse.

The width of the tree determines whether a given saddle fits a horse. Horses with wide shoulders need saddles with wide trees; horses with narrow shoulders need narrow trees. For more information, see the later section titled "Fitting a horse."

- **Pommel:** The pommel is the front of the saddle.
- **Seat:** The seat is the center of the saddle where you sit.
- **Cantle:** The back of the seat of the saddle is the cantle.
- **Stirrups:** All riding saddles have stirrups for the rider's feet. The *fenders* (Western) or *leathers* (English) are the part of the stirrup that attaches to the saddle.

Leather is the most common outer material for saddles, although synthetic material is also catching on. But that's where the similarities end. The shape of the tree, the style of stirrups, and the general shape of the saddle determine whether the saddle's Western or English.

The Heavy Hitters: Western Saddles

Western saddles are easy to tell apart from English saddles (which I cover later in this chapter). Their size and shape varies considerably from the English saddle, as does their purpose. Every Western saddle has

- ✔ A deep seat
- ✔ A high pommel
- ✔ A *horn,* or part of the saddle that projects upward from the pommel
- ✔ A high cantle
- ✔ Wide fenders

Some Western saddles have a flank cinch in addition to a front cinch. *Cinches* are the straps that hold the saddle on the horse. The stirrup is usually made from wood and covered with leather or synthetic material if the rest of the saddle is synthetic. See the earlier "Going Over the Basic Makeup of a Saddle" section for info on saddle parts.

Western saddles are notoriously heavier than English saddles, and they can weigh anywhere from 15 to 50 pounds, depending on the type of saddle, what it's made from, and what kinds of adornment it features.

Most Western saddles have *tooling,* another word for decorations etched into the saddle leather. Some saddles have very elaborate tooling; others have barely any at all. Western saddles also have *conchos,* or metal studs placed in various positions on the saddle. Conchos often serve as anchors for *saddle strings,* leather straps that hang from the saddle and can be used to tie on accessories such as rain ponchos, saddle bags, and other items. In fancy Western show saddles, conchos are sterling silver.

Most Western saddles come in different tree (frame) sizes:

- ✔ Semi–Quarter Horse trees, the narrowest of the three, are for horses with high withers and narrow shoulders.
- ✔ Quarter Horse trees are medium width and are for horses with medium-sized withers and shoulders.
- ✔ Full Quarter Horse trees are the widest of all and are meant for horses with low withers and wide shoulders.

 The actual measurement of each tree width varies from brand to brand, so unfortunately, no tree-width standard exists. The only way to know whether a saddle fits a particular horse for certain is to try it on the horse's back. I explain how to fit saddles later in this chapter.

To the untrained eye, all Western saddles look basically alike. They may vary in color depending on the stain of the leather (anything from black to pale tan) or the dyed color of the synthetic material, but overall, telling one type of Western saddle from another can be difficult.

The truth is that Western saddles come in several different styles, depending on their projected use. Each of these saddles has features that make it a better choice for certain activities. The most common Western saddle types are the pleasure saddle, the barrel racing saddle, the roping saddle, and the trail saddle; I cover them all in the following sections.

If you're just beginning to ride, any one of these saddles can suit you fine. As you progress in your riding and get involved in competitive equine activities, you may want to choose another saddle as your primary one. Your instructor or trainer can advise you on the type of saddle most suited to your activity.

The pleasure saddle

Pleasure saddles are used not only for trail riding but also for show. These saddles are usually lighter in weight than other Western saddles because they don't need to be as strong as working saddles (such as barrel racing or roping saddles).

Riders using a pleasure saddle find themselves balanced toward the back of the saddle. This design gives the rider more comfort when riding on trail. Check out a pleasure saddle in Figure 8-1.

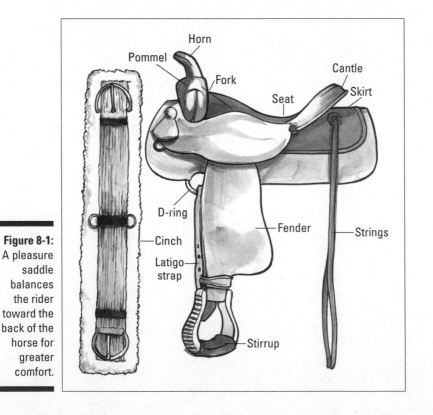

Figure 8-1:
A pleasure saddle balances the rider toward the back of the horse for greater comfort.

The barrel racing saddle

Barrel racing saddles are so named because their design makes them a top choice for gymkhana riders, where sharp turns around poles or barrels at high speed are the norm.

Barrel racing saddles have a very deep seat to help keep the rider in the saddle when the horse is running fast and turning sharply. The horn on a barrel racing saddle is higher, too, giving the rider something to grab onto during turns if needed. Many barrel racing saddles also have a seat made from rough material, which gives the rider better grip. Figure 8-2 shows a barrel racing saddle.

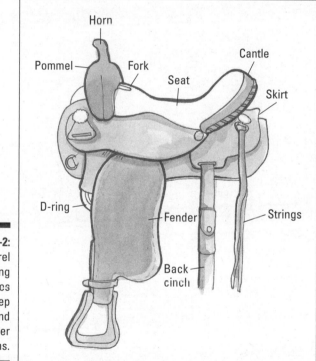

Figure 8-2: Barrel racing saddles have deep seats and higher horns.

The roping saddle

As the name suggests, roping saddles (see Figure 8-3) are a favorite of riders who rope cattle. Here's why:

✔ The saddle is designed to help balance the rider when he or she is standing up in the saddle, throwing the rope.

✔ After roping the calf, the rider ties the other end of the rope to the horn of the saddle; the saddle's horn and tree are made to be very strong so the pull of the calf doesn't break them.

✔ The *swells* of the saddle — that is, the contoured shape of it — are made so the rope has the least possible leverage on the horn when a calf is at the end of it.

✔ The seat is rough to help keep the rider in place.

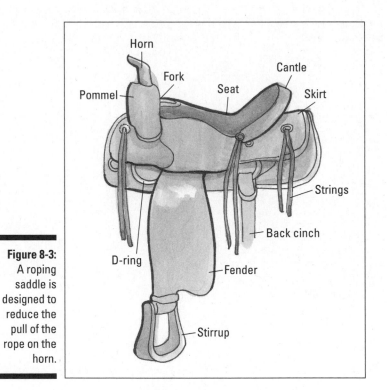

Figure 8-3:
A roping saddle is designed to reduce the pull of the rope on the horn.

The trail saddle

Although all Western saddles are designed for comfort on long rides, the trail saddle (see Figure 8-4) pays particular attention to this feature. The seat is deep to help keep the rider secure in various types of terrain. Many trail saddles give wider swing to the *fenders* (parts of the stirrup attached to the saddle) to enable riders to put their legs behind them when going uphill and in front of them when going downhill.

Trail saddles are also designed to provide maximum comfort to the horse when worn for long periods of time. They're lighter than many other Western saddles and allow the horse to cool off more quickly because they have shorter skirts.

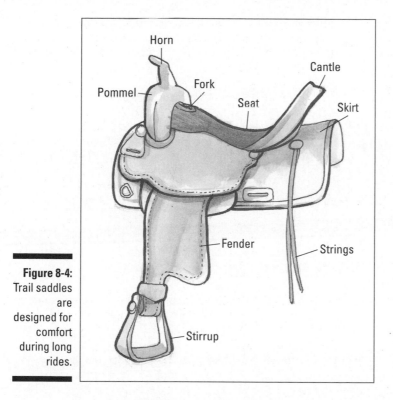

Figure 8-4:
Trail saddles are designed for comfort during long rides.

On the Smaller Side: English Saddles

English saddles are considerably smaller than Western saddles, and they can be harder to stay in for many riders because their seats aren't as deep. However, if you learn to ride in an English saddle, you're unlikely to have problems staying on a horse in a Western saddle. English riders rely a lot on balance to stay mounted.

"Going Over the Basic Makeup of a Saddle," earlier in this chapter, can tell you more about parts. All English saddles have

- A pommel
- A cantle
- A *flap,* or large piece of leather that rests under rider's leg
- A *skirt,* or piece of leather that covers the stirrup bar
- *Panels,* or cushioning between the saddle's seat and the horse

To keep the saddle on the horse, a *girth* is added. Separate from the saddle, it attaches to either side of the saddle and goes under the horse's belly.

Some English saddles have knee rolls, which help keep the rider's leg in the proper position. The shape of the saddle differs, depending on the type of English saddle, and the depth of the seat can vary. On English saddles, the stirrup, called an *iron,* is metal, usually stainless steel.

English saddles come in different tree sizes for horses with different shoulder widths: narrow, medium, and wide. They vary from brand to brand.

The colors of English saddles are generally the same — dark brown — although many dressage saddles also come in black. Synthetic English saddles are usually black as well, even if they're not dressage saddles.

In the following sections, I describe three popular English saddles: the all-purpose saddle, the close-contact saddle, and the dressage saddle.

The all-purpose saddle

Hunt seat riders who do a lot of trail riding but also like to do jumping and *flatwork* (basically working in the arena without jumping) often prefer an all-purpose saddle.

All-purpose saddles (you can see one in Figure 8-5) have a flap that's cut far forward to accommodate riders who want to jump but don't do it often enough to require a close-contact jumping saddle (see the next section). These saddles are more comfortable for trail riding than a close-contact saddle because the seat is slightly deeper and the rider's position is less forward.

The close-contact saddle

Hunt seat riders may use close-contact saddles. These saddles do as their name suggests: They allow close contact between the horse and rider. The rider is better able to cue the horse with his or her legs because the saddle provides very little interference.

Riders use close-contact saddles for jumping. The seat is shallow, which enables the rider to lift him- or herself out of it when going over an obstacle. The design of the saddle also helps the rider stay in a forward position, which is necessary for jumping. Check out a close-contact saddle in Figure 8-6.

The dressage saddle

People who study the discipline of dressage usually ride in a dressage saddle (see Figure 8-7), although some riders at the lower levels use an all-purpose saddle instead (see the earlier section on this saddle).

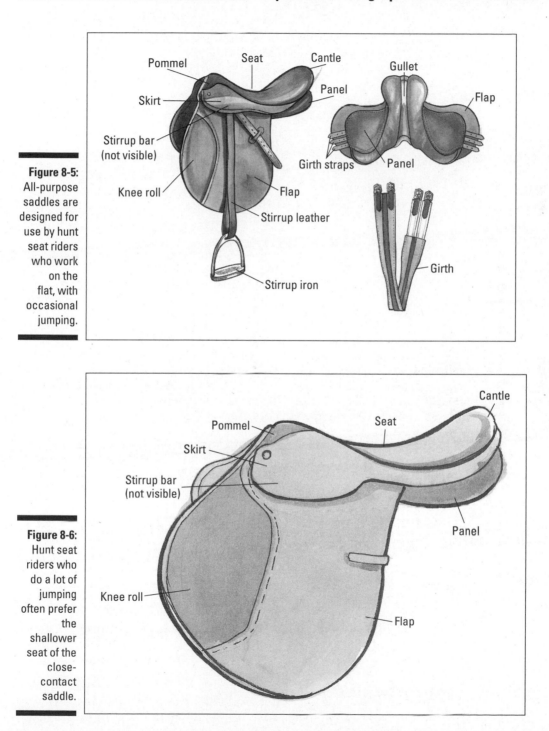

Figure 8-5:
All-purpose saddles are designed for use by hunt seat riders who work on the flat, with occasional jumping.

Figure 8-6:
Hunt seat riders who do a lot of jumping often prefer the shallower seat of the close-contact saddle.

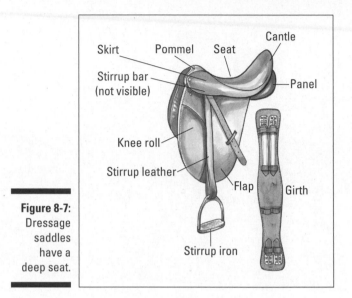

Skirt Pommel Seat Cantle

Stirrup bar
(not visible)

Panel

Knee roll

Stirrup leather

Flap Girth

Figure 8-7:
Dressage
saddles
have a
deep seat.

Stirrup iron

Dressage saddles are designed with a deep seat that allows the rider to sit more deeply on the horse, a necessity for this discipline (see Chapters 13, 14, and 15 for more information on the dressage position). Riders wear the stirrups on a dressage saddle slightly longer than those of an all-purpose or close contact saddle, although stirrups still have to be short enough for riders to effectively cue with their legs.

Dressage saddles feature flaps that have a squared off shape rather than the rounder shape of all-purpose or close-contact saddles. Because the seat is deeper, the pommel and cantle are higher too.

Setting Yourself Up with Saddle Pads

All saddle types in this chapter require saddle pads. These pads fit between the saddle and the horse to protect a horse's back from chafing and saddle sores and to aid in distributing the rider's weight.

Western, all-purpose, close-contact, and dressage saddles all use specific pads because of differences in the shape of the saddles as well as in the pressure points on the horse's back. Here's a rundown of how the pads vary (see Figure 8-8):

✓ **Western pads:** Pads for Western saddles are usually about an inch thick or thicker, and they're made from synthetic fleece, wool, or felt. Some contain other synthetic materials designed to provide more cushion between the horse's back and the saddle. Wool or synthetic fleece pads come in a variety of patterns and colors. If you like Native American designs, you can also use a synthetic or wool pad and put a thin Navajo-style blanket on top of it.

✔ **All-purpose and close-contact pads:** Hunt seat riders typically use white synthetic fleece pads underneath all-purpose or close-contact saddles, which are basically the same shape as the pad. These pads are made from fleece or another synthetic material and are designed to help reduce pressure on the horse's back. They're usually about an inch thick, and they typically come in white or off-white, although you may be able to find other colors.

✔ **Dressage pads:** Dressage riders usually use square, quilted, cotton pads. Dressage pads don't provide much cushion between the horse and saddle, although they do serve to protect the saddle from sweat and prevent chafing on the horse's back. These pads are about half an inch thick, and they usually come in white, although solid colors and even fun patterns are showing up more often in these pads.

Figure 8-8: Western, all-purpose, and dressage saddle pads are specially designed for use in corresponding saddles.

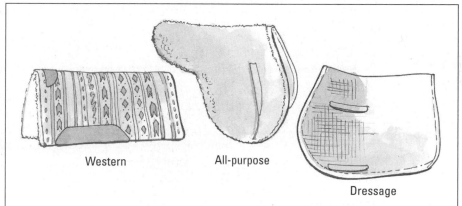

Western   All-purpose

Dressage

Playing Matchmaker as You Fit Saddles

Making a match between horse and saddle takes skill. Although some horses have easy-to-fit backs, others can be tricky. Fitting the rider is a bit easier, although seat size and other subtle nuances can mean the difference between a comfortable ride and a more painful one.

Fitting a horse

One of the most difficult aspects of horsemanship is making sure the saddle fits the horse. Because horses' backs differ from one another, you can't just toss any old saddle on a given horse. Doing so only gets you a horse with a sore back, impaired performance, and even a bad attitude. Ensuring that the horse is wearing a saddle that fits right takes practice.

If you're taking lessons on a school horse, your instructor should have enough concern for his or her horses that saddle-fitting is a priority. Hopefully, your instructor is using saddles that fit the horses in his or her care. (For info on choosing an instructor, see Chapter 3.)

If you're shopping for a saddle for your own horse (could happen someday! — see Chapter 18), get the help of an experienced horse person — preferably a horse trainer — to find the right saddle for your horse.

In the following sections, I tell you how to fit Western and English saddles on a horse.

Western saddles

To make sure that a Western saddle fits correctly, follow these steps:

1. **Place the saddle on the horse's back with a 1-inch-or-so-thick saddle pad underneath it (see Figure 8-9).**

2. **Tighten the cinch so that the cinch is snug but comfortable.**

3. **Have a rider sit in the saddle with his or her feet in the stirrups.**

4. **Examine the width of the saddle's tree, or frame, as it sits on the horse; compare it to the shape of the horse's back.**

Figure 8-9:
Fit a Western saddle with a pad already on the horse.

You can place your fingers sideways (on a flat hand) between the saddle and the top of the horse's shoulder to help determine the width of the tree. Be sure you can fit at least three fingers between the arch of the pommel and the horse's withers (Chapter 2 includes a diagram showing the withers and other parts of the horse). If the fit is so tight that you can't squeeze your fingers between the saddle and the top of the horse's shoulder, the tree is too wide for your horse. If you can put your entire hand between the saddle and the top of the horse's shoulder, the tree is too narrow.

English saddles

To determine whether an English saddle fits a particular horse, follow these steps:

1. **Put the saddle on the horse without using a saddle pad.**

2. **Tighten the girth so that the saddle is comfortably secure.**

3. **Have someone sit in the saddle with his or her feet in the stirrups.**

4. **Using a flat hand, slide your fingers underneath the pommel, near the horse's withers.**

   Your fingers should fit comfortably between the horse and saddle. Be sure that you can place at least three fingers between the horse's withers and the arch below the pommel. See Chapter 2 for a diagram showing the withers and other parts of the horse.

5. **Have a helper lift the horse's left foreleg and pull it forward while your fingers are between the top of the horse's shoulder blade and the pommel.**

   As the horse's shoulder moves, check that the saddle doesn't impede shoulder movement. Perform the same test on the horse's right side.

6. **Stand behind the horse and look through the saddle.**

   If the saddle fits, you should see a tunnel of light shining through. If you don't see any light, the saddle is too snug. Also, make sure that the saddle isn't too long for the horse. The seat panel shouldn't reach past the main part of the back onto the loins.

After checking the saddle for size, you can put the saddle on with a saddle pad underneath and get ready to ride (see Figure 8-10). Chapter 11 tells you how to saddle up.

Fitting yourself

After determining that a saddle fits a particular horse (see the preceding section), your next task is to make sure it fits *you*. If it doesn't, you'll be uncomfortable and off balance when you ride. Luckily, finding a saddle that suits you is much easier than finding one that suits the horse. I explain how to fit yourself on Western and English saddles in the following sections.

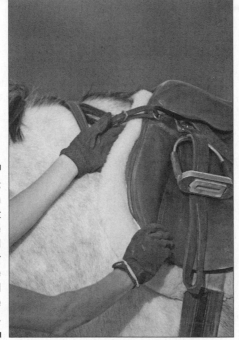

Figure 8-10:
With English saddles, put on the saddle pad only after you've determined that the saddle fits.

The seats of Western and English saddles are measured in inches. If you're taking lessons in a particular saddle that you like, find out the inch measurement of the seat. Armed with this information, you can rule out saddles that don't have the same seat measurement. You can also sit in different saddles in a tack shop and take note of which size suits you best. Ask whether a saddle fitter is on staff to help you determine fit, because deciding on your own can be tough.

Here's how to find a saddle that fits your body:

- **Western saddles:** Adjust the stirrups to the proper length (see Chapter 11 for information on how to do so). Sit in the saddle with your feet in the stirrups, and judge the comfort of the saddle. You should have about 4 inches between the front of your body and the pommel. Your derriere needs to rest against the base of the cantle but not be squashed against the rise of the cantle. Ride in the saddle for half an hour to determine whether it still feels comfortable after you've been in it awhile.

- **English saddles:** Sit in the seat with your stirrups at the length you prefer (see Chapter 11 for information on determining the right stirrup length) and gauge how comfortable the saddle feels. You should have about 4 inches in front of your body and 4 inches behind it. Ride in the saddle while a trainer or another person experienced in English riding watches you and points out any apparent problems with the saddle.

Chapter 9

Getting a Heads-Up on Bridles

A crucial piece of equipment when you're riding — in addition to saddles, which I cover in Chapter 8 — is the bridle. This horse headgear serves as an important line of communication between you and the horse. With the bridle, you can give instructions that would otherwise be hard to get across.

In this chapter, I go over the basic makeup of a bridle. I also show you Western and English bridles and bits. (For info on how to put a bridle on a horse, see Chapter 11.)

Breaking Down the Basic Parts of a Bridle

A *bridle* is the headgear you use on the horse during riding. Each riding discipline has its own style of bridle, and styles vary within those. Figure 9-1 shows basic Western and English bridles.

Your riding instructor can tell you which bridle to use on your lesson horse. The training level and disposition of the horse you're riding determine what kind of bridle he should wear. Your skill level also has something to do with the choice of bridle, because beginning riders need styles that are easier to handle. A standard-sized bridle can fit most horses; ponies and draft horses need bridles sized especially for them.

A bridle consists of the following basic parts:

- ✔ **A bit (or bit substitute):** The piece that goes inside the horse's mouth (or a substitute for a bit, such as a *hackamore,* which puts pressure on the horse's nose; see "Nosing around hackamores," later in this chapter)

- ✔ **A headstall:** The part that goes over the ears and connects to the bit; the headstall includes the crownpiece and cheekpiece (which, naturally, go over the horse's crown and cheeks); the straps have buckles on them and are adjustable

- ✔ **Reins:** The leather straps that the rider holds, connecting to the bit

One of the most overwhelming and confusing aspects of the horse world is the subject of bits. Go into any tack store and you'll see so many bits, your head will spin. Over the centuries, horse people seem to have tried to invent a bit for every riding problem ever imagined.

The purpose of a bit (which is usually metal but can also be rubber or another synthetic material) is to apply pressure to the horse's mouth and thus send the message to stop, slow down, turn, and so on. The shape of the mouthpiece determines how you apply that pressure. Some bits are mild, meaning that they apply minimal pressure. Others are harsh, demanding the horse's undivided attention by stricter means.

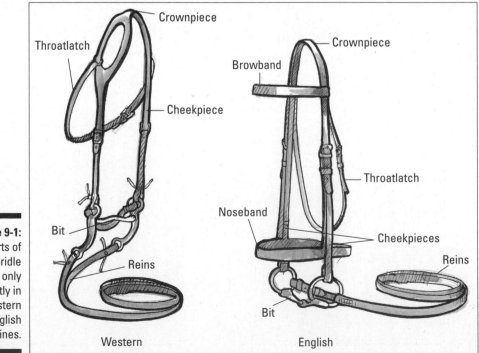

Figure 9-1: The parts of the bridle vary only slightly in the Western and English disciplines.

Bitting a horse (choosing the right bit for a given horse) is a very complex process that should be left to professionals. Using the wrong bit, or one you aren't skilled enough to use, can harm a horse. Should the time come when you need to choose a bit for your horse, consult a professional trainer for advice on which bit to use.

Gearing Up with Western Bridles and Bits

You can see all kinds of Western bridles in the tack store: leather bridles, synthetic bridles, black bridles, brown bridles, purple bridles. Despite all the differences in color and material, the basic designs are the same. In the following sections, I describe several popular Western headstalls, bits, and hackamores.

Looking at Western headstalls

Western bridles consist of a headstall and reins. If the bit you use has a *curb shank* (a long, curved piece between the bit and the part where the reins attach; see the next section), then a curb chain or strap under the chin is included.

Facing up to hard mouths

If you've ever ridden a horse who pulls back when you try to slow him down or completely ignores your rein cues, you have a horse with a hard mouth. The term *hard mouth* conjures up images of horses with concrete jaws and steel gums, bracing themselves against a skinny little bit that has no hope of making an impression. In reality, hard mouth is less of a physical issue and more of a training problem. Horses with hard mouths have simply learned to resist the bit instead of giving in to it.

Riders who overuse their hands and don't know how to use their legs when riding tend to cause this problem to start. Hard mouth can even develop in well-trained horses who are constantly exposed to riders who rely too much on their hands for control instead of using their legs and seat. This problem is most common in beginning riders because using the hands, arms, and upper body for control offers a greater feeling of security in controlling the horse. However, don't feel guilty if you're a beginner; even experienced riders can put their horses at risk for developing a hard mouth. These riders sometimes have a habit of *locking* the reins in their hands (holding them tight and not providing any give as the horse moves his head), causing the horse to stiffen against the bit.

A horse with a hard mouth needs to be retrained to be responsive to the bit. If you find yourself riding a horse with a hard mouth, talk to your instructor about how you can help the horse take a different attitude about the bit. The instructor may suggest switching to a different bit and make suggestions on how to teach the horse to respond differently.

The traditional Western bridle consists of a split-ear, double-ear, or browband headstall design with a bit attached. Here are the headstalls (see Figure 9-2):

- ✔ **Split ear:** This bridle is so-called because a strap on the headpiece allows one ear to fit through it. The other ear stays in front of the crownpiece.

- ✔ **Double ear:** Double-ear headstalls have individual straps on the head-piece for each ear.

- ✔ **Browband:** This bridle has a strap that goes across the horse's fore-head, through which the ears protrude.

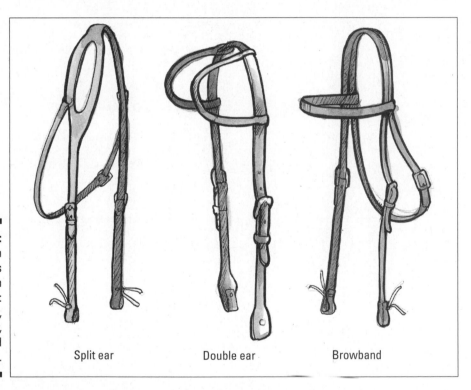

Figure 9-2:
Western headstalls come in three styles: split ear, double ear, and browband.

Split ear   Double ear   Browband

Gaining leverage with Western bits

The most common bits in Western riding are the curb bit and variations on it. Read the following descriptions and refer to Figure 9-3 to see what these three common Western curb bits look like:

- ✔ **Curb bit:** Curb bits have *shanks* (curved pieces between the bit and reins) and a curb chain, and they work by putting leverage on the horse's mouth. This leverage means the rider has to use a much lighter touch on the reins than he or she would with a non-leverage bit. The leverage of the curb bit pulls the horse's muzzle down when the rider applies pressure to the reins.

- **Curb bit with roller:** Some curb bits have rollers attached, which are spinning barrels in the center of the bit. These barrels encourage the horse to salivate and relax the mouth.

- **Tom Thumb bit:** Tom Thumb bits look like snaffle bits (see the upcoming section titled "Directing attention to English bits"), but they have shanks attached to them. They provide the rider with leverage while exerting a bit less pressure on the horse's tongue than the curb bit.

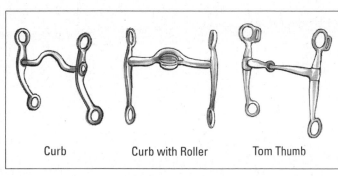

Figure 9-3: Three common Western bits are the curb, curb with roller, and the Tom Thumb.

Curb   Curb with Roller   Tom Thumb

Nosing around hackamores

Hackamores, which are used with Western headstalls, are substitutes for bits. The *hackamore* is essentially a nosepiece that allows the rider to control the horse without placing a bit in the horse's mouth.

A hackamore in untrained hands can be harsh on the horse. Consult a professional trainer before switching to a hackamore — different theories exist about when using a hackamore is appropriate and when it isn't.

Hackamore bridles come in two types (see Figure 9-4):

- **Bosal:** This hackamore is a rolled leather or braided rawhide training device used to school young horses. Attached to a headstall, the bosal goes over the bridge of the horse's nose. Reins are attached underneath.

- **Mechanical:** Used for both training and regular riding, the mechanical hackamore consists of metal shanks attached to a rolled leather noseband. The reins attach to the bottom of the shanks, allowing the rider to control the horse by putting pressure on the nose, chin, and *poll* (the area on the horse's neck just behind the ears). The entire hackamore piece is attached to a Western headstall.

Figure 9-4:
Hackamores
work by
putting
pressure on
the horse's
nose.

Bosal   Mechanical

Examining English Bridles and Bits

English bridles haven't changed much over the centuries. They're almost
always leather, and they come in black, dark brown, and light brown. The bridles vary slightly from one English subdiscipline to the next (see Chapter 8
for general info on English riding). I describe a few common English headstalls and bits in the following sections.

Some levels of dressage don't allow competitors to use certain bits and nose-
bands. If you intend to show in dressage, contact the ruling dressage federation in your country to find out the latest rules.

Discovering English headstalls

English bridles consist of a headstall and reins. The headstall always has a
browband (which goes across the forehead), *throatlatch* (which attaches
under the horse's jowl), and *noseband* (which goes across the nose and
under the jaw). Some English bridles come with special attachments such as
a drop noseband or a flash noseband; these two attachments keep the horse
from opening his mouth and evading the action of the bit.

Two popular English headstalls are dressage and single-rein (see Figure 9-5):

 ✓ **Dressage (double bridle):** Riders at the upper levels of dressage use a
   double bridle, which is similar to a snaffle bridle except the headstall has

an additional cheekpiece to hold another bit (see the next section for info on the snaffle bit). This bridle has two sets of reins, which the rider must use individually because each set corresponds to a different bit.

✔ **Single-rein:** This headstall consists of a single headstall strap, browband, throatlatch, and noseband. The bridle uses only one rein that attaches on one side of the bit, goes over the horse's neck, and attaches to the other side of the bit. Hunt seat riders — and many dressage riders, especially at the lower levels of the sport — use these bridles, often with a snaffle bit.

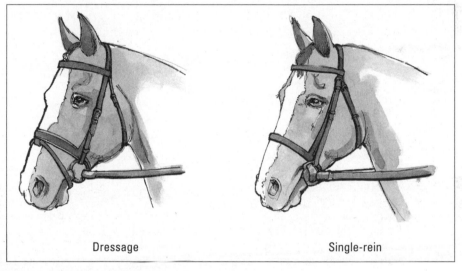

Figure 9-5:
English bridles come in dressage and single-rein varieties.

Dressage   Single-rein

Directing attention to English bits

The snaffle bit and variations on it are the most common bits in English riding. Snaffles come in different thicknesses and with varying cheekpieces, each with a specific effect on the horse's mouth (see Figure 9-6 to see what three common English curb bits look like):

✔ **Snaffle:** This bit, which has a ring on either side, consists of two pieces attached to each other in the middle at a joint. The snaffle bit comes in a variety of widths and mouthpiece styles.

✔ **Weymouth:** This bit is used on double bridles, usually with a separate snaffle bit. The Weymouth features a curb-type mouthpiece (see "Gaining leverage with Western bits") with long shanks and a curb chain.

✔ **Full-cheek snaffle:** This type of bit has large cheekpieces that help keep the mouthpiece in place.

Figure 9-6: Three bits in English riding are the popular snaffle, the Weymouth, and the harsher twisted-wire full-cheek snaffle.

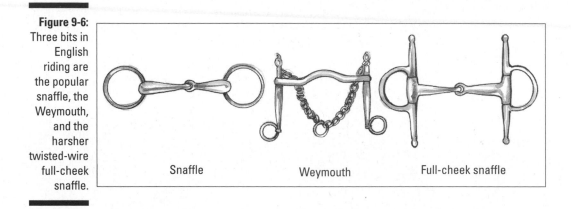

Snaffle   Weymouth   Full-cheek snaffle

Shopping around for bridles and bits

When you're taking riding lessons, your instructor provides the bridle and bit that your lesson horse wears. However, that doesn't mean you shouldn't go bit and bridle shopping — or at least go window shopping for bits and bridles. Who knows? If you get your own horse someday, you'll have to go bit and bridle shopping for real. Use the following sources to get an idea of what different bridles and bits look like:

✔ **Tack and feed stores:** Most communities that have horses also have at least one tack and feed store. These places sell not only food for horses but equipment, too. Take a stroll through the bit and bridle departments and see what's out there. Don't be afraid to touch or pick up the equipment. If you hold it in your hand, you can get a better sense of the effect it must have on the horse (imagine having *that* in your mouth!). Also, if the bit or bridle isn't labeled, ask the sales staff to tell you what the piece of equipment is. Employees in tack stores often enjoy talking about this stuff — most of them are horse people themselves.

✔ **Mail-order catalogs:** The horse world has been blessed with a number of quality mail-order companies that deal exclusively in equine equipment. These catalogs are a great way to study and find out about bits and bridles without salespeople hovering around. See the Appendix for a list of equine mail-order catalogs.

✔ **Consignment shops:** Less common than regular tack and feed stores, equine consignment shops deal almost exclusively in used tack. They often have a great selection of bits because horse owners tend to change bits frequently.

✔ **Other horse owners:** Ask your friends to show you the bits and bridles they use on their horses. Have them explain the equipment to you and why they chose a particular combination. You can discover a lot just by asking other horse people questions. In fact, that's how most horse people learn about tack and equipment.

Chapter 10

Equipping Yourself with Other Important Gear

In This Chapter

▶ Discovering casual riding apparel

▶ Checking out show ring attire

▶ Spurs and whips: Getting the lowdown on artificial aids

A big part of riding is all the great clothes and cool accessories you get to use. Looking the part is important, not only for safety reasons but also because other riders expect it. After all, when you ride a horse, you're keeping a tradition that has existed for thousands of years, and your fellow riders are more likely to take you seriously if you dress like you're part of the club. Riding accessories in the form of artificial aids, such as spurs and whips, can also be crucial for communicating with your horse.

In this chapter, you discover the different types of riding apparel for English and Western riders. You also find out about the artificial aids.

Dressing in High Style

In riding, you have two options within your chosen discipline in terms of dressing: schooling clothes or show apparel. You wear schooling clothes when you're just riding a horse in the arena for practice or are simply out on the trail for a relaxing ride. If you're taking a horse in a show, you wear — naturally — show clothes. You can see big differences in these types of clothing if you pay attention.

In the following sections, I explain the importance of wearing the right riding gear and delve into the details of Western and English attire.

Choosing clothes for safety and comfort

Why do riders wear special clothes, anyway? Won't an oversized t-shirt, shorts, and a pair of sneakers do? Well, no, not unless you want to be unsafe, feel uncomfortable, and give the impression you don't know what you're doing. Riding apparel, whether for Western or English riders, serves a few purposes:

- ✔ It helps you avoid getting caught on tack or having a foot slide through the stirrup.
- ✔ It keeps you free from chafing and saddle sores.
- ✔ It protects you from the whims of Mother Nature.

Here's an overview of how each piece of riding apparel helps riders:

- ✔ **Hats and helmets:** With their wide brims, Western hats protect your face and the top of your head from the sun. In cold weather, Western hats also keep you warm.

   Helmets, which English riders and some Western riders wear, protect your skull from damage should you fall off your horse (which is bound to happen sooner or later). Helmets with visors also protect your face from the sun. If you're trail riding (see Chapter 21), a helmet can keep low tree branches from scratching you.

- ✔ **Riding pants:** Whether jeans (Western) or breeches (English), riding pants are designed to protect your skin from rubbing against unforgiving leather. Breeches also have an elastic component that keeps your knees from being restricted when you're in the stirrups.

- ✔ **Boots:** Riding boots are designed to protect your feet from clumsy hooves fitted with metal shoes should a horse step on your foot. They also keep your foot from getting caught in the stirrup in case you fall off your horse — you don't want to be dragged.

There's no regulation top for riders. Some wear t-shirts, some wear tanks tops, some wear sweatshirts — all depends on the person's preference. Check out Chapter 5 for additional information about dressing appropriately for your safety.

Following tradition: Western dress

The tradition of Western apparel comes from the days of the Old West. Modified somewhat from olden times, this style has changed very little in the last 150 years. In the following sections, I describe Western apparel for both schooling and shows.

Western schooling and trail clothes

Some subtle differences tend to crop up throughout the decades. These days, Western riders wear the following items when schooling their horses or going on trail rides (see Figure 10-1):

- **Western hats:** Western riding hats are made from felt or straw, and they come in a variety of colors, from camel to black. Some have *stampede straps,* strings that hold the hat in place under the chin.

- **Helmets:** Although most Western riders don't wear safety helmets, they should. Helmets aren't part of the Western tradition, so Western riders often don't include them in the wardrobe. However, some riders are putting safety ahead of vanity and are wearing lightweight, vented trail helmets when riding, particularly out on the trail.

- **Shirts:** The original cowboys almost always wore long-sleeve shirts to protect themselves from the sun and from brush they encountered on the range. These days, Western riders who are schooling their horses wear everything from t-shirts to tank tops. If you wear a shirt that's blousy, be sure to tuck it in for safety's sake.

- **Jeans:** Blue jeans are the staple of Western riding apparel, and you can see them on just about every Western rider out there. As for style, a boot cut is essential so the jeans fit over riding boots. Wear jeans on the longer side, because they ride up when you're in the saddle.

  Although few companies are producing jeans made especially for riding (these have an elastic component that makes them fit more snugly than regular jeans), some of the larger jeans manufacturers market certain loose-fitting styles specifically to riders.

- **Boots:** Western riders wear — guess what — Western boots! Equestrians don't wear the kind you go line dancing in, however. Western riding boots have a lower heel than Western dress boots, which helps keep your foot from getting caught in the stirrup should you fall off your horse. Variations on the traditional boot also abound — they include Western-style paddock boots and riding shoes.

Figure 10-1:
Casual
Western
riders often
wear jeans
and a long-
sleeve shirt
or t-shirt.

Western show clothes

With Western show clothes, riders have a stricter mandate to follow. Show ring trends change, and five years from now, some of the following items may be obsolete. But right now, they're hot as can be (see Figure 10-2):

- ✔ **Western hats:** Western riders in the show ring wear felt hats mostly in black, white, or camel.

- ✔ **Shirts:** Men wear long-sleeve, button-down shirts in Western cut, in solids or subtle patterns, with a Western scarf. Women wear fitted, long-sleeve, button-down shirts in Western cut. These shirts are often colorful, with glittery patterns that sometimes match perfectly with solid-colored jeans.

- ✔ **Jeans:** Men usually wear black jeans; women wear starched, colored jeans that match their blouses.

- ✔ **Chaps:** Both men and women wear fringed chaps that go with their out-fits. These can be black, camel, blue, or whatever color works.

- ✔ **Boots:** The boots are Western, of course, and usually match the jeans in color.

- ✔ **Accessories:** The women wear jewelry — subtle necklaces worn under the shirt or stud earrings — although you may see some more sparkle as trends change. Both sexes wear belts, usually with large Western belt buckles. In certain Western riding classes, such as Western pleasure and equitation, riders wear gloves.

For details on shows and competitions, see Chapter 22.

Figure 10-2:
Western show apparel includes a dressy shirt, jeans, and fringed chaps.

Staying conservative: English dress

The dress of English riders has changed very little over the past 100 years, although the astute observer may notice subtle difference in color and styling. The name of game in English apparel is *conservative,* especially in the show ring. In the following sections, I give you the scoop on English schooling and show clothes.

English schooling and trail clothes

English riders who are schooling their horses or hacking out on the trail dress much more casually than their show ring counterparts. Schooling apparel for English riders includes the following (see Figure 10-3):

- ✔ **Helmets:** English riders who are schooling their horses usually wear lightweight schooling helmets, in any variety of colors.

- ✔ **Shirts:** Everything from long-sleeve shirts to t-shirts to tank tops are a go for schooling in English apparel.

- ✔ **Breeches or tights:** Breeches are the traditional riding pants of the English discipline; they're stretchy and sometimes have a padded seat and knee patches. Some riders prefer riding tights to breeches for schooling, however, because they can be less expensive and more comfortable. Riding tights usually have pads on the insides of the knees.

✔ **Boots and chaps:** English riders who are schooling wear tall boots or *paddock boots* (boots that come just above the ankle). If they wear paddock boots, they need something to protect their legs from rubbing on the *stirrup leathers* (the strap that attaches the stirrup to the saddle). This protection comes in the form of *full chaps,* which cover the leg from the hip to the ankle, or *half chaps,* which cover the leg from just below the knee to the ankle.

Figure 10-3: Casual English riders often wear breeches and a t-shirt.

English show clothes

English show apparel is much more formal than schooling apparel. Although elements such as color and helmet style in hunt seat and lower-level dressage may subtly change, the basics stay the same. These days, English show apparel looks like this (see Figure 10-4 for hunt-seat show clothes and Figure 10-5 for dressage show clothes):

✔ **Headwear:** Hunt seat and lower-level dressage riders wear black velvet-covered helmets. Upper-level dressage riders wear a derby.

✔ **Shirts:** English riders wear show shirts under a jacket. These tailored shirts are designed to allow movement needed in the shoulders for jumping. They're button-down, have a collar, and are usually white or a very light color, such as pale pink or blue. Some shirts are short sleeved; others are sleeveless.

✔ **Jackets:** All English show riders wear jackets. Hunt seat and lower-level dressage riders wear tailored jackets in solids or pinstripes; upper-level dressage riders sport a black *shadbelly* — a tailored, short-waisted jacket that has tails.

✔ **Breeches:** All English riders wear breeches in the show ring. Breeches are form-fitting, and they extend just below the calf.

In hunt seat and lower-level dressage, color is prone to trends, including everything from rust to hunter green. Tan is usually a staple, although it's a good idea to go to a show and scope it out to see what's fashionable in your region at any given time. Upper-level dressage riders always wear white breeches.

✔ **Boots:** Hunt seat and dressage riders wear tall, black boots at shows.

✔ **Accessories:** In the show ring, English riders usually wear black gloves, although upper-level dressage riders wear white gloves.

Chapter 22 can tell you more about the world of horse shows.

Figure 10-4: In shows, hunt seat gear features breeches, tall boots, gloves, and a jacket.

Figure 10-5:
Upper-level
dressage
riders wear
white
breeches,
white
gloves, and
tailored
jackets in
competition.

Reviewing Artificial Aids

For many riders, the equipment that makes up the artificial aids is almost like part of their riding wardrobe. This equipment includes spurs and whips. Although they may sound like torture devices, properly used artificial aids help foster the communication between rider and horse. Not all horses need the aids in the following sections, but many do.

Talk to your instructor before donning your first pair of spurs and mounting with a whip, because you need to have good control and use of your legs and hands before you can use these tools.

A leg up: Spurs

Spurs are metal devices worn on the rider's heels, and they're attached with leather or nylon straps. Although the style of Western and English spurs differs, the function is the same: to provide a strong signal to the horse. Riders apply spurs to the horse's girth area with a gentle squeezing motion. Spurs should not be used to punish a horse.

Here are the differences between Western and English spurs (you can see both types in Figure 10-6):

✔ **Western:** Western spurs look much fancier than their English counterparts and come in many more styles. Western spurs have *rowels,* or sharp-toothed wheels, located at the end of a shank. Some wheel rowels are smooth, which makes them milder. The type of rowel you choose depends on how much contact you want to make with the horse. The sharper the rowel, the stronger the contact. Western spurs come in simple stainless steel or, for those with bigger budgets, engraved silver.

✔ **English:** English spurs come in several different knob styles and lengths, which means that the end of the spur that comes in contact with the horse can be longer or shorter, rounded or elongated. The longer the spur, the more contact you make. English spurs are simple in design, usually made from stainless steel.

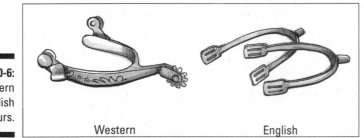

Figure 10-6:
Western and English spurs.

Western   English

Never ride a horse with spurs without professional supervision when you're first learning. If you aren't well-versed in how to use spurs, you may hurt the horse, who may in turn hurt you by running away with you, bucking you off, or doing something else unpleasant.

Tap it out: Whips

Although most people think of whips as instruments of punishment, good riders don't use them this way. Instead, whips provide an extra means of communication from the rider to the horse. If a horse is properly trained, a gentle tap on the rear with a whip is all you need to send the message across. Messages vary according to discipline.

Both Western and English riders may use whips. The type of whip depends on what they're trying to do with the horse and, to some degree, the riding discipline (see Figure 10-7):

- **Crop:** Crops, which some riders call *sticks* or *bats,* are medium-sized whips, usually measuring anywhere from 22 to 27 inches in length. They feature a leather *popper* at one end and a hand strap at the other. Both Western and English riders use crops. Because they're short, these whips are easy for riders to handle.

- **Fly whisk:** Western riders seem to prefer fly whisks, which often feature a leather handle, a wooden shaft, and horsehair bristles at the end. These aids measure about 21 inches in length.

- **Dressage whip:** Dressage whips are longer than crops, usually measuring anywhere from 36 to 45 inches. They have a leather hand grip with a capped end and a short lash at the other end. Hunt seat and dressage riders use dressage whips.

- **Quirt:** A quirt is a thick, braided leather strap around 30 inches long with a loop handle on one end and two or more leather straps at the other. This type of whip is used exclusively by Western riders.

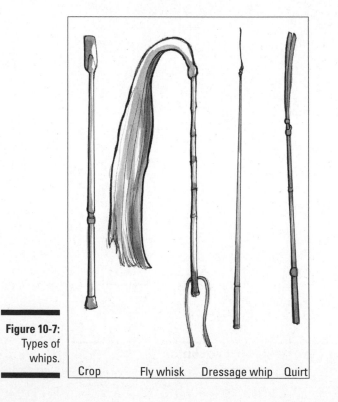

Figure 10-7:
Types of
whips.

Crop   Fly whisk   Dressage whip   Quirt

Part III

Settling into the Saddle and Easing into Riding

The 5th Wave   By Rich Tennant

"He prefers it to trotting."

In this part . . .

Time for the really good stuff! The chapters in Part III give you pointers on how to handle horses from the ground, how to saddle and bridle, and how to mount and dismount. You also discover the correct way to ride the walk, trot or jog, and canter or lope. If you're so inclined, you can also make the leap into jumping.

Chapter 11

Working from the Ground, Saddling, and Bridling

*B*efore you can get on a horse, you have to do plenty of work from the ground. The activity of riding starts with handling the horse while your two feet are planted firmly on Mother Earth. For your safety and for that of the horse, you have to know what you're doing in this part of horse handling.

In this chapter, you discover how to handle a horse before you mount up. You also find out the safest and most effective ways to deal with horses when approaching them and how to halter, lead, and tie them. Finally, you get details on how to saddle and bridle a horse so you can mount and start riding. (For more safety tips on working with horses from the ground, see Chapter 5.)

When you first start riding, your riding instructor guides you through the various steps of preparing your horse. Expect your instructor to help you the first few times. After that, you may be on your own. Read this chapter as a refresher before you head out for your lessons!

Handling Horses from the Ground

Horses are large creatures, so skill and knowledge are paramount when working around them. The vast majority of horses are gentle and would never deliberately hurt a person, but because horses are so large, accidents can happen. Staying aware and knowing how to handle these big animals can minimize the risk. In the following sections, I explain how to approach, halter, lead, and tie a horse safely.

Play catch: Approaching horses

A *halter* is a harness of sorts designed to fit on the horse's head for the purpose of leading and restraining the horse (not riding); a ring under the horse's jaw lets you clip a lead rope to the halter. Well-trained horses who are used to being handled a lot are easy to approach and catch with a halter; however, practicing safety measures whenever you approach a horse in a stall or pasture is still a good idea — particularly if you don't know the horse.

In the stall or paddock

Catching a horse in a stall or *paddock* (a fenced area smaller than a pasture and without grass for grazing) simply means going up to the horse and placing a halter on his head. In most cases, you can just walk up to the horse without a problem. The following method is safe and effective for most horses in a stall or paddock:

1. **Have your halter with you with the lead rope attached.**

2. **Speak to your horse to let him know you're there before you enter the stall or paddock.**

   If the horse is facing away from you, make sure he sees you before you approach him.

3. **Enter the stall or paddock and approach the horse at his left shoulder rather than directly at his face.**

4. **As you get close to the horse, extend your hand, palm down, and let the horse sniff you.**

5. **Loop the lead rope around the horse's neck.**

6. **Slip the halter over the horse's head and buckle the strap that comes from behind the ears (see "Buckle up: Haltering horses" for details).**

In the pasture

You may discover that catching a horse in a pasture is a little more difficult than catching one in a stall or small paddock, especially if the horse doesn't want to be caught. Happy, well-trained horses stand quietly when you approach them for haltering, even in a big pasture, but some horses don't. The ones who don't want to work take off walking, trotting, or running, making it impossible to slip halters over their heads.

Your body language and approach can make a difference when trying to catch a horse in a pasture. Use the following technique to capture a pastured horse, especially if other horses are out there with him:

1. **With your halter and lead rope in hand, walk quietly toward the horse with your hands at your side.**

2. **Approach the horse at his left shoulder, never directly from the front or back.**

3. **When you reach the horse, gently pat or scratch his neck, speaking softly.**

4. **Place the lead rope around the horse's neck in a loop.**

5. **Holding the noosed lead rope, put on the halter as I describe in the following section.**

If the horse doesn't want to be caught, don't give up — letting him get out of it just teaches him that his evasion tactics work. If the horse is yours, talk to a trainer about teaching him to allow himself to be caught.

If the horse is alone in the pasture, you can try taking a treat out there with you to entice him to be caught; however, if other horses are in the pasture too, having treats in your hand may prove hazardous to your health. The horses may get nasty and competitive with one another over the treats, leaving you vulnerable to a misplaced bite or kick.

Buckle up: Haltering horses

The most important tools you have for handling your horse on the ground are the halter and lead rope. A horse who has been properly trained offers no resistance when you slip a halter on his head.

The hardest thing about putting a halter on a horse is figuring out where all those straps are supposed to go. Take a look at a horse wearing a halter before you attempt to put one on the horse you're going to catch. If you understand the way the straps go on the horse's head and then hold the halter in your hand, imagining the horse's head inside it, you should have an easier time putting it on the horse.

Your instructor should guide you through the haltering process the first one or two times to make sure you know how to do it right. Follow these steps:

1. **Stand at the horse's left shoulder, facing the same direction your horse is facing.**

2. **Place the lead rope in a loose loop around the middle of the horse's neck and hold it together with your right hand.**

   This step secures the horse and keeps him from walking away.

3. **Check to make sure that the crown strap of the halter is unbuckled.**

   The *crown strap* is the piece of the halter that goes behind the horse's ears and buckles at the horse's left cheek.

4. **With the buckle side of the strap in your left hand and the crown strap in your right hand, slip the horse's nose through the noseband of the halter by reaching your right hand underneath the horse's neck, as shown in Figure 11-1.**

5. **When the horse's nose is through the halter, bring the crown piece up behind the horse's ears and buckle it so the halter fits comfortably — not too tight and not too loose.**

   It's too tight if you can't fit a finger between the nose strap and cheek strap.

6. **Take the lead rope from around the horse's neck and fold it in your left hand, with your right hand holding the attached rope just below the halter.**

Figure 11-1:
Halter a
horse from
the left side.

Follow me: Leading horses

After you've haltered a horse, you want to lead him out of his stall or pasture so you can tie him and put on his tack (I cover all these tasks later in this chapter). Use the following method to lead your horse safely in any situation (also see Figure 11-2):

1. **Stand on the horse's left side.**

2. **Hold the end of the lead rope closest to the horse's head in your right hand, with your thumb pointing up toward the horse's head.**

   Your hand should be about 6 inches from the halter. If the lead rope has a chain at the end, hold the rope just below the chain so it doesn't injure your hand if the horse pulls back. If you find you need more control when leading your horse, move your hand closer to the halter.

3. **In your left hand, hold what's left of the lead rope folded up.**

   Don't coil the remainder of the rope around your hand. If you do and the horse pulls back, the coil can tighten, trapping your hand.

4. **Before you ask the horse to move forward, stand at his left shoulder, facing ahead, your hands holding the lead rope as I describe in the preceding steps.**

   Hold out your arm on the side of the horse to make sure he doesn't step into you when you start to move.

5. **As you begin to walk forward, give the lead rope a gentle pull with your right hand.**

   The horse should begin walking, keeping pace with you so you remain at his shoulder.

6. **To turn the horse while leading him, push your right hand to the right or pull your hand to the left and step in the direction you want to turn.**

   Keep an arm's distance between you and the horse if you ask the horse to move to the left to ensure he doesn't step on your heel. The horse should follow your lead.

7. **To stop the horse, say "whoa!" and stop walking, giving a very slight backward tug on the rope with your right hand.**

When leading your horse, keep in mind that your horse doesn't know which way you intend to go at any given moment. Remember that your horse is much bigger than you and can't turn as fast or stop as quickly as you can. You know you're about to turn or stop, but your horse doesn't.

Horses are very adept at picking up body signals. They also learn voice commands quickly. Give your horse a warning before you turn or stop. Slow your pace as you start to turn, and say "whoa" as you begin to stop. Your horse will appreciate the warning.

Also, as you lead the horse, look where you're going, not at the horse. Doing so helps the horse have confidence in you and keeps him from getting confused about what he's supposed to do.

Figure 11-2:
Lead a horse at his left shoulder and look where you're going.

Take care of loose ends: Tying horses

Tying a horse isn't as simple as it may sound: You can't just tie a horse to any object with a regular knot and walk away. That's a recipe for disaster! Some horses, being nervous Nellies, are prone to pulling back when tied. When a horse pulls back, he may panic at having his head constrained and throw all his weight onto his hindquarters, practically sitting on his rear end.

If you tie a horse to a strong object (such as a hitching post or a large tree out on the trail), the horse won't be able to pull the object out should he panic. Also, tying the horse with a safety knot enables you to pull the loose end of the rope and quickly release the panicked horse's head before he can do damage. Figure 11-3 shows you one method of tying a safety knot. You essentially create a loop (Step 1), pull a second loop behind the dangling rope and through the first loop (Step 2), and then pull to tighten (Step 3).

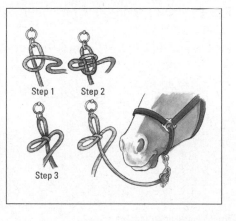

Figure 11-3:
Tie a safety knot when securing a horse for a quick release.

Step 1   Step 2

Step 3

When tying a horse, follow these rules for safety:

✔ Whenever possible, tie a horse in cross-ties. *Cross-ties* are two ropes or chains, one on each side of the horse, that attach to the sides of the horse's halter with metal clips and then to poles on either side of the horse's head. Cross-ties should at least as high as the top of the horse's shoulders. Figure 11-4 shows a horse tied to cross-ties.

Make sure the horse you're working with is familiar with being cross-tied before you secure him, because if he's not, he may panic when he feels himself restrained in this way. Also, make sure that the cross-tie clips have a breakaway feature so the horse won't get hung up in the ties if he panics. A breakaway feature releases the horse should he put extreme pressure on the cross-ties.

✔ Tie a horse only by a halter and lead rope or halter and cross-ties. *Never* tie a horse by the reins of a bridle. If the horse pulls back, the reins can break and the bit may damage the horse's jaw.

✔ Tie a horse only to an immovable object. The rope or chain should be tied so its height is stable and won't slip down toward the ground. Horses should be tied to

• Solid fence posts

• Hitching posts made for this purpose

• Horse trailers hooked to a truck

• Cross-ties

• Strong, secure tree trunks (if on the trail)

✔ Tie a horse with the knot about level to the horse's withers (where the shoulder blades meet), with no more than 3 feet of rope or chain from the post to the halter. Doing so keeps the horse from getting the rope or chain over his head or from getting a leg caught in it. Figure 11-5 shows a horse safely tied to a hitching post.

✔ Don't tie a horse with a chain shank run through his halter. If the horse pulls back, the chain can injure him.

✔ Never leave a horse alone and unsupervised when tied up. Horses are experts at getting into trouble, especially when no one is watching.

Figure 11-4:
A horse secured in cross-ties with a chain on each side.

Figure 11-5:
Short ropes ensure that a horse remains safe when tied to a hitching post.

Putting on a Saddle Properly

Tacking up a horse, especially putting on the saddle, takes practice. Become familiar with the process in this section and then ask an experienced horse person (such as your riding instructor or trainer) to help you the first few times you try it. Making sure the saddle goes on right is important because you don't want it to slip off while you're riding. Correctly positioning and fastening the saddle on the horse's back are also essential for the horse's safety and comfort; an improper saddling job may hurt the horse, which can result in rearing or bucking.

 The horse should be tied by the halter when you're putting on the saddle (see the earlier section "Handling a Horse from the Ground" for info on catching, haltering, leading, and tying). The saddle and pad go on before the bridle, and you remove the halter after you put on the bridle (I cover bridling later).

Before you saddle up the horse, do the following:

- ✔ Tie the horse securely by his halter to a hitching post using a quick-release knot or cross-ties. I discuss tying horses in detail in the preceding section.

- ✔ Groom the horse thoroughly, being careful to brush down the hairs on the back and the girth area (see Chapter 19 for grooming instructions). Make sure no dirt, bedding, or other objects are stuck to these areas.

- ✔ Check the saddle blanket and girth or cinch to make sure that no burrs, sticks, or other items are clinging to the underside.

Western saddles

Before you start, familiarize yourself with the parts of the Western saddle (see Chapter 8). Be sure to have your saddle pad ready, too. Follow these steps to saddle your horse:

1. **Lay the pad on the horse's back.**

   Stand on the horse's left side and position the front of the pad a few inches in front of the horse's withers, at the base of the neck.

2. **Slide the pad backward a couple of inches so the front edge of the pad is still covering the withers.**

   If you need to move the pad forward, don't slide it, because doing so ruffles the hairs underneath, which can irritate the horse while you ride. Instead, lift the pad to move it forward. Check both sides of the horse to make sure that the amount of pad is even on the left and the right.

3. **Prepare the saddle.**

   On a Western saddle, the cinch is attached to the right side. Before you approach the horse with the saddle, flip the cinch up and place the ring at the end over the saddle horn. Take the right stirrup and loop it over the saddle horn on top of the cinch ring. This step keeps the cinch and the stirrup out of your way when you put the saddle on the horse.

4. **Bring the saddle to the horse.**

   Grasp the front of the saddle in your left hand and the back of the saddle in your right. Approach the horse's left side.

   Lift the saddle up to the height of the horse's back a couple of times to get a sense of the weight of the saddle before you hoist it onto the horse's back.

5. **Place the saddle on the horse's back.**

   From the left side of the horse, swing the saddle up and over, and place it gently on the horse's back. The saddle should sit in the hollow just below the withers with about 3 inches of the pad showing in front and the in back. To determine whether the saddle is correctly positioned on the horse's back, look to see whether the cinch, when attached to the saddle, will fit just behind the horse's elbows (see Figure 11-6 for the correct position of a Western saddle).

6. **Walk around to the right side of the horse, unloop the stirrup from the saddle horn, and let it hang; undrape the cinch so it hangs down as well.**

7. **Go back to the left side of the horse and secure the saddle with the cinch.**

   From the left side of the horse, reach underneath and take up the cinch. Run the latigo strap through the ring of the cinch, starting from the side closest to the horse, and then feed the strap through the same D-ring on the saddle where it's attached (see Chapter 8 for a diagram showing the parts of the Western saddle), making sure the strap is flat and free of twists. Continue to loop the latigo strap through the two rings until you have about 12 inches of free strap coming from the ring attached to the saddle.

8. **Make sure the cinch is snug enough that the saddle won't move but not so snug that you can't fit the fingers of a flat hand between the cinch and the horse's body.**

   To tighten the cinch, loosen the knot and pull up on the outside layer of strap between the D- and cinch rings.

Check the cinch again after walking your horse a little and before mounting. You may need to retighten the cinch.

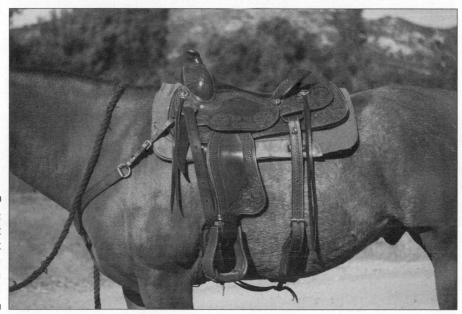

Figure 11-6:
Correct
placement
of a
Western
saddle.

English saddles

You need to be familiar with the parts of an English saddle before you start saddling up; see Chapter 8 for details. Then follow these steps to safely saddle a horse with an English saddle (have your pad and girth ready to go):

1. **Lay the pad on the horse's back.**

   Stand on the horse's left side and position the front of the pad a few inches in front of the horse's withers, at the base of the neck.

2. **Slide the pad backward a couple of inches so the front edge of the pad is still covering the withers.**

   Don't slide the pad forward if you need to reposition it because doing so ruffles the hairs underneath, which can irritate the horse — lift the pad instead. Check both sides of the horse to make sure that the amount of pad is even on the left and the right.

3. **Pick up the saddle.**

   Grasp the front of the saddle in your left hand and the back of the saddle in your right. Make sure you've pushed the stirrup irons up to the top of the stirrup leathers so they don't flop around while you lift the saddle.

4. **Place the saddle gently on the horse's back in the hollow just below the withers.**

   After placement, about 3 inches of the pad should be showing in front and back of the saddle. To ensure you've done it right, look to see whether the girth, when attached to the saddle, will fit just behind the horse's elbows (see Figure 11-7 for the correct position of an English saddle).

5. **Slide the girth straps on the left side of the saddle through the *tab,* the loop on the side of your saddle pad, from the top down.**

   Go to the other side of the horse and repeat the process.

6. **Fasten the girth to the right side of the saddle.**

   Three girth straps, also known as *billets,* hang on the right side of the saddle, but you need to use only the outer two. The third one is present just in case one of the other straps breaks.

   Bring the girth to the right side of the horse and fasten the girth's buckles to the two outside girth straps hanging from the saddle. (Girths vary, so get help from your instructor regarding which side of the girth to fasten to which side of the saddle.) Fasten the buckles about halfway up each girth strap.

7. **Fasten the girth to the left side of the saddle.**

   Move to the horse's left side and reach underneath the horse to grasp the girth. Follow the same buckling procedure that you did in Step 6. Before you attach the girth, be sure it rests just behind the horse's elbows and that it isn't twisted or covered with debris. Make the girth snug.

8. **Gradually tighten the girth on the left side over a period of several minutes.**

   Doing so gradually is kinder to the horse. Make it snug enough that the saddle doesn't move dramatically if you grab the pommel and move it from side to side.

   If you run out of holes on your left-side girth straps, begin tightening the buckles on the right. Ideally, you should have the girth attached at the same notch on both sides or as close as possible for even pressure.

9. **Check your stirrup length.**

   Before you mount (which I discuss in Chapter 12), determine whether your stirrups are the correct length. One way to check whether you're close is to slide your right hand, palm down, under the flap of the saddle where the stirrup leather attaches to the *stirrup bar* (the metal bar holding the stirrup leathers to the saddle); if your horse has already been bridled, hold the reins in your left hand while doing this. Using your left hand, grasp the stirrup iron and pull it toward the crook of your outstretched right arm, allowing the stirrup leather to lay flush against the bottom of your arm. If the stirrup iron fits snugly in the crook of your arm, the stirrups are most likely the correct length for your leg.

If your stirrups need lengthening or shortening, adjust them by using the buckle on the stirrup leather. After you're finished, slide the stirrup leather buckle so it's under the skirt and won't rub on your leg when you're riding.

Figure 11-7:
The girth fits well when you position an English saddle correctly.

Before you can mount, you may need to repeat Step 8 after leading your horse around. The girth may loosen after the horse starts moving. Before you get on, make sure that the girth is snug enough that it feels tight if you put your fingers between it and the horse's body. If you can't get your fingers in there, the girth is too tight and needs to be let out a notch.

Saving the Bridling for Last

The bridle is the tack that goes on last. After you bridle your horse, you can't tie him up again until you finish your ride. Before bridle your horse, do the following:

- ✔ Tie the horse securely by his halter to a hitching post (using a quick release knot) or cross-ties. I explain how to tie horses in "Wrap it up: Tying horses," earlier in this chapter.

- ✔ Groom and saddle the horse (see Chapter 19 for grooming details and the preceding section for saddling info).

- ✔ Check the bridle to make sure that the *noseband* (the part that goes around the nose) and *throatlatch* (the strap that fastens around the horse's jowls) on an English bridle are unbuckled. If you have a throatlatch on a Western bridle, make sure that it's unbuckled, too.

- ✔ Have an experienced horse person (such as your riding instructor or trainer) help you determine whether the bit size is correct and how short the straps on the headstall should be if your horse has never worn this particular bridle.

The steps for putting on an English and Western bridle are nearly the same. Familiarize yourself with the parts of both bridles before you begin (see Chapter 9 for more on bridles). Then follow these steps to put on the bridle:

1. **Secure the horse with the halter.**

   Standing at the horse's left side, unbuckle the halter, slide the noseband off, and then rebuckle the halter around the horse's neck (see the earlier section on haltering for details).

2. **Put the reins over the horse's head so they lie on the horse's neck.**

3. **Hold the bit and headstall and stand at the left side of your horse's head, facing the same direction that your horse is facing.**

   Grasp the top of the headstall in your right hand and the bit in your left hand. Let the bit lie against your outstretched fingers. Stand next to the horse's head, still facing the same direction as the horse.

4. **Place your right hand (still holding the headstall) just on top of the horse's head, in front of his ears.**

   If you can't reach above the horse's head, you can instead reach your arm under the horse's jaw and around to the right side of the horse's head so your right hand and the headstall are just above the horse's forehead or above the bridge of his nose.

5. **Open the horse's mouth and insert the bit.**

   With your left thumb, gently press down on the inside corner of the horse's lip to open his mouth and gently guide the bit into the horse's mouth, being careful not to bang it against his front teeth. Raise the headstall in your right hand until the bit slides all the way in to the horse's mouth. If the bridle has a curb chain, make sure it rests behind the horse's chin.

6. **Gently slide the headstall over the horse's ears.**

   Adjust the browband so it sits evenly on the horse's forehead, or make sure the horse's ear or ears fit comfortably through the one- or two-ear loops. The bridle is now in place.

7. **Buckle the throatlatch and noseband, if any.**

   - **Western bridle:** Figure 11-8 shows a horse with a Western bridle. You probably won't have a noseband to tighten. If the bridle has a throatlatch, make sure that two fingers fit between the horse and the strap.

   - **English bridle:** Figure 11-9 shows a horse with an English bridle. The throatlatch and noseband should be snug but not so tight that you can't get three fingers between them and the horse.

Figure 11-8:
Putting on a Western bridle.

Figure 11-9:
Putting on
an English
bridle.

If a curb chain or strap is attached to the bit, make sure that it's loose when you let the reins go slack but that it makes contact with the horse's chin when you pull the bit shanks back at a 45-degree angle.

8. Unbuckle the halter from your horse's neck.

If you plan to mount where you are, leave the reins over your horse's neck. If you want to lead your horse to another area for mounting, remove the reins from around your horse's neck and lead the horse by the reins. Chapter 12 has full details on mounting your horse.

Chapter 12

Mounting and Dismounting

You can't do much riding until you've gotten on your horse, and you can't get on with the rest of your life until you get off. Thus, mounting and dismounting are important factors in the sport of horseback riding.

In this chapter, I tell you what you need to know before you get on a horse. I also give you the details on how to get yourself into the saddle — and how to get yourself out of it. Your riding instructor will help you develop these skills as well.

Get Set: Preparing to Mount

If you've watched a lot of Hollywood Westerns, your idea of how to mount a horse may be a running leap from behind. In real life, I hope no one mounts a horse like this. The running-leap-mount is and should remain a specialty of Hollywood stunt riders.

Although mounting correctly is a lot easier than the way they do it in the movies, hauling your body up and into a saddle can be a challenge. Doing it right requires a little preparation. In the following sections, I explain what you need to do before you mount: examine your tack and select a place for mounting.

Checking tack

Regardless of whether you ride English or Western, checking your tack before you mount is important. You want to make sure everything is in proper working order and attached to the horse securely before you get on.

You may want to review the parts of the saddle in Chapter 8 and the parts of the bridle in Chapter 9 before you start. Follow these steps — in any order — to check your tack:

- **Examine the bridle.** Make sure all the buckles are securely fastened and that the leather isn't unduly worn in a particular spot. If you're riding Western, check the Chicago screws that hold your bridle together to make sure they're tight.

- **Examine the cinch (on a Western saddle) or girth (on an English saddle) for wear.** Look at the leather straps that attach the cinch or girth to the saddle to make sure they're not worn and prone to breaking when pressure's applied (as it surely will be while you're riding). Check to see whether the buckles or knots are securely fastened.

- **Check your cinch or girth for proper fit.** Before you put your foot in the stirrup to get on, check your cinch or girth one more time. It should be snug, securely holding the saddle in place. (See Chapter 11 for more details on tightening a cinch or girth.)

Choosing a mounting location

Unlike movie cowboys, real riders need a safe place to mount. Choose a place

- Where you have plenty of room to maneuver yourself into the saddle and where your horse is comfortable (so she'll stand still)

- That isn't near an open gate or barn door, which may prove too tempting for your horse — she may move off as you get on!

Remember, too, that your horse should be bridled when you mount, not tied to a fence or cross-ties, for safety reasons.

When you're riding English, your stirrups are on the shorter side, which puts them higher. English riders can mount from the ground, though you may want to use a mounting block to get a leg up. A *mounting block* is a 1-to-2-foot-high wooden or plastic platform that has two or three steps. You can see a mounting block in Figures 12-5 through 12-7.

Western riders sometimes use mounting blocks or mount directly from the ground. Mounting from the ground is easier in Western than in English because the stirrups are longer.

When mounting from the ground, use your environment to help you get on. Position your horse on a slope so she's downhill from where you're standing to mount, as shown in Figure 12-1. The higher ground makes you instantly taller and shortens your reach to the stirrups.

Figure 12-1:
Using high ground to mount can give you an advantage.

If you're out on the trail and need to dismount and then get back on again, using higher ground can be a huge help because you don't have access to a mounting block. Consider using other objects you see in your environment as well, including large rocks, logs, or fence posts. Just be sure that whatever you stand on is stable and can support your weight.

Get on Up: The Mechanics of Mounting

Horsemen and horsewomen have taken hundreds of years to develop the safest, easiest way to get onto the back of a horse. This protocol has been well established in the horse community, and just about all riders practice it. Western and English riders do have slightly different ways of mounting, as you find out in the following sections.

Never release the reins while you're mounting. You need to keep control of your horse at all times.

Western mounting

Mounting in a Western saddle is easier than mounting in an English one because Western riders wear stirrups longer, making them easier to reach. Western saddles are also less likely to slip than English saddles during mounting. Plus, you have more saddle to hold onto as you climb aboard.

Follow these steps to mount Western-style:

1. **Lead your horse to the area where you want to mount.**

   If you want to use a mounting block, place it next to the saddle about a foot from the side of the horse.

2. **Position yourself and stay in control of the horse.**

   Place the reins over your horse's head, maintaining your grip on the reins. Stand at the horse's left shoulder, facing the back end of the horse (see Figure 12-2). The reins should be in your left hand. With the same hand, grab hold of the saddle horn.

3. **Using your right hand, grasp the stirrup, turn it toward you, and place your left foot in the stirrup (see Figure 12-3).**

Figure 12-2:
Face the back of the horse as you stand at the horse's left shoulder.

Figure 12-3:
Grab the stirrup with your right hand and put your left foot in it.

4. **Swing into the saddle.**

   Turn your body toward the horse as you grasp the cantle with your right hand. Bounce on your right foot three times and then launch yourself up. Try to hoist yourself up more by using propulsion from your leg than by pulling your body weight up with your arms. Swing your right leg over the horse's hindquarters, being careful not to touch them, and land gently in the saddle (see Figure 12-4).

5. **Place your right foot in the stirrup and adjust the reins.**

   Be careful not to squeeze the horse with your legs as you try to get your foot in the right stirrup; squeezing may cue the horse to go forward before you're ready.

Figure 12-4:
Swing your right leg over the horse's hindquarters without touching the rump.

English mounting

Mounting in an English saddle is easiest if you use a mounting block or higher ground to stand when hoisting yourself into the saddle. See the earlier section "Choosing a place to mount" for more information.

To mount English style, follow these steps:

1. **Lead your horse to the area where you want to mount.**

   You may want to place a mounting block next to the saddle, about a foot from the horse's left side.

2. **Position yourself and stay in control of the horse (see Figure 12-5).**

   Place the reins over your horse's head and rest them on her neck. Stand at the horse's left shoulder, facing the side of the horse. The reins should be in your left hand. Grab a handful of mane at the base of the horse's neck with the same hand.

Figure 12-5: Grab a handful of mane in your left hand as you hold the reins.

3. **Using your right hand, grasp the stirrup iron and turn it toward you; place your left foot in the stirrup (see Figure 12-6).**

4. **Swing into the saddle.**

   Grasp the cantle with your right hand. Bounce on your right leg two or three times and then launch yourself up into the air. Try to hoist yourself up using the power from your leg more than the strength of your arms. Swing your right leg over the horse's hindquarters, being careful not to touch them, and land gently in the saddle (see Figure 12-7).

Figure 12-6:
Still hanging onto the reins, place your foot in the stirrup.

Figure 12-7:
Turn your
body toward
the horse as
you take
hold of the
cantle with
your right
hand and
launch into
the air.

5. **Place your right foot in the stirrup and adjust your reins.**

   Don't squeeze the horse with your legs as you try to get your foot in the right stirrup, or else you'll cue the horse to go forward before you're ready.

Wrap It Up: Preparing to Dismount

You've had a great ride, but before you can do anything else in your life, you have to get off the horse. Dismounting is much easier than mounting because you don't have to battle gravity. However, you still need to dismount correctly for your own safety and the comfort of your horse, and you need to perform a couple of tasks before you even think about dismounting.

Unlike Hollywood stunt riders, you can't leap off just anywhere, and you need your horse to be standing still before you get out of the saddle. Save running dismounts for the professionals.

As with mounting, pick a safe place to dismount. Follow these guidelines:

- Find a spot where you have plenty of room to land when you step out of the saddle without being close to a wall, fence, or another horse. If you're dismounting on the trail, pick a flat area free of trees and other objects so you have a lot of elbow room.

- Choose a place where your horse is comfortable and unlikely to spook or start moving, such as inside an arena or in front of a hitching post or cross-ties.

- Aim to land on sturdy ground. Mounting blocks can tip over.

- Avoid dismounting near an open gate or barn door, which may be too tempting for your horse to resist. You don't want her to start walking off while you're trying to dismount.

Of course, you have to stop before you can get off. The way you stop your horse depends on the gait you choose: walk, trot or jog, or canter or lope. All involve cues with the reins and seat. For details on how to stop your horse at the different gaits, see Chapters 13, 14, and 15.

Get Down: The Mechanics of Dismounting

Dismounting is similar for both Western and English riders, with only slight variations. The key to figuring out how to get off the horse is remembering the process in steps; I explain both processes in the following sections.

Always maintain your hold on the reins while you're dismounting so you can keep control of your horse.

Talk to your instructor about learning an *emergency dismount,* a way to safely get off your horse in a hurry if you need to. He or she should be willing to teach you this safety procedure. Also, ask for advice on "involuntary dismounts" so you know how to stay safe when you fall.

Western dismounting

Dismounting Western style is fairly easy because the stirrups are longer and the saddle has more to grab onto should you need help with balance. Follow these steps when dismounting Western:

1. **Bring your horse to a complete stop.**

2. **Take your right foot out of the stirrup, hold the reins in your left hand, and grasp the saddle horn with this same hand.**

3. **Swing your right leg over the horse's hindquarters — being careful not to touch the horse as you do — and at the same time, move your right hand to the cantle and your left hand, still holding the reins, to the pommel (see Figure 12-8).**

Figure 12-8: Swing your right leg over the horse's hind-quarters as you move your right hand to the cantle.

4. **Turn so your stomach is against the side of the saddle and your legs are next to one another; free your left foot from the stirrup (see Figure 12-9).**

5. **Gently lower both feet to the ground (see Figure 12-10).**

Figure 12-9:
Turn so your stomach is against the side of the saddle.

Figure 12-10:
Still holding onto the cantle and pommel, lower yourself to the ground.

English dismounting

Dismounting English style is a bit different from Western because English saddles are built differently. Follow these steps to dismount from an English saddle:

1. **Bring your horse to a complete halt.**

2. **Take your right foot out of the stirrup and position your hands.**

   Put the reins in your left hand and grasp the horse's mane at the base of the neck with the same hand. Put your right hand on the pommel.

3. **Swing your right leg over the horse's hindquarters — be careful not to touch the horse as you do — and at the same time, move your right hand to the cantle (see Figure 12-11).**

Figure 12-11:
Swing your right leg over the horse's hindquarters and move your right hand to the cantle.

4. **Turn so your stomach is flat against the side of the saddle and your legs are next to one another; remove your left foot from the stirrup (see Figure 12-12).**

Figure 12-12:
After your stomach is flat against the side of the saddle and your legs are next to one another, remove your left foot from the stirrup.

5. **Slowly slide down until your feet are touching the ground.**

Chapter 13

Enjoying the Walk

As a new rider, the first gait you master is the walk. Because the walk is the slowest gait, you have more time to think about the cues you're giving the horse. How convenient! It's the easiest gait to ride and the one you'll use the most, especially if you plan to trail ride.

The *walk* is a gentle, rocking gait that's easy on your seat. When a horse walks, his legs move in the following order: left rear, left front, right rear, right front. Three legs are on the ground pretty much at the same time (see Chapter 2 for a figure showing the walk). Most horses walk at about 4 miles per hour.

In this chapter, I tell you what you need to know to ask the horse to walk. You discover how to ride the walk in the Western and English disciplines as well as how to make the horse change directions, move backward, circle, and stop. At the end of the chapter, you find exercises you can try to build your riding skills at the walk. But to start you off, I describe the natural aids that horseback riders use when they ride all gaits.

When riding the walk in any discipline, maintaining correct position with your body, hands, and legs is important. Keeping the proper *equitation*, as people call it, helps you stay balanced and communicate more effectively with the horse. Your riding instructor can help you with this and everything else mentioned in this chapter.

Body Language: Helping Your Riding with the Natural Aids

The walk is the first gait where you hear about the natural aids. The *natural aids,* which are your primary tools when riding a horse, include the following:

- ✔ Hands
- ✔ Legs
- ✔ Seat
- ✔ Voice

As I explain in the following sections, you use the natural aids to let the horse know what you want him to do. As you read through this chapter and Chapters 14 and 15, you can see many references to using your hands, legs, seat, and voice. These natural aids are an integral part of your riding. (For info on artificial aids, see Chapter 10.)

Your hands

A very important means of communication is your hands. Your hands hold a direct connection to the horse's mouth via the reins and bit. The way you use your hands determines how well you send signals to the front part of your horse. These signals help communicate direction and speed. In more advanced riding, the hands may communicate more-complex messages.

The discipline you ride in determines how much contact your hands should have with your horse's mouth. In dressage, for example, you keep a fairly taut (but not tight) rein that enables you to have direct contact with the bit. In Western, your reins should have a little more slack unless you're stopping the horse.

Your legs

Your legs are a crucial instrument among your riding communication tools. They cue the horse in a number of different ways, indicating things such as speed and direction. In essence, your legs control the horse's hind end.

The way you use your legs depends on whether you ride Western or English. Stirrup length is specific to each discipline, and along with riding style, it can have a bearing on which part of your leg makes the most contact with the horse's sides.

Your seat

The seat is a vital but sometimes overlooked natural aid in communicating with the horse. Basically, your *seat* is your weight and the way you shift it in the saddle. Although this natural aid can be tricky for beginning riders to understand at first, you need to know how to use your seat effectively when you ride.

Riders in the various disciplines use their seats differently. Dressage riders use their seats to cue their horses to perform a variety of maneuvers; riders in some Western disciplines use their seats to keep their horses at a slow, steady pace. All riders use their seats to slow their horses to a stop, which makes the seat a particularly important tool.

Your voice

Voice is the aid that's easiest for novice riders to master. Through your words and tone of voice, you can communicate a number of messages to the horse, including how fast you want to go (slow or fast) and praise or correction.

Riders in all disciplines use voice when working with their horses. Dressage riders aren't allowed to use voice in competition, so many avoid it when training so they don't get into the habit of using it. Trail riders, however, use voice quite a bit to reassure a horse who sees something he finds scary on the trail.

Asking a Horse to Go for a Walk

Your first task if you want to ride a horse at the walk is to cue him forward. The way you cue him varies according to discipline, although the differences are subtle.

Each horse is different, and some are more responsive than others. You may find that your cues to ask one horse to walk may need to be "louder" than the same cue on another horse. The rule of thumb is to ask quietly first and increase the volume (intensity) if you don't get a response.

As I describe how to get a horse to walk forward in the following sections, I assume you've just gotten on and are at a stop. Chapter 12 outlines the steps for mounting a horse.

Western cues

When riding Western, you ask a horse to walk by gently squeezing the horse's sides with your calves (keeping your knees in place). Maintain this pressure until the horse moves forward. After you feel the horse respond, relax your calves.

If the horse doesn't respond at first, increase the pressure until you get a response. You may need to use your voice to encourage the horse to go. For horses, clucking with your tongue is a fairly universal signal to move forward.

When asking the horse to go forward, be sure your reins are somewhat slack. Keep your body position in mind as the horse starts to move forward. I describe correct Western body position at the walk later in this chapter.

English requests

English riders ask a horse to walk by using leg pressure. Squeeze the horse forward with your calves (not your knees) by pressing in on his sides and maintain this pressure until the horse moves forward. After the horse responds, relax your calves. Be careful not to take your calves completely off the horse, because you want to maintain some contact with your legs.

When asking the horse to walk when riding hunt seat, your reins should be neither too tight nor too slack. Traditionally, you want to keep a straight line in the reins from bit to elbow. If you're riding dressage, you should have some contact with the bit, which means you have slight tension in your reins.

In hunt seat riding — but not in dressage — you can also use your voice to encourage the horse to go forward if you don't get an immediate response to your leg pressure. You do this by clucking.

Riding the Walk in Western

In Western riding, the walk is a slow, easy gait that's comfortable to ride for long periods of time. Because the Western discipline is the one most commonly used for trail riding (see Chapter 21), the walk is the gait that Western riders use most often.

When you're in correct position, your body is relaxed, the reins are about 2 inches above the horse's withers, and the balls of your feet are squarely in the stirrups. Figure 13-1 shows a Western rider at the walk. Read the following sections for details on how to position yourself correctly. See Chapter 2 for info on horse anatomy; Chapter 8 includes images of saddles.

Figure 13-1: Stay relaxed when you ride the walk in Western.

Positioning your body

Relaxation is key when riding Western; however, you do need to keep yourself in the proper position without being stiff or unnatural. Here's what that position entails (refer back to Figure 13-1):

✔ When riding Western, remember to "sit deep." This phrase means that your weight is on your seat bones. Relaxing your pelvis and lower back can help you achieve a deep seat.

✔ Sit up straight, but don't sit like you have a board in your back. Your shoulders should be relaxed but not slumped forward.

Tip: To help get a sense of where your shoulders should be, take a deep breath and exhale. Keep your shoulders in the position they land in when you let the air out.

✔ Make sure you aren't leaning to one side of the horse or another. In other words, sit square in the saddle. Use the saddle horn as a guide to make sure you're centered. The horn should be directly in front of you if you're in the right spot.

✔ Keep your elbows relaxed but at your sides. Avoid a common pitfall of beginners: letting your elbows stick out like you're about to imitate a chicken!

✔ Don't forget your head. Many beginners have a tendency to stare at their horse's ears. To maintain your balance, keep your chin up and your eyes directed at where you're going.

Trying your hand at holding the reins

Western riders have two different ways of holding the reins. These styles originated in different parts of the country, and riders usually prefer one style over another. I explain both styles to you, but the one you use will most likely depend on what your riding instructor prefers:

✔ **California:** Because I grew up in Southern California, I learned to ride Western using the California style of holding the reins. This style is common in many parts of the Western United States.

California requires that you hold the reins in the left hand. The reins come up through the bottom of your hand, with one rein going up between your pinky and your ring finger and the other rein pressed against your palm. Your thumb should be on the top of the reins facing upward (see Figure 13-2).

✔ **Traditional:** Riders in many parts of the country hold the reins traditional style, which means they use either their right or left hand. You hold one rein between the thumb and the index finger and the other between the index finger and the middle finger. The thumbnail faces upward and the thumb points toward the horse's neck. The reins exit your hand between your pinky and palm (see Figure 13-3).

Figure 13-2:
In California style, hold the reins in your left hand with your thumb facing up.

Figure 13-3:
In traditional style, hold the reins between fingers with your thumb pointed toward the horse's neck.

In both styles, you hold the reins about 2 inches above the horse's withers (see Chapter 2 for a diagram of the horse). Your hand should be in front of the saddle horn.

What about your other hand? In Western riding, you usually have the option of putting the unused hand on the same-side thigh or letting it hang alongside your leg, completely relaxed.

Putting your legs in position

Your stirrups are long when riding Western, which is good if you plan to be in the saddle a long time. Longer stirrups are easier on the knees.

When your horse is walking, you should have the balls of your feet in the stirrup and your heels should be down. Your toes should be pointed forward so your foot is parallel to the horse's body. If your stirrups are set at the correct length (your riding instructor can help you with this), you should have a slight bend in your knees, and your legs should go alongside the cinch. (Refer to back Figure 13-1 to see how to position your legs.)

Moving with the Western horse

As the horse walks, you feel his motion beneath you. Tune in to this motion and feel its rhythm. See whether you can sense how the horse's left shoulder and then his right shoulder move. Feel in sync with the rhythm as you let your body relax while still holding your position. Let the horse's movement gently rock your hips. If you get in tempo with your horse, you should start to feel at one with the big creature beneath you.

Riding the Walk in Hunt Seat

In hunt seat, the walk is the gait you use primarily to warm up to the faster gaits. Horses whom people choose for hunt seat riding often have big strides, making their walks feel "bigger." For this reason, the walk is a good gait for beginners to focus on. Mastering this gait helps you develop balance and rhythm with the horse.

You should have a slightly forward seat, your hands should be 2 to 3 inches apart, and your calves should rest just behind the girth. Figure 13-4 depicts the proper alignment for riding the walk in hunt seat; you can also check out the following sections to figure out how to position yourself correctly. Chapters 2 and 8, respectively, can show you figures of the parts of a horse and saddles.

Figure 13-4:
A rider at the walk in hunt seat is slightly forward.

Positioning your body

Hunt seat is a formal type of riding that requires a distinct position in the saddle. The challenge is to maintain the proper position while staying relaxed and moving freely with the horse (refer back to Figure 13-4):

✔ Your body position in hunt seat riding is slightly forward. This means you have a gentle bend at the hips (not the waist), which gives you a *closed hip angle.* Your weight in the saddle is on your seat bones.

✔ You have a slight, natural arch in your lower back, with the rest of your back flat. In other words, don't force an arch or tuck in your pelvis.

✔ Your shoulders are squared and back rather than hunched forward.

✔ Your elbows are close to your body, your chin is up, and your eyes are lifted, looking ahead at where you're going.

With both hands: Holding the reins

In hunt seat, you hold the reins in two hands with your palms down. Have your fingers closed in a relaxed fist; the reins go between your thumb and your index finger and exit the hand between your pinky and ring fingers.

Hold your hands 2 to 3 inches apart from each other, about 3 inches above the horse's withers. Have the reins relaxed but taut enough that someone looking at you from the side could draw a straight line from the bit to your elbow (refer back to Figure 13-4).

Putting your legs in position

In hunt seat, your stirrups are fairly short, giving you a significant bend in your knee. To know what length your stirrups should be, take your feet out of your stirrups while you're in the saddle. The bottom of the irons should rest at your ankle bone. If they come below it, they're too long. Above it, they're too short. Your riding instructor can help you determine whether your stirrup length is correct. If the stirrups are too short or too long, your instructor will adjust them for you or you'll need to dismount to adjust them yourself.

When you're in the saddle, your calf should rest just behind the girth. The balls of your feet should be in the stirrup, and your heels should be down. Let your weight rest on the balls of your feet. Your toes should point forward at a slight outward angle of about 15 degrees. (Refer back to Figure 13-4.)

When the horse is walking, your knee should have contact with the saddle. A good way to judge how much pressure to apply is to imagine a sponge between the inside of your knee and the saddle. You want to keep the sponge in place without squeezing any water out of it.

Moving with the hunt-seat horse

When the horse is walking in hunt seat, you need to keep your forward position. Move with the movement of the horse while keeping your shoulders back and your hips relaxed. Feel the horse move underneath you, allowing his movement to gently rock your hips back and forth.

When the horse is moving, pay attention to your legs. Make sure they don't slide forward or backward. They should stay just behind the girth.

Riding the Walk in Dressage

The walk is an important gait in dressage, especially at the lower levels. If you intend to compete in dressage in the future, you have to perform most maneuvers at this gait.

You should sit deep in the saddle, your hands should be 2 inches above the horse's withers, and your calves should be about 1 inch behind the girth (see Chapter 2 for images of the parts of a horse, Chapter 8 for saddles). Figure 13-5 shows the proper position for a dressage rider at the walk, and the following sections explain how to position yourself correctly.

Figure 13-5:
A dressage rider at the walk sits deep in the saddle.

Positioning your body

Dressage riders use the following body position (refer back to Figure 13-5):

✔ In dressage, riders sit deep in the saddle. This means your weight drops down into your rear end. You sit on your seat bones and sink into your hips.

✔ Your shoulders are open and square yet relaxed.

✔ Your back is flat — you don't want any arch.

✔ Your chin is up and your eyes are forward, looking where you're going.

Get a grip: Holding the reins

In dressage, you hold the reins in two hands, palms down. Your fingers are closed in a relaxed fist, and the reins go between your thumb and your index finger and come out between your pinky and ring fingers.

Your hands should be 3 to 4 inches apart, about 2 inches above the horse's shoulders. You want slight tension in your reins so you have contact with the horse's mouth. (Refer back to Figure 13-5.)

Putting your legs in position

When riding dressage, your stirrups are longer than they'd be in hunt seat but shorter than in Western. Your riding instructor can help you determine the correct stirrup length.

At the walk, your calf should be about 1 inch behind the girth. Your heel should be in line with your hip, and your knees should have considerable contact with the saddle without pinching the horse. The balls of your feet are in the stirrups, and your heels are down. Your toes point forward so your feet are parallel to the horse's body. (See Figure 13-5.)

Moving with the dressage horse

In dressage, riding should look effortless. When the horse is in motion, your body should move with him as you sit deep in the saddle.

Make sure your hips are relaxed and that you hold the body position described earlier in this chapter. The horse's motion gently rocks your hips while the rest of your body stays where it should.

Maneuvering the Horse at the Walk

In the following sections, I describe a variety of helpful maneuvers at the walk. You want to be able to stop a horse after you've put him in motion (for info on how to start a horse, see the earlier section titled "Asking a Horse to Go for a Walk"). And unless you plan on riding in a straight line all the time, you need to know how to turn your horse and possibly move backward. Circling is another important skill you should develop on horseback, especially if you ever want to compete.

Pulling out all the stops

The stop is an important maneuver that both horses and riders need to know well. Stopping is important in every discipline because it gives the rider considerable control — and makes your eventual dismount a bit less daunting!

A horse responds to specific stopping cues depending on how he's been trained, which differs slightly between disciplines. I explain the cues in the following sections.

Western stops

For beginning riders, the stop from the walk is a basic maneuver that you learn in the first lesson. To stop a horse from a walk in Western riding, follow these steps (and see Figure 13-6):

1. **Say "whoa" as you put tension on the reins while moving your hand slowly backward toward your belly button.**

   Keep in mind that when using a leverage bit (such a curb bit — see Chapter 9 for details), even the slightest pull on the reins puts considerable pressure on the horse's mouth. For this reason, use your hands gently and carefully when riding with a leverage bit.

2. **When the horse stops walking, release the tension in the reins.**

Figure 13-6:
To stop a horse in Western riding, say "whoa" as you put tension on the reins.

English stops

In hunt seat and dressage, you request the stop in a manner similar to how you do it in Western (see the preceding section), though you also use your weight to help bring the horse to a halt. To stop a horse from a walk in English riding, follow these steps (see Figure 13-7):

1. **Sink your weight into the saddle without slouching your shoulders and put more tension on the reins.**

    In hunt seat, put more tension on the reins while moving your hands backward and say "whoa." In dressage, where you already have considerable contact (tension) on the reins, increase that tension. Do not use your voice; the horse should stop without your using this aid.

2. **When the horse stops walking, release the tension in the reins.**

Figure 13-7: To stop a horse in English riding, sink your weight into the saddle as you add tension to the reins.

Turning left and right

Horses understand certain cues about changing direction. The differences in cues are subtle, yet horses well-trained in a particular riding discipline recognize these subtleties. Pay attention to the directional cues for the discipline you plan to ride in. Although executing these cues takes concentration at first, they'll eventually become second nature.

When first figuring out how to turn a horse, you start in an arena. The side of your horse next to the rail is called the *outside,* and the side away from the rail is called the *inside.* You need to know these terms because your riding instructor may make references to your outside leg, your inside leg, and in English riding, your inside rein and your outside rein.

Western turns

In Western riding, something called neck reining is the most common way to turn a horse. *Neck reining,* or cueing the horse to turn using rein pressure against the neck, can happen only when you hold the reins in one hand (see "Trying your hand at holding the reins," earlier in this chapter). Still, don't be surprised if you see Western riders using what looks like an English bridle; when horses are first being trained in Western riding, they learn the direct rein method, which is the same method that English riders use at all levels.

Beginning riders usually pair up with seasoned horses, so you'll probably use neck reining. When riding Western, turn your horse either to the left or right, using your reins and your legs, in the following manner (see Figure 13-8):

1. **To turn your horse to the inside of the arena (away from the rail), move the hand holding the reins to the inside so that the outside rein is lying across the horse's neck; at the same time, apply pressure with the calf of your outside leg.**

   The horse moves away from the pressure, encouraging him to turn to the inside.

2. **When the turn is complete, move your rein-hand back to the center of your horse and release the pressure from your outside leg.**

Figure 13-8:
When turning in Western riding, use neck reining to cue the horse.

English turns

In English riding, when you want your horse to turn either to the left or right, use your reins and your legs in the following manner (see Figure 13-9):

1. **To turn your horse to the inside of the arena (away from the rail), increase the tension on the inside rein; at the same time, apply pressure with your outside leg.**

   If you're riding hunt seat, pull the rein out slightly to the inside. If you're riding dressage, pull the rein back slightly. The horse moves away from the leg pressure, which encourages him to turn to the inside.

2. **When the turn is complete, release the pressure on the inside rein and return it to its normal position; release the pressure from your outside leg as well.**

Figure 13-9:
In English riding, increase the tension on the inside rein when turning your horse.

Circling the horse

All novice riders find out how to turn a horse in a large circle in their riding lessons. Circling is an important maneuver because it helps you build both communication with your horse and your riding skills.

Equestrians often use circling in arena riding for a variety of reasons. In Western riding, circling is part of reining competition. Hunt seat riders use the skills they develop through circling when negotiating a jumping course. And in dressage competition, circling is part of the tests at all levels.

The cues you use to circle a horse depend on your riding discipline and the gait you're using. The differences are subtle, but a horse well-trained in a particular discipline understands specific cues.

Western circling

When circling a horse at the walk in Western riding, you neck rein (as I describe in the earlier section "Turning left and right"), using one hand on the reins. The following steps take you through a circle (see Figure 13-10):

1. **Start riding straight along the rail.**

2. **To turn to the inside (away from the rail), move the hand holding the reins to the inside so that the outside rein is lying across the horse's neck; at the same time, apply pressure with the calf of your outside leg.**

   The horse moves away from the pressure, which encourages him to turn to the inside.

3. **Maintain the rein and leg pressure as the horse turns.**

   When the horse is moving into the circle pattern, apply pressure with both legs to guide him through the circle.

4. **When the circle is complete (when you end up back where you started, on the rail), move your rein-hand back to the center of your horse and release the pressure from your legs.**

Figure 13-10:
To circle in Western riding, use neck reining and leg pressure.

English circling

When circling a horse at the walk in hunt seat and dressage, you use direct reining, with two hands on the reins. The following steps take you through a circle (see Figure 13-11):

1. **Start riding straight along the rail.**

2. **To circle your horse to the inside of the arena, increase tension on the inside rein; at the same time, apply pressure with your outside leg.**

   If you're riding hunt seat, pull the rein out slightly. If you're riding dressage, pull the rein back slightly. The horse moves away from the pressure of your leg, encouraging him to turn to the inside.

3. **Continue to maintain the rein and leg pressure as the horse turns.**

   When the horse is moving into a circle pattern, apply pressure with both legs to guide him through the circle.

4. **When the circle is complete (when you're back on the rail), move your hands back to the center of your horse.**

   Reduce the amount of pressure from your legs, but be sure not to take your legs off the horse completely. In both hunt seat and dressage, you need to maintain leg pressure to keep the horse moving forward — kind of like keeping your foot on the gas pedal!

Figure 13-11: To circle a horse in English riding, put tension on the inside rein while applying pressure with the outside leg.

In reverse: Calling for backup

Asking a horse to back up is a simple task that everyone who wants to ride should master. In the show ring, judges often ask for a back-up, and on the trail, backing up can become a necessity.

As with most cues, the directions for backing up differ slightly between disciplines, as you find out in the following sections. Keep in mind that backing up is not a very natural maneuver for the horse and thus requires some effort on his part.

Always do the backup from a standstill, never from a walk or faster gait. Why? Because suddenly going into reverse while moving forward is too hard and confusing for a horse. You wouldn't shift your car into reverse without first applying the brakes, right? For information on how to do that stop, see the earlier section called "Pulling out all the stops."

Western

In Western riding, backing up is particularly important. Roping-horses and horses working cattle in a ranch environment use this maneuver. It's also a vital movement for trail horses in rough terrain. You never know when you'll find yourself in a tight spot on the trail and need to put the horse in reverse!

To back up your horse when riding Western, follow these steps (also see Figure 13-12):

1. **Slide your hand up the reins toward the horse's neck and create some tension in the reins.**

   Pull the reins gradually backward toward your belly button.

2. **If the horse doesn't start to back up, apply pressure with both of your calves while maintaining backward tension on the reins.**

3. **After the horse has taken several steps backward (your situation determines how far back you want to go), stop his movement by sending your hands forward toward his neck and releasing leg pressure.**

Figure 13-12:
When backing a horse in Western riding, slide your hand up the reins to create tension.

English

In the hunt seat discipline, riders sometimes use backing up in the show ring, and both hunt seat and dressage riders use it when out on the trail. Although not used as frequently in the English disciplines as it is in Western riding, backing up is an important maneuver that all English riders should know.

To back your horse when riding English, follow these steps (and see Figure 13-13):

1. **Gather up your reins a few inches so you have less rein between your hands and the horse's mouth.**

   Create some tension in the reins by pulling them back gradually toward your hips.

2. **If the horse doesn't start to back up, alternately pull back gently on each rein.**

   If this movement doesn't get a response, apply pressure with both of your calves while continuing to apply alternating tension on the reins.

3. **After the horse has taken several steps backward (your situation determines how far back you want to go), stop his movement by sending your hands forward toward his neck and releasing leg pressure.**

Figure 13-13: To back up in English riding, gather up your reins and create tension by pulling back gradually.

Trying a Couple of Walking Exercises

A good way to develop your riding skills is to practice. Get on a horse and use the cues you've been taught. The following sections describe some exercises to try. You can suggest these to your riding instructor or do them when you're riding on your own in an arena.

Using barrels in Western riding

A great walking exercise for Western riders uses barrels. The stable where you ride probably has barrels set up in the arena or may have them on the property and let you use them with permission. You can use poles if barrels aren't available.

This exercise, which has you weave in and out of the barrels, helps you both turn and circle your horse, letting you develop the coordination you need between your rein-hand and your legs (Figure 13-14 shows the pattern in which you should move):

1. **Line up three barrels, approximately 12 feet apart, in the center of the arena.**

2. **Start at one end of the arena facing the barrels; walk the horse straight toward the barrels.**

3. **When you're in front of the first barrel, turn the horse slightly to the right and make a tight counterclockwise circle around the barrel.**

   Walk all the way around till you're facing the second barrel, and then walk straight.

4. **Go to the next barrel and turn your horse slightly to the left of that barrel so you can circle it clockwise.**

5. **After completing your circle, move on to the next barrel and circle counterclockwise.**

6. **When you've finished the circle on this barrel, continue back to the middle barrel and circle it again.**

   Continue this routine back and forth through the barrels three times altogether.

Figure 13-14:
In Western, use barrels to practice turning and circling at the walk.

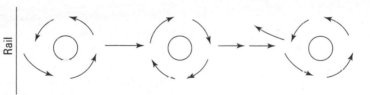

Figure 13-15 shows a rider performing the exercise.

Figure 13-15:
Practice
going
around the
barrels
three times
total.

Crazy eights: Turning a figure eight in English riding

The figure eight is a good exercise for hunt seat and dressage riders to practice at the walk. It helps you figure out how to turn and circle your horse, and it develops the coordination you need between your legs and hands. You can do this exercise in any riding arena (Figure 13-16 shows the pattern you want to make):

1. **Start on the rail, and turn your horse to the inside as though you were going to make a circle.**

2. **When you get halfway through your circle, straighten your horse.**

3. **Ask the horse to change directions to make a connecting circle in the opposite direction.**

   If your first circle was clockwise, the second will be counterclockwise.

4. **After the horse completes the circle, straighten him again and then begin a connecting circle in the opposite direction.**

   Here, you're completing the half-circle you made in Steps 1 and 2.

5. **Continue walking through this pattern four to six times.**

Figure 13-16:
In English,
riding a
figure eight
is a good
way to
practice
turning and
circling.

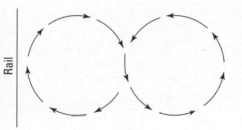

Chapter 14

Bumping Up Your Skills with the Jog or Trot

. . . .

In This Chapter

▶ Asking a horse to jog or trot

▶ Riding the "bouncy" gait in different disciplines

▶ Practicing stops, turns, and circles

▶ Getting in some exercises

. . . .

*W*estern riders call it the jog; English riders call it the trot. No matter what you call it, this intermediate gait — between the walk (in Chapter 13) and the canter or lope (in Chapter 15) — is one that every rider needs to master. For most new riders, the jog or trot is the most challenging gait to ride. This gait tends to be bouncy, especially for those who haven't developed the skills to ride it. However, after you master this gait, the experience can be exhilarating.

When a horse *jogs* or *trots,* a front foot and the opposite hind foot come down at the same time, making a two-beat rhythm (see Chapter 2 for a figure of a horse at the trot). Most horses travel at around 9 miles per hour at the trot.

In this chapter, you discover how to ride the jog or trot in the Western and English disciplines, as well as how to make the horse change directions, circle, and stop from this gait. At the end of the chapter, I present exercises you can try to help build your riding skills.

When riding the jog or trot in any discipline, make sure you maintain correct position with your body, hands, and legs. Keeping the proper *equitation* (your overall position in the saddle) helps you stay balanced and improves the effectiveness of your communication with your horse. Your instructor can help you master the proper form at this gait.

Asking the Horse to Pick Up the Pace

The horse typically moves from the walk into the jog or trot. You can also ask your horse to jog or trot from the lope or canter when you begin more advanced riding, but in this chapter, I discuss only taking your horse from a walk to a jog or trot. As I explain in the following sections, the way you cue the horse to speed up depends on your riding discipline, although the difference are subtle.

When you give cues, ask quietly first and increase the intensity if you don't get a response. Each horse is different, and some are more responsive than others. You may find that your cues to ask one horse to jog or trot may need to be "louder" than the same cue on another horse.

Western jog requests

When riding Western, you ask a horse to jog by gently squeezing the horse with your calves to go forward. Maintain this pressure until she breaks into a jog. After you feel the horse respond, relax your calves.

If the horse doesn't respond at first and continues to walk instead of jog, increase the pressure with your legs until you get a response, being careful not to lean forward as you do so — continue to sit up straight. You may need to use your voice to encourage the horse to jog. For horses, clucking with your tongue is a signal to increase speed.

When asking the horse to jog, be sure your reins are loose and keep your body position in mind as the horse starts to move forward. I describe correct body position at the jog later in this chapter.

English trot cues

English riders ask a horse to trot using leg pressure. Squeeze the horse into a trot with your calves and maintain this pressure until the horse begins trotting. After the horse responds, relax your calves. Be careful not to take your calves completely off the horse because you want to maintain some contact with your legs.

When asking the horse to trot in hunt seat or dressage, you should have some contact with the bit, which means you maintain a slight tension in the reins. You can move your hands forward slightly to allow the horse to move on, but you don't want any swing in the reins. Be careful not to pull back on the reins or raise your hands, which sends mixed messages if you're asking the horse to go forward.

In hunt seat riding — but not in dressage — you can also use your voice to encourage the horse to trot if you don't get an immediate response to your leg. You do this by clucking.

Riding the Jog in Western

In Western riding, the jog is a slow, collected (controlled) gait that shouldn't be too bouncy. The slower the jog, the less bounce you get.

Figure 14-1 shows the jog in Western. In correct position, riders are relaxed and sit deep in the saddle. The reins are loose and the legs are relaxed at the horse's sides. Read the following sections to discover how to position yourself correctly.

Figure 14-1:
A relaxed Western rider sits deep in the saddle during the jog.

Positioning your body

(REMEMBER icon)

Before you can tackle more speed and master the lope (see Chapter 15), you need to develop your body position at the jog. Here's how to hold your body (refer to Figure 14-1):

- ✔ Even though the horse is moving faster than she is at a walk, your body should stay relaxed. Keep yourself in the proper position without being stiff or unnatural.

- ✔ Remember to sit deep. Keep your weight on your seat bones and your pelvis relaxed.

- ✔ Sit up straight, but don't sit like you have a board in your back. Your shoulders should be relaxed, but don't slouch.

- ✔ Make sure you aren't leaning to one side of the horse or another as the horse jogs. Sit square in the saddle, using the saddle horn as a guide; the horn should be directly in front of you if you're sitting in the right spot.

- ✔ Have your elbows relaxed at your sides, not sticking out and bouncing off your body. Proper elbow position lets you remain balanced and gives you sufficient control of your hands. Keeping your shoulders relaxed can help keep your elbows in the right place.

- ✔ Because the horse is going faster, you may find yourself wanting to look down toward her ears. To avoid losing your balance, keep your chin up and your eyes directed on where you're going.

Holding the reins in Western

When jogging in Western riding, you hold the reins about an inch above the horse's *withers* (where the shoulders come together — see Chapter 2 for a diagram of the horse). This position reduces leverage on the *shank* of the bit (the piece between the bit and where the reins attach) and encourages the horse's forward movement. Hold your hand forward on the horse's neck, about an inch in front of the saddle horn (refer back to Figure 14-1).

Regardless of whether you hold the reins in California style or traditional style (see Chapter 13 for details), keep your other hand on the same-side thigh or hanging alongside your leg, completely relaxed, as you do with walking.

Putting your legs in position

In Western riding, leg position is the same in the jog as it is in the walk: When your horse is jogging, you should have the balls of your feet in the stirrup and your heels should be down. Your toes should be pointed forward so each foot is parallel to the horse's body.

You'll have a slight bend in your knees if your stirrups are set at the correct length (your riding instructor can help you with this), and your legs should be situated alongside the cinch. Refer back to Figure 14-1 for correct leg position.

Sit deep in the saddle while also sitting up straight. This posture helps keep your legs from slipping forward and out of place.

Moving with the Western horse

Sit deep as the horse jogs, keeping your arms relaxed, and sink down into the saddle with the horse's rhythm. Don't let your body stiffen — relax your lower back, buttocks, and thigh muscles, too. You want your lower body to move with the horse as the upper body maintains its upright position to keep you balanced.

If the jog starts to get too bumpy, slow the horse down. Put slight tension in the reins until the jog becomes easier to ride.

Riding the Trot in Hunt Seat

The trot is an important working gait in hunt seat. When you're first figuring out how to jump — as most hunt seat riders do — you take the jumps at the trot (Chapter 16 can help you out when you're ready to start working on your jumping skills). The trot is also used a lot in the show ring and on the trail.

Horses used for hunt seat riding often have big, bouncy trots. For this reason, hunt seat riders often *post the trot,* which means they rise up and down in the saddle with the rhythm of the gait. Hunt seat riders can alternatively *sit the trot* (remain seated), which takes both skill and balance. Sitting the trot is something you learn a bit later in your lessons after you've mastered the posting trot. The basic position for both posting and sitting the trot is the same.

Positioning your body

Beginning riders often find maintaining the proper body position while sitting or posting the trot to be a challenge. Proficiency comes with practice and learning to feel the horse's rhythm. Here are some guidelines to start you off:

- ✔ At the trot, your body position is more forward than it is at the walk; you have a greater bend at the hips (not the waist).
- ✔ When you're sitting the trot, your weight in the saddle is on your seat bones. When you're posting, your weight rises up and out of the saddle.

✔ You have a slight, natural curve in your lower back, with the rest of your back flat.

✔ Your shoulders are squared and back rather than hunched forward.

✔ Your elbows are close to your body, your chin is up, and your eyes are lifted, looking ahead at where you're going.

Holding the reins

In hunt seat, you hold the reins in two hands. Close your fingers in a relaxed fist, with the reins going between your thumb and your index finger and coming out between your pinky and ring fingers before going to the bit.

Hold your hands 2 to 3 inches apart from each other, about 2 inches above the horse's withers, which is a bit lower than where you'd hold them at the walk. This position gives the horse more room to extend her neck as she trots. Your hands are also forward on the horse's neck to allow freedom of movement for the horse's head. Keep slight tension in the reins.

Positioning your legs in hunt seat

When riding the trot, your leg position is the same as at the walk. In other words, the calf should rest just behind the girth (see Chapter 8 for saddle info). The balls of your feet should rest in the stirrup, and your heels should be down. Your toes should point forward so each foot is at a slight outward angle of about 15 degrees.

As with the walk at hunt seat, a good way to judge how much pressure your knees should apply is to imagine a sponge between the inside of your knee and the saddle. You want to keep the sponge in place without squeezing any water out of it.

Your calves should have contact with the horse's sides as they do at the walk, with just slight pressure to "support" the horse at the trot. This pressure also helps you keep your legs in position, which can be more difficult to do at the trot.

Moving with the hunt seat horse

When the horse is trotting in hunt seat, you can either post or sit, as I explain in the following sections. Posting to move with the horse is easier, and it's best used when you're asking the horse for an extended (longer-strided) trot. You can sit the trot when you're asking the horse for a more collected (shorter-strided) trot.

Whether you're posting or sitting the trot, pay attention to your legs. Make sure they don't slide forward or backward. They should stay just behind the girth.

Posting the trot

When you're posting the trot, bouncing does have its advantages. With each trotting stride, one side of the horse's back rounds as the other flattens. As one front leg moves forward and that side of the horse's back rises, you can get a nice lift right out of the saddle. When that side flattens out, you make your (gentle) landing.

To post, follow these steps (see Figure 14-2):

1. **Place your weight in the stirrup irons and let yourself to be lifted up out of the saddle as one side of the horse's back rounds.**

    As the horse trots, the sides of the horse's back alternately round and flatten, and the movement can help push you up out of the saddle. Allow yourself to rise in rhythm with the horse's gait.

2. **On the next stride, lower your seat back into the saddle as that side of the horse's back flattens.**

    Don't drop your weight; rather, gently lower yourself until the horse's back rounds again and pushes you up.

Figure 14-2: To post, lift yourself out of the saddle when one side of the horse's back is rounded.

Knowing when to rise and when to sit when posting takes practice. You can learn the basics of *knowing your diagonals* by looking down at the horse's shoulders to see which front leg is moving forward and which is moving back (the term *diagonal* comes from the fact that at the trot, the horse's legs move in diagonal pairs). When the horse's outside foreleg, the one along the rail, is forward (you know because the shoulder appears forward from your vantage point in the saddle), that side of the horse's back is rounded. That's when you should rise. If you need help, count out "one-two, one-two" as you ride in rhythm with the trot. Sit down on the *one,* when the inside leg is forward, and allow yourself to be lifted out of the saddle on the *two.*

In arena riding, you should rise out of the saddle only on the correct diagonal, when the outside leg is forward. Posting on the correct diagonal helps the horse balance as she turns around the corners of the arena; she can bear your weight better when moving on a curve or while circling. If you rise out of the saddle when the horse's outside leg is forward, your weight is off the horse's back when her inside hind leg pushes all her weight forward, and that's a good thing. When showing in certain hunt seat classes (and in dressage as well), the judge will mark you down if you're on the wrong diagonal.

Sitting the trot

To move into the sitting trot from the posting trot (see the preceding section), slow the horse down by applying tension on the reins and placing your weight in the saddle. Sitting the trot is much easier when the trot is slower. When the horse responds by slowing down, sink deep into your seat bones and relax your hips. You should remain in the saddle. Figure 14-3 shows the sitting trot.

Figure 14-3: Sitting the trot in hunt seat requires that you relax your hips.

At the sitting trot, your body position should remain the same as when you were posting. Sit up straight with shoulders relaxed, head forward, and chin straight ahead. Your legs should also be in the same position that they were in at the posting trot (see the earlier "Positioning your legs" section).

Riding the Trot in Dressage

Riders use the trot at all levels of dressage competition (see Chapter 22 for info on shows). The official dressage tests require riders to perform a number of maneuvers at this gait. The trot is also the gait at which you do much of your early training in this discipline. I explain the proper alignment and movements for riding the trot in dressage in the following sections.

Positioning your body

In dressage, body position is very important. The way you hold your body and use your weight sends messages to the horse. At the higher levels of dressage, the ability to communicate with the horse using your body is even more imperative.

In dressage, the following body position is standard:

- ✔ Riders sit deep in the saddle when they're sitting the trot and when they're in the down position during posting. In other words, your weight drops down into your rear end. You sit on your seat bones and sink into your hips.
- ✔ Your shoulders are open and square yet relaxed.
- ✔ Your back is flat — you don't want any arch.
- ✔ Your chin is up and your eyes are forward, looking where you're going.

Holding the reins

In dressage, you hold the reins in two hands. The reins go between your thumb and your index finger and come out between your pinky and ring fingers before going to the bit.

Hold your hands 2 to 3 inches apart from each other, which is closer than you'd have them at the walk (see Chapter 13). Your hands should about 2 inches above the horse's withers and forward on the horse's neck to allow freedom of movement for the horse's head. Keep your fingers closed in a relaxed fist, and make sure your reins have slight tension, giving you contact with the horse's mouth.

Putting your legs in dressage position

Your leg position at the trot is similar to your position at the walk (see Chapter 13). At the trot, your calf should be about 1 inch behind the girth. Your heel should be in line with your hip, and your knees should have considerable contact with the saddle without pinching the horse.

In correct position, the balls of your feet are in the stirrups and your heels are down. Your toes point forward so each foot is parallel to the horse's body. You should maintain light pressure with your calves on the horse's sides.

At the trot, you may find that your legs want to slip forward on the horse's sides. Have your instructor help you keep your legs in position by adjusting whatever flaws you have in the rest of your body position that may be causing your legs to slide forward.

Moving with the dressage horse

When the horse is trotting in dressage, you can either post or sit, as you find out in the following sections:

✔ Posting — or *rising to the trot,* as it's sometimes known in dressage — makes moving with the horse easier; use it when you're asking the horse for an extended (longer-strided) trot.

✔ You can sit the trot when you're asking the horse for a collected (shorter-strided) trot.

As with hunt seat (which I cover earlier in this chapter), pay attention to your legs while posting or sitting. Make sure they don't slide forward or backward. They should stay just behind the girth (see Chapter 8 for saddle images).

Posting the trot

Follow these steps to post the trot in dressage (check out Figure 14-4):

1. **Place your weight in the stirrup irons and lift your hips up out of the saddle, pushing your belly button forward and out.**

   Stretch into your heels and feel your weight in them. Do this in rhythm with the horse's gait. If you rise at the right moment in the horse's stride, one side of the horse's back will round as she trots, helping push you up out of the saddle.

2. **On the next stride, lower your seat into the saddle as that side of the horse's back seems to flatten.**

   Don't drop your weight, but gently lower yourself until the horse's back rounds again and pushes you up.

Figure 14-4:
When posting in dressage, place your weight in the stirrup irons and lift your hips up.

Knowing when to rise and when to sit when posting in dressage takes practice. Check out the tips that I give in the earlier section on posting the trot in hunt seat; they apply to dressage, too.

Sitting the trot

Begin with posting the trot (see the preceding section). To sit the trot, slow the horse down by adding tension on the reins and sinking your weight in the saddle. Keep your hips open by rounding your lower back. Sink deep into your seat bones so you can absorb the impact of the horse's trot and thus remain seated. (See Figure 14-5 for the sitting trot.)

Figure 14-5: Sink deep into your tailbone when sitting the trot in dressage.

Maneuvering the Horse at the Jog or Trot

Riders often change direction or circle at the trot (otherwise, the horse would just run into things more quickly!), so you have to know how to ask your horse for this cue. Stopping from the trot is also important, and it requires more finesse than stopping from the walk. I explain how to perform all these maneuvers in the following sections.

Stopping the horse

Although you're moving faster at the jog or trot than you are at the walk, the horse should still stop for you on command. Remember that the cue to stop a horse differs slightly between disciplines, as you find out in the following sections.

Stopping a horse from a jog or trot looks just like stopping a horse from the walk; check out Chapter 13 for figures depicting the stopping maneuver.

Western stops

Most Western horses perform a simple, quick stop without sliding. To stop a horse from a trot in Western riding, following these steps:

1. **Say "whoa" as you put tension on the reins while moving your hand backward toward your belly button; sink deep into the saddle and release all leg pressure from the sides of the horse, all at the same time.**

2. **When the horse comes to a stop, release the tension in the reins.**

English stops

In hunt seat and dressage, the horse walks before coming to a complete stop from the trot. Here's how you stop a horse from the trot in English riding:

1. **Sink your weight into the saddle.**

2. **Increase tension on the reins.**

   Sit tall with your heels down and your lower back and hip muscles relaxed. In hunt seat, put more tension on the reins while moving your hands backward and saying "whoa." In dressage, where you already have considerable contact (tension) on the reins, further increase that tension.

   In dressage, don't use your voice. The horse should stop without your using this aid.

3. **The horse breaks from a trot to a walk and eventually stops; when the horse stops walking, release the tension on the reins.**

   When the horse stops, try not to let your weight come forward in a whiplash effect. If you're sitting deep in the saddle, you'll be more likely to hold your position as the horse stops.

Turning left and right

When you master turning at the trot, you know you're really advancing in your riding. Turning the horse at a trot is a bit more challenging than turning at a walk because the additional speed requires you to remember how to cue your horse more quickly. Making tighter circles is easier for the horse if she's trotting.

In an arena, the side of your horse next to the rail is called the *outside,* and the side away from the rail is the *inside.*

Western turns

In Western riding, you use neck reining to turn the horse. Turn your horse either to the left or right, using your reins and your legs, in the following manner (see Figure 14-6):

1. **To turn your horse to the inside of the arena, away from the rail, move the hand holding the reins to the inside so that the outside rein is lying across the horse's neck.**

2. **At the same time, apply more pressure with your outside leg than you would at the walk.**

This leg pressure encourages the horse to turn to the inside while staying at the trot (and not breaking into a walk). The amount of pressure you apply depends on how the horse responds. Start with the least amount of pressure and increase it until the horse responds.

3. **When the turn is complete, move your rein hand back to the center of your horse and release the pressure from your outside leg.**

Figure 14-6:
Turning the horse at the jog requires more leg pressure than you'd apply at the walk.

English turns

In English riding, when you want your horse to turn either to the left or right at the trot, use your reins and your legs in the following manner (see Figure 14-7):

1. **To turn your horse to the inside of the arena, increase tension on the inside rein.**

   If you're riding hunt seat, pull the rein out slightly to the inside. If you're riding dressage, pull the rein back slightly.

2. **At the same time, apply pressure with your outside leg.**

   You should use more pressure here than you did at the walk to encourage the horse to maintain the trot as she turns to the inside. The amount of pressure you apply depends on how the horse responds. Start with the least amount of pressure and increase it until the horse responds.

3. **When the turn is complete, release the pressure on the inside rein and return it to its normal position; release the pressure from your outside leg as well.**

Figure 14-7: When turning at the trot in English, use your legs to maneuver the horse's body.

Circling the horse

Most of the circling you perform in riding lessons is at the jog or trot. Circling is an important maneuver because it helps you build communication with your horse as well as your riding skills. In the following sections, I explain the subtle cues you use to circle your horse in a Western jog and an English trot.

Jogging around in Western

When circling a horse at the jog in Western riding, you neck rein, using one hand on the reins. The following steps take you through a circle at the jog (see Figure 14-8):

1. **To circle your horse to the inside of the arena, start along the rail.**

   Move the hand holding the reins to the inside so that the outside rein is lying across the horse's neck.

2. **At the same time, apply pressure with your outside leg.**

   This pressure should be greater than what you'd use when circling at the walk. The horse moves away from the pressure, which encourages her to turn to the inside while maintaining the jog. Start with light pressure and increase it until the horse responds.

3. **Continue to maintain the rein and leg pressure as the horse turns.**

   When the horse is moving into a circle pattern, apply pressure with both legs to guide her through the circle and keep her from making the circle smaller than you want it.

4. **When the circle is complete (you know because you're back where you started, on the rail), move your rein hand back to the center of your horse and lighten the pressure from your legs.**

   Don't release the pressure completely or the horse may break into a walk.

Figure 14-8:
For Western
riding,
maintain
leg and
neck-rein
pressure
when
circling.

Rounding out English trots

When circling a horse at the trot in hunt seat and dressage riding, you use direct reining, with two hands on the reins. The following steps take you through a circle (see Figure 14-9):

1. **To circle your horse to the inside of the arena, (the only direction you'd turn in a circle), increase tension on the inside rein.**

   If you're riding hunt seat, pull the rein out slightly. If you're riding dressage, pull the rein back slightly.

2. **At the same time, apply pressure with your outside leg.**

   Use more pressure than you'd apply when circling at the walk. The horse moves away from the pressure, which encourages her to turn to the inside and maintain the trot. Start with light pressure and increase it until the horse responds.

3. **Continue to keep rein and leg pressure as the horse turns.**

   When the horse is moving into a circle pattern, apply pressure with both legs to guide her through the circle and keep her from making the circle smaller than you'd like.

4. **When the circle is complete (when you're back where you started), move your hands back to the center of your horse.**

   Reduce the amount of pressure from your legs only slightly, being sure not to take your legs off the horse completely. In both hunt seat and dressage, you need to maintain some contact with the horse's sides.

Figure 14-9: In English, apply pressure with both legs after the horse has begun the circle.

Trying Some Exercises

A good way to develop your jogging or trotting skills is to practice turns and circles. I give you some exercises to try in the following sections. You can suggest these to your riding instructor or do them when you're riding on your own in an arena.

Following a serpentine pattern in Western riding

Western riders can develop their skills at the jog using a winding pattern. This pattern allows you to change directions and straighten the horse often in the confines of an arena so you can become coordinated at using your reins and legs together.

This exercise has you and your horse jog up and down the arena, performing a serpentine pattern (see Figure 14-10):

1. **Start at one end of the arena, on the rail, at the jog.**

2. **When you get to the rail at the other end of the arena, turn the horse to the inside and make a half-circle (or as drivers like to call it, a U-turn).**

3. **As soon as the horse is facing opposite direction, ask her to go straight so you're parallel to the rail you're next to but farther away from it.**

4. **Jog down the length of the arena, and when you reach the end, turn the horse to the inside again so you complete a half-circle.**

   When the horse is facing the way you just came from, straighten her out and jog her forward.

5. **Complete this pattern up and down the entire arena until you reach the other side.**

   Then repeat and go back the way you came. I recommend doing the serpentine as many as five times.

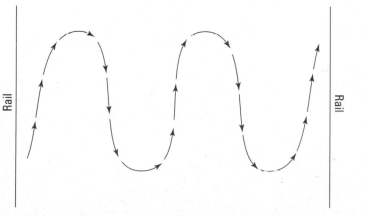

Figure 14-10: Jogging a serpentine pattern is a good way to practice turning and straightening the horse.

Circling jump poles in English riding

Remember riding the horses on the merry-go-round? Well, here's your chance to put all that circling to good use. A good exercise for hunt seat and dressage riders to practice at the trot involves moving over jump poles laid on the ground.

Before you do this exercise, talk to your instructor to make sure you're ready for this level of riding. Ask your instructor to help you with this exercise and supervise your progress.

By laying jump poles on the ground and trotting over them in a circular pattern, you can practice turning and keeping your horse straight at the trot. You can perform this exercise at either the sitting or posting trot:

1. **Lay four poles down in the center of the arena so they form a cross shape but don't touch each other.**

   The ends of the poles that are across from each other should be about 10 feet apart. In other words, you should have a 10-foot hole in the middle of the cross.

2. **Approach one of the poles at its center, trotting over the middle of the pole.**

3. **Turn the horse so she trots over the center of the next pole.**

4. **Repeat for the next two poles and then go back to the first pole (see Figure 14-11).**

   Continue the circle about five times.

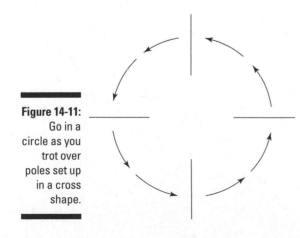

Figure 14-11:
Go in a circle as you trot over poles set up in a cross shape.

Figure 14-12 shows a rider trotting over the poles.

Figure 14-12:
Trotting over
poles in a
circle.

Chapter 15

Getting on the Fast Track with the Lope or Canter

For most new riders, the lope (Western) or canter (English) is one of the most exciting and enjoyable gaits to ride. Next to an all-out gallop, this smooth gait is the fastest you can go on a horse. Combining speed with rhythm, the lope or canter makes the wind ruffle your hair and gives you the sensation of being one with the horse.

The *lope* or *canter* is a three-beat gait. When a horse is cantering or loping *on the right lead,* his left hind leg comes down first, followed by his right hind leg and left foreleg together, and then his right foreleg follows. When a horse is *on the left lead,* the legs are reversed.

As the horse moves, he extends his forelegs while also gathering his hind legs beneath his body. The legs move rhythmically with each other in the same general direction. In one phase of this gait, all four hooves are off the ground at the same time (see Chapter 2 for a diagram showing the lope or canter). This gait can be a slow as 10 miles per hour or as fast as 20 miles per hour.

In this chapter, I tell you what you need to know to ask the horse to lope or canter. You find out how to ride the lope or canter in the Western and English disciplines, as well as how to make the horse stop, turn, and circle at this gait. At the end of the chapter, you find exercises that can help build your riding skills. (I don't discuss the gallop, a four-beat gait, because it's best attempted by experienced riders. After you've learned to ride, your instructor can help you ride the fastest gait.)

When riding the lope or canter, maintaining correct body position as well as correct leg and hand position are key. The proper position keeps you balanced as the horse races forward.

Cueing the Horse to Lope or Canter

Horses typically go from the walk (see Chapter 13) or jog or trot (see Chapter 14) into the lope or canter. Most beginning riders move their horses into a lope or canter from the walk, so this chapter describes moving from the slowest gait to the fastest one I cover in this book. As you find out in the following sections, the way you cue the horse to lope or canter depends on your riding discipline.

Ask the horse quietly first and increase the intensity of the cue if you don't get a response.

Western: Telling your horse you want to lope

When riding Western, you ask a horse to lope by moving the hand holding the reins forward to create more slack and by squeezing the horse forward with the calf of your outside leg (in an arena, the leg closest to the rail). Maintain this pressure until the horse steps into a lope. After you feel the horse respond, relax your calf. Keep your body position in mind as the horse starts to move forward (I describe body position at the lope later in this chapter).

If the horse doesn't respond at first and starts to jog, don't chase him into the lope by leaning forward and trying to make him go faster. Instead, bring him back to a walk and ask for the lope again, this time with greater pressure from your outside leg until you get a response. You may need to use your voice to encourage the horse — for many horses, a kissing sound is the cue to lope.

English: Requesting a canter

When riding hunt seat or dressage, ask a horse to canter by moving the inside rein (the rein closest to the center of the arena) slightly up, back, and out, all at the same time. In hunt seat, your outside rein (the rein closest to the rail) should be slightly slack and the inside rein should be slightly taut.

As you move the inside rein, squeeze the horse with the calf of your outside leg, and maintain this pressure until the horse begins cantering. After the horse responds, relax your leg. You want to maintain some contact with your legs, so don't take your legs completely off the horse.

In hunt seat riding — but not in dressage — you can also use your voice to encourage the horse to canter if you don't get an immediate response to your leg. You do so by making a kissing noise.

Riding the Lope in Western

In Western riding, the lope is a slow, collected gait (well, it's slow compared to a faster English canter or a gallop, but it's still the second-fastest gait). In highly trained Western pleasure horses, the lope is almost as slow as a jog.

In the show ring, the lope is used in pleasure and horsemanship classes (see Chapter 22 for info on shows). It's also the gait of choice for riders competing in reining classes, where collection and sensitivity to the rider are paramount.

Figure 15-1 shows riding the lope in Western. In correct position, riders have relaxed arms and a straight back, and they sit deep in the saddle. The legs are relaxed as well, and the rider holds the rein hand just above the withers. Read the following sections to discover how to position yourself correctly.

Positioning your body for Western

You get some speed with the lope, but you should still be relaxed. Maintain the following position (and refer back to Figure 15-1), but avoid becoming stiff. If you stiffen up, you may bounce in the saddle instead of moving with the horse (if you really want to bounce, the jog may be your ideal gait — see Chapter 14):

- ✔ When riding Western at the lope, sit deep in the saddle while also sitting tall. Your weight should be on your seat bones. Allow your body to rock gently with the movement of the horse.

- ✔ Sit up straight but not straight as a ramrod. Your shoulders should be relaxed, but don't slouch.

- ✔ Make sure you aren't leaning to one side of the horse or another as the horse lopes. Sit squarely in the saddle, using the saddle horn as a guide. The horn should be directly in front of you.

- ✔ Keep your elbows relaxed but at your sides. Don't let your elbows stick out and flap in the wind.

- ✔ Because the horse is going faster than he would at the trot, you may find yourself looking at the back of the horse's head. Doing so affects your balance, so instead get in the habit of looking straight ahead at where you're going.

Figure 15-1:
A Western rider has a deep seat, relaxed arms, and a straight back.

Holding the reins

At the walk or jog, you hold the reins about an inch or two over the horse's withers; however, when loping, you hold the reins even lower (refer to Figure 15-1). Your rein hand should be just in front of the pommel. This placement gives the horse's head the freedom of movement it needs at the lope.

Regardless of whether you hold the reins in California or traditional style (see Chapter 13 for the scoop on holding reins), keep your other hand on the same-side thigh or hanging alongside your leg, completely relaxed, as you do at the slower gaits.

Putting your legs in loping position

In Western riding, leg position is the same at the lope as it is at the walk and jog. When your horse is loping, have the balls of your feet in the stirrups and your heels down. Point your toes outward only slightly.

You should have a slight bend in your knees if your stirrups are set at the correct length (your riding instructor can help you there), and your legs should go alongside the cinch. The back part of each calf should fall just behind the cinch. After the horse responds to your cue and moves into the canter, each leg should have contact with the horse but not be pressing on him. (Refer back to Figure 15-1 for correct leg position.)

Because the lope is a faster gait than the walk or jog, keeping your legs in place as the horse moves forward takes more effort. Imagine that your calves are glued to your horse's sides so they can't move. That image can help you keep your legs still.

Moving with the Western horse

The lope is a faster gait than the jog, but it's a lot smoother. The rocking motion you feel when you lope is pleasant and easy to sit. To help yourself move with the horse's body, stay relaxed, sit deep in the saddle, and keep your arms loose. Allow your hips to move with the rhythm of the horse. Your upper body should be able to remain upright.

Riding the Canter in Hunt Seat

After mastering the trot in hunt seat (see Chapter 14 for more about riding the trot), you move on to the canter. The canter is an important working gait in hunt seat, and you'll do a lot with your horse at this gait after you advance in your riding. Plus, the canter is a lot of fun! The speed and rhythm of this gait are a real joy.

When riding the canter in hunt seat, you lean forward slightly at the hips, your legs are stable, and your hands are low. Figure 15-2 shows the canter in hunt seat; keep reading for the full scoop on positioning yourself correctly.

Figure 15-2:
Riding the canter in hunt seat warrants a forward bend at the hips.

Positioning your body for hunt seat

Stick to the following guidelines for proper body position when you're riding the canter in hunt seat (refer to Figure 15-2):

✔ When the horse is cantering, lean forward from the hips (not the waist), with a greater degree of bend than you'd have at the walk. Refer to Figure 15-2 to get a feel for the correct angle.

✔ Hold your hands about an inch above the horse's neck, which is slightly lower than where you'd hold them at the trot. This placement allows the horse to have more freedom of movement through his head and neck.

✔ When cantering in hunt seat, you should have a slight, natural arch in your lower back, with the rest of your back flat.

✔ Keep your elbows close to your body.

✔ Keep your shoulders back and your chin up.

Holding the reins

In hunt seat, you hold the reins in two hands. The reins go between your thumb and your index finger and come out between your pinky and ring fingers before going to the bit.

At the canter, hold your hands 2 to 3 inches apart from each other about an inch above the horse's neck and in front of the withers (toward the horse's head). Your hands are forward to allow freedom of movement for the horse's head, your fingers are closed in a relaxed fist, and your reins are snug but not tight against the horse's mouth. (Refer back to Figure 15-2.)

Putting your legs in cantering position

When riding the canter, your calves rest just behind the girth. The balls of your feet are in the stirrup, and your heels are down. Your toes should point slightly outward to help you maintain light contact with your calves on the horse's sides. Evenly distribute your weight through your seat, thighs, and feet. (Refer back to Figure 15-2 for the best leg position.)

When the horse is cantering, each knee has light contact with the saddle. Imagine that you're trying to use your knee to keep a wet sponge against the saddle without squeezing any water out.

At this gait, your calves have contact with the horse's sides as they do at the walk and trot, but add pressure to keep the horse moving at the canter. The amount of pressure you need depends on your horse. If your horse is very responsive, you maintain the same amount of pressure as you would at the trot (see Chapter 14 for info on trotting).

When cantering, concentrate on keeping your legs still. You don't want them to rock back and forth independently of the horse's sides. Pretend your legs are glued to the horse to help keep them stable.

Moving with the hunt seat horse

When the horse is cantering in hunt seat, lift your body up and slightly out of the saddle. This posture is called a *half seat* position. (**Note:** Your instructor may not use this method of riding the canter and instead suggest that you sit firmly in the saddle with a relaxed lower back.) Roll with the motion of the horse as he canters, finding his rhythm. Your legs should be glued to the horse's sides so they don't move on their own. Your hands should move up and back with the rhythm of the horse's head, but be careful not to exaggerate this movement by pumping your hands back and forth.

Riding the Canter in Dressage

The canter is used at most levels of competition in dressage (see Chapter 22 for info on horse shows). If you intend to compete in dressage in the future and go above the introductory level, you need to know this gait. Besides, riding the canter can be a blast!

In dressage, you sit deep in the saddle, relax your lower back, keep your legs still at the horse's sides, and hold the reins in both hands. Figure 15-3 depicts the canter in dressage. Read on for details on proper body position.

Positioning your body for dressage

Stick to the following guidelines for the best body position when you ride the canter in dressage (refer back to Figure 15-3 for a look):

- ✔ Sit deep in the saddle when you're cantering; let your weight drop down into your rear end, sit on your seat bones, and sink into your hips.

- ✔ Your shoulders are open and square yet relaxed.

- ✔ Your back is flat — you don't want any arch.

- ✔ Keep your elbows close to your body.

- ✔ Your chin is up and your eyes are forward, looking where you're going.

Figure 15-3:
Dressage
riders sit
deep in the
saddle at
the canter.

Holding the reins

In dressage, you hold the reins in two hands. The reins enter between your thumb and your index finger and exit between your pinky and ring fingers before heading to the bit.

Hold your hands 2 to 3 inches apart from each other, about 3 inches above the withers. At the canter, put your hands closer to your hips than you would at the trot (at the trot, your hands are forward on the horse's neck — see Chapter 14 for details). You want to prepare your horse for the canter in dressage, and you do so in part by creating more tension on the reins. Keep your fingers closed in a relaxed fist. (Refer back to Figure 15-3 for hand positioning.)

Putting your legs in position

At the canter in dressage, your calves stay about 1 inch behind the girth. Your heels are in line with your hips, and your knees have considerable contact with the saddle without pinching the horse. (Refer back to Figure 15-3.)

Leg position at the canter in dressage is similar to position at the walk and trot. The balls of your feet are in the stirrups, and your heels are down. Your toes point forward so your feet are parallel with the horse's body. You don't want your weight to rest in the stirrup irons, however; keep the pressure on the stirrups light.

Maintain firm pressure with your calves to keep the horse moving forward at the canter. The amount of pressure you apply depends on the horse. Your instructor can help you determine the right amount of pressure for the horse you're riding.

Keep your legs still. Think of them as being glued to your horse's sides to keep them from moving back and forth independently of the horse.

Moving with the dressage horse

In dressage, you want to sink into the horse's canter. Your hips should move with the rhythm of the horse, causing your rear end to "polish" the saddle as you ride.

Maneuvering the Horse at the Lope or Canter

In the following sections, I describe several important maneuvers for riding a horse at the lope or canter. After mastering this gait on the rail, beginning riders discover how to circle or turn their horses, so you have to know how to ask your horse for this move. Stopping from this gait is also important (you have to get off the horse *eventually*), and it requires more finesse than stopping from the walk or trot.

Whoa, Nelly! Stopping the horse

Although you're moving faster at the lope or canter than you are at the jog or trot, the horse should still stop for you on command. The cue to stop a horse differs slightly between disciplines, as you discover in the following sections. The way the horse stops also depends on the horse's training.

Stopping a horse from a lope or canter looks just like stopping a horse from the walk; check out Chapter 13 for figures depicting the stopping maneuver.

Western stops

Upon request, horses highly trained in the Western sport of reining can slide to a stop. However, most Western horses — especially those that beginners ride in a lesson program — perform a simple, quick stop without sliding. In most cases, a Western horse will take a couple of steps at a walk before coming to a complete stop from a lope.

To stop a horse from a lope in Western riding, following these steps:

1. **Sink deep into your seat and prepare to stop.**

   When preparing to stop from a lope, sit tall with your heels down and head up. Imagine drilling a hole through the seat of your saddle with your tailbone, and sink your body weight into the hole you just drilled.

2. **As you sink your body weight down, take your leg pressure off the horse's sides, pull the reins toward your belly button, and say "whoa."**

3. **When the horse comes to a stop, release the tension in the reins.**

English stops

In hunt seat and dressage, the horse trots and then walks a couple of strides before coming to a complete stop from the canter. Here's how to stop a horse from the canter in English riding:

1. **Sink your weight into the saddle and increase tension on the reins.**

   In hunt seat, say "whoa" and put tension on the reins while moving your hands backward; in dressage, where you already have contact (tension) on the reins, increase that tension.

   In dressage, don't use your voice. The horse should stop without using this aid.

2. **The horse breaks from a canter to a trot and goes into a walk.**

   Expect a couple of strides at each of these gaits before you get to a complete stop.

3. **When the horse stops walking, release the tension in the reins.**

   Try not to let your weight come forward in a whiplash effect. When you're sitting deep in the saddle, you're more likely to hold your position as the horse stops.

Turning in an L-pattern

Unlike with walking or trotting, a beginning rider at the canter usually isn't asked to change the horse's direction so that he's going the opposite way; the horse would need to *switch leads* (reverse which front leg extends first) to change directions at this gait, and riders find out how to get the horse to switch leads only at more-advanced stages of riding.

However, beginning riders can turn their horses in an L-pattern at the canter without changing directions (the classic move of the knight in chess — minus the jumping, of course). Take a look at the directional cues in the following sections for the discipline you plan to ride. Although executing these cues takes concentration at first, they can become second nature.

In an arena, the side of your horse next to the rail is called the *outside,* and the side away from the rail is the *inside.*

Western turns

In Western riding, you use neck reining to turn the horse at a lope. Use your reins and legs in the following manner to turn your horse either to the left or right (see Figure 15-4):

1. **To turn your horse to the inside of the arena, away from the rail, move the hand holding the reins to the inside so that the outside rein is lying across the horse's neck.**

Figure 15-4: When turning the horse in an L-pattern in Western, move the reins to the inside.

2. **At the same time, apply more pressure with your outside leg than you would at the jog.**

   This leg pressure encourages the horse to turn to the inside while staying at the lope and not breaking into a jog. If the horse doesn't respond to light pressure, add more until you get a response.

3. **When the turn is complete, move your rein hand back to the center of your horse and release the pressure from your outside leg.**

English turns

In English riding, when you want your horse to turn to the left or right at the canter, use your reins and legs in the following manner (see Figure 15-5):

1. **To turn your horse to the inside of the arena, away from the rail, "take a feel" of the inside rein.**

   In other words, pull the rein out slightly to the inside if you're riding hunt seat. If you're riding dressage, pull the rein back slightly.

Figure 15-5: Pull the rein out slightly to the inside when turning a horse in hunt seat.

2. **At the same time, apply pressure with your outside leg.**

   Use more pressure here than you would at the trot to encourage the horse to maintain the canter as he turns to the inside. Start with light pressure and increase until you get the response you're looking for.

3. **When the turn is complete, release the pressure on the inside rein and return it to its normal position; release the pressure from your outside leg as well.**

Circling the horse

As you progress in your riding, your instructor may ask you to circle your horse at the lope or canter. Circling helps you build communication with your horse as well as your riding skills. In the following sections, I explain the cues you use to circle your horse in a Western lope and an English canter.

Western circling

When circling a horse at the lope in Western riding, you neck rein, using one hand on the reins. The following steps take you through a circle at the lope (see Figure 15-6 for a Western rider circling at the lope):

1. **To circle your horse to the inside of the arena, start along the rail.**

2. **Move the hand holding the reins to the inside, away from the rail, so the outside rein is lying across the horse's neck; at the same time, apply pressure with your outside leg.**

   Apply more pressure than you'd use when circling at the jog. Start with slight pressure and increase until you get a response. The horse moves away from the pressure, encouraging him to turn to the inside while maintaining the lope.

3. **Apply pressure with both legs and continue to maintain the rein and leg pressure as the horse turns.**

   When the horse is moving into a circle pattern, apply pressure with both legs to guide him through the circle and keep the circles from getting smaller. This pressure also keeps the horse from moving straight and breaking the circle. Use more leg pressure here than you'd use at the jog.

4. **When the circle is complete (when you're back where you started, on the rail), move your rein hand back to the center of your horse and lighten the pressure from your legs.**

   Don't release the pressure completely or the horse may break into a jog.

Figure 15-6:
Hold the reins to the inside while applying leg pressure when you circle at the lope.

English circling

When circling a horse at the canter in hunt seat and dressage, you use direct reining, with two hands on the reins. The following steps take you through a circle (see Figure 15-7 for an English rider circling at the canter):

1. **To circle your horse to the inside of the arena, away from the rail, "take a feel" of the inside rein.**

   In other words, if you're riding hunt seat, pull the rein out slightly away from the horse's neck; if you're riding dressage, pull the rein back slightly toward your hip.

2. **At the same time, apply pressure with your outside leg.**

   Use more pressure than you'd apply when circling at the trot. Start with slight pressure and increase until you get a response. The horse moves away from the pressure, turning to the inside and maintaining the canter.

3. **Apply pressure with both legs and continue to keep rein and leg pressure as the horse turns.**

   When the horse is moving into a circle pattern, apply pressure with both legs to guide him through the circle and to keep the circle from getting smaller or breaking. Use more leg pressure than you would at the trot. Start with light pressure and increase until you get a response.

4. **When the circle's complete, move your hands back to the center of your horse.**

   Only slightly reduce the amount of pressure from your legs, being sure not to take your legs off the horse completely.

Figure 15-7: Maintain rein and leg pressure at the canter in English to keep the horse turning in a circle.

Trying a Couple of Balancing Exercises

A good way to develop your riding skills is to practice circles at the lope or canter on the lunge line. The *lunge line* (also called a *longe line*) is a long rope that attaches to the horse's bridle; your instructor or another person familiar with the task holds the other end of the rope, standing in the center of the circle created by the horse's movement. In some cases, the person holding the lunge line also holds a lunge whip as a visual cue to encourage the horse to move forward in the circle.

Your riding instructor can help you with the exercises in the following sections by controlling the horse on the lunge line as you practice your balance at the lope or canter. That way, you can focus on what you're doing with your body and rather than on making the horse go forward.

Look, Ma, no hands! Western lunge line work

The following exercise (in Figure 15-8) teaches you balance at the lope and discourages you from using the reins to balance:

1. **With the horse on the lunge line, the instructor asks the horse to pick up the lope.**

Figure 15-8: With your instructor holding the lunge line, keep your arms at your sides as the horse lopes.

2. **When the horse is loping, place the reins on his neck or over the pommel of the saddle and allow your arms to hang loosely at your sides.**

   Drop the reins completely. Let go!

3. **The horse lopes in a circle around your instructor as you practice balancing without having your hands on the reins.**

One-handed English lunge line work

A good way for hunt seat and dressage riders to learn balance without depending on the reins is to canter on the lunge line (see Figure 15-9):

1. **With the horse on the lunge line, the instructor asks the horse to pick up the canter.**

2. **When the horse is cantering, you place the reins in one hand; rest this hand on the horse's withers and extend the other arm outward away from your body.**

   You can start by extending the arm on the inside of the circle and then switch to the other arm for a continuation of this exercise if your instructor so chooses.

3. **The horse canters in a circle around your instructor as you practice balancing with one arm out and the other holding loose reins.**

Figure 15-9:
Extend one arm away from your body while your instructor controls the horse's movement.

Chapter 16

Making the Leap into Jumping

*J*umping isn't part of the Western and dressage disciplines, but for most hunt seat riders, jumping is the ultimate goal. The feeling of soaring over a fence on the back of a horse is exhilarating. After you try it, it's hard not to get hooked.

In this chapter, I tell you about the different types of competitive jumping and the various types of fences. I also detail how to ask a horse to jump, how to position your body when jumping, and how to ride over multiple jumps. Finally, I cover common jumping problems and how to deal with them.

Safety is an important issue, especially during the learning process. Make sure your instructor is present when you practice your jumping, and always wear an ASTM/SEI-approved safety helmet. (See Chapter 5 for more information on helmets.) Also, if you're just figuring out how to jump, you should be studying with an experienced jumping instructor and riding an experienced jumping horse, one known for her ability and willingness to jump with an inexperienced jumper rider on her back.

Delving into Different Types of Jumping

Jumping is exciting in the schooling arena, but it's even more of a rush in competition. Most hunt seat riders work toward the eventual goal of jumping in one of several types of competitions. Each of the competitions in the following sections offers different challenges and requires certain types of horses and riders. (For an introduction to horse competitions, head to Chapter 22.) You can also learn jumping just for the fun of it, although most riders who study jumping soon get the urge to compete.

On the inside: Arena jumping

The most popular type of competitive jumping takes place in an arena. Riders can compete in two basic types of arena jumping: show jumping (also called stadium jumping) and hunters.

Show jumping

If you've ever watched the equestrian events during the Olympic Games, you've probably seen show jumping (check out Figure 16-1). Show jumping can take place in a stadium as big as Madison Square Garden or in the arena of your local boarding stable. The rules are essentially the same, regardless of the venue. Only the experience and skill levels of the horses and riders — and the winning prize — differ from one setting to the next.

In *show jumping,* horse and rider teams have to negotiate a series of jumps within a certain amount of time. The team that finishes the course in the shortest amount of time with the fewest faults is the winner. Teams accumulate faults when the horse knocks down parts of the jump, when the horse refuses to take a jump (I discuss refusals later in this chapter), or when the rider jumps the fences in the wrong order.

Fences for beginners often start at 2 feet, 6 inches. At the higher levels, which include the Olympics, fences can be as high as 8 feet or more.

Figure 16-1:
Show jumping, also called stadium jumping, is a timed event.

Hunters

Based on the British tradition of foxhunting, *hunter classes* consist of a series of jumps that horse and rider have to negotiate in a particular order. Unlike show jumping, hunter classes are not timed. Instead, judges rate the horse on her manners and how she looks when going over the fences. The fences are also lower in hunter classes.

In hunter classes, riders are expected to dress a certain way (see Chapter 7 for more information about hunt seat apparel) and to groom their horses accordingly. Hunter horses usually have braided manes and tails and are impeccably groomed.

Beginning hunters can start out with a crossrails class, which consists of a course made up of crossrails only, the smallest of jumps (I describe crossrail jumps later in this chapter). Many schooling shows offer hunter classes with fences as low as 12 inches. At the upper levels of hunters, fences get as high as 4 feet.

Out there: Cross-country jumping

Cross-country jumpers are the daredevils of the jumping world. They jump over just about anything in their way. You can find competitive cross-country courses at all levels, from novice to the Olympics. Cross-country may be part of a competition called *three-day eventing* (dressage and show jumping are the other two events), or it can stand on its own as a separate, single competition.

Cross-country events take place out in the open (see Figure 16-2). The courses consist of a series of jumps presented over several miles, and the level of competition determines the number of miles and jumps. Unlike arena jumping, which is made up of non-solid jumps that fall down when the horse hits them, cross-country jumps are solid and don't fall, making this sport a bit riskier than arena jumping.

The jumps in cross-country consist of a variety of objects, including telephone poles and ditches that must be jumped over and water obstacles that require the horse to land in a small pond. The horse and rider have to complete the course within a given time frame. Horse-and-rider teams receive faults if the horse refuses the jump or the rider falls off.

Cross-country jumps can start at as low as a telephone pole on the ground and work their way up to 11 feet, 10 inches for *ditch drop jumps* (jumps that require the horse to land lower than where she took off) in the more advanced divisions. Because cross-country jumps vary so much, some obstacles are long rather than tall, meaning the horse has to jump farther rather than higher.

Figure 16-2: Cross-country jumping tests the stamina and courage of horses and riders.

Checking Out Types of Fences

If you plan to ride hunt seat and learn to jump, you need to know some of the common types of fences you may have to negotiate. As I explain in the following sections, each fence type offers its own set of challenges — and learning experiences — for both horse and rider. Figure 16-3 depicts five popular types of fences: crossrails, verticals, oxers, walls, and cross-country jumps. Riding instructors start students on the easiest fence first and move them to more advanced fences when they're ready.

X marks the spot: Crossrails

A crossrails fence is considered a warm-up fence, and it's the first fence you jump when you're learning this skill. *Crossrails* consist of two rails in an X shape placed between two *jump standards,* or the vertical poles that hold up the horizontal poles (refer to Figure 16-3 for an illustration of a crossrails fence).

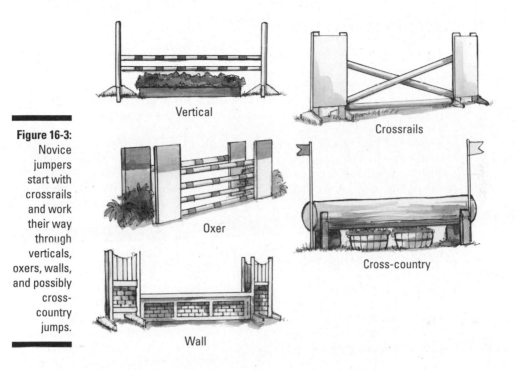

Figure 16-3:
Novice
jumpers
start with
crossrails
and work
their way
through
verticals,
oxers, walls,
and possibly
cross-
country
jumps.

Vertical

Crossrails

Oxer

Cross-country

Wall

Crossrails are designed to encourage the horse to jump in the center of the jump, the lowest point. This fence is the best one for beginners because it teaches them to gauge where the center of the jump is. For novice jumpers, jumping off to the side of the crossrails rather than in the center is a common mistake. Also, horses sometimes *leave too early* with crossrails, meaning they jump sooner than they should to properly clear the barrier.

Get some air: Verticals

A vertical fence is more advanced than a crossrails fence (see the preceding section), but it's still suitable for beginning jumpers. *Vertical fences* consist of two jump standards (vertical poles) and one or two poles laid out horizontally between them, kind of like a split rail fence (refer back to Figure 16-3).

Verticals are ideal for helping riders figure out how to judge distance — to know where the horse should take off for the jump. For new riders, vertical fences are more challenging than crossrails because verticals don't provide a lot of visual definition for the horse. The horse may have trouble determining the best place to start to jump, so the rider needs to provide guidance. This responsibility can be difficult for new jumpers, who are just figuring out how to judge distance themselves. The result may be that the horse takes off too soon or too late to jump the obstacle. (See the later section "Taking the jump" for more information about the jumping process.)

Go the distance: Oxers

More advanced than vertical fences, oxers provide a more three-dimensional obstacle for horses. *Oxers* have two sets of jump standards (vertical posts) and two sets of horizontal poles, making them deeper than verticals. *Even oxers* have horizontal poles at the same level; *uneven oxers* have the front set of poles lower than the other. Refer to Figure 16-3 for an image.

Students negotiate oxers after they've mastered the skill of correctly judging distance with crossrails and verticals. Because the horse has to jump width as well as height when negotiating an oxer, this jump teaches horse and rider to take off from the right place; the added dimension helps the pair estimate distance more accurately.

Not as scary as they look: Walls

Walls are the most intimidating of the jumps because they appear solid and therefore bigger. A *wall* is just what it sounds like: a wall built between two jump standards (vertical poles). Of course, the wall in this case is just a series of unattached, lightweight blocks stacked on top of each other. The lack of mortar enables them to come down easily if the horse strikes them with her legs. (See Figure 16-3 for an image.)

To jump a wall, you need a confident horse who's not easily frightened by jumps. Some horses become hesitant when jumping a wall because the jump looks more difficult to negotiate and because they can't see what's on the other side.

These fences can be daunting to horses, so you need to exhibit confidence in yourself to encourage your horse to take the leap of faith. Jumping walls helps you become a "brave" jumper. The more walls you jump, the more confident you'll be; in turn, you'll pass that confidence on to your horse.

A test of stamina: Cross-country jumps

When beginning to jump cross-country, riders encounter relatively easy obstacles — compared to what the upper levels are jumping, that is. These obstacles can be anything from telephone poles to low shrubs, from verticals to oxers (which you may have encountered in your arena lessons — see the earlier sections on these types of fences). In Figure 16-3, the long wooden pole at the bottom right is an example of a cross-country jump.

When jumping cross-country obstacles, you test your stamina and that of your horse. You also put all the skills you learned in arena jumping to the test while you're out in the great wide open.

Making Your Way through the Jumping Process

Horses are amazing for many reasons, one of which is their ability to jump. Jumping comes naturally to horses, although they need to be taught proper technique. Proper jumping involves good *form over fences* (the way the horse carries herself), obedience to the rider (in order to take direction), and courage (to jump over something intimidating when asked).

In the following sections, I describe the two-point position, which is crucial in successful jumping. I also take you through a single jump step-by-step.

Practicing the two-point position

Before you can take a horse over a jump, you need to know how to hold your body while the horse is in the air. Called the *two-point,* this position enables you to stay balanced while taking your weight off the horse's back to assist her in clearing the jump.

Your riding instructor should give you plenty of practice at the two-point position before you start jumping. Regularly practicing this position can build up the muscles in your legs so you can adequately hold yourself in two-point over a series of jumps.

Follow these guidelines for the two-point position (and see Figure 16-4). In one motion, make sure you

- ✔ Bend forward from the hips (not your waist) so your chest is at a 45-degree angle to your horse's body.
- ✔ Put your weight in your heels, which are pointing down. Keep contact on the saddle with your knees without squeezing.
- ✔ Lift yourself slightly but not completely from the saddle.
- ✔ Keep your hands low, almost resting on the horse's neck.
- ✔ Keep your head straight ahead with eyes looking forward.

Figure 16-4:
A rider in two-point position rider bends forward from the hips while lifting her weight out of the saddle.

Taking the leap

So exactly how do you get a horse to jump over a fence? Essentially, you aim the horse toward the fence and ask her to go forward, and the horse takes the jump. Your job as the rider is to

✔ Keep the horse centered as she approaches the jump

✔ Control her speed so she approaches the jump in a controlled manner

✔ Assume a correct body position to allow the horse to jump without interference

The horse does the rest!

When jumping more than one fence in succession (see the later section called "Riding over Multiple Jumps"), you also need to measure the horse's strides and control her speed so she takes off for the jump from the right spot. Some horses are naturally good at figuring out this distance and timing for themselves, but your job as a rider is to influence the horse and guide her.

Before you start jumping, warm up your horse. Walk and trot her in the arena for at least 10 minutes so her muscles are ready to work.

Keeping your horse obedient and brave

Although jumping is a natural behavior for a horse, jumping with a rider on board is not. You can do a lot to make sure your horse is willing to jump with you on her back.

First, encourage your horse to be obedient. Before you start jumping, spend time riding your horse in the arena and practice turns and circles at the different gaits as I discuss in Chapters 13, 14, and 15. This practice is a good way of "turning up" your horse before you start jumping.

Next, work on your own confidence to help your horse be brave. Horses are very sensitive, and they pick up on a rider's feelings. If you're riding a horse who doesn't have a lot of confidence and experience in jumping and you're fearful as you approach a jump, you may scare your horse. The good news is that most lesson horses are brave on their own and don't need the rider to exude a lot of confidence to take a jump. A horse like this can help you build your own confidence when riding, enabling you to take that confidence to any horse you ride.

When you're ready to jump, follow these steps:

1. **Ask the horse to trot (see Chapter 14 for details on trotting).**

   Make sure you like the speed the horse is going and that you feel balanced and comfortable. Then turn her toward the fence. Make sure you have at least four horse-lengths worth of distance between you and the fence when you start your approach.

2. **Keep your legs on the horse for contact as you approach the fence and aim the horse at the center of the jump.**

   More than likely, your horse's ears will go up when she sees the fence in anticipation of taking the jump.

   Keep your eyes forward and resist the urge to look down at the jump. Doing so may throw you off balance.

3. **Just as you approach the base of the jump, assume the two-point position (see the preceding section), keeping contact with your legs.**

   If your horse is a bit on the sluggish side, you may want to add a little more pressure with your calves just as you hit the spot where she needs to take off. You'll have a sense of where this spot is as you get close to the jump.

4. **As the horse goes over the jump, maintain the two-point position and prepare yourself mentally for landing.**

   By staying in position and maintaining your balance, you help the horse make it over the jump.

5. **When the horse lands, stay in the two-point position for a couple of strides and then slowly sit back in the saddle.**

   Keep your eyes up and focused at the end of the arena to help you maintain your balance.

   If you feel like you're being left behind when your horse lands after the jump, grab some mane in one of your hands just before the horse jumps. This grip can help you balance and keep you moving with the horse when you land.

   To get an idea of what your body should look like as you go over a fence, see Figure 16-2, earlier in this chapter.

Riding over Multiple Jumps

After you master jumping a single fence, your riding instructor may start you on multiple fences. Different multiple-fence patterns, such as the ones in the following sections, teach you specific jumping skills. Your instructor will watch you go over each series of fences and give you advice on your jumping as you practice.

Getting on the grid

One of the first fence patterns you may jump in your training is called a grid. Designed to help you learn balance when jumping, a *grid* consists of two to four fences (or poles on the ground) in a row, usually with poles also laid on the ground perpendicular to these fences to serve as guides. These poles help keep the horse moving straight toward the jump on the approach. The fences in a grid are easy jumps, such as crossrails (which I describe earlier in this chapter). See Figure 16-5 for a photo of a grid.

The grid pattern is laid out to create measured strides between fences. When strides are unmeasured, as in lines and courses, a horse may have difficulty deciding on the right place to negotiate the jump; the horse needs guidance from the rider on the proper number and length of strides between fences (see the later sections called "Staying in line" and "Being on course" for info on other types of multiple jumps).

However, the premeasured distances in a grid make jumping multiple fences easier on the rider. You don't have to figure out how many strides the horse needs to take between jumps. A grid may require one stride between two fences and then two strides between two others. Because the strides are already measured between fences, the grid teaches the rider where he or she and the horse must take off in order to successfully clear a fence.

Figure 16-5:
Riders learn
to judge
distances
between
fences
when
jumping a
grid.

Staying in line

Besides the grid (see the preceding section), another simple fence pattern for novice jumpers is a line. Consisting of two or three fences in a row, often crossrails, a *line* has unmeasured distances between the obstacles. In other words, the jumps weren't designed so that the horse has to take a specific number of strides between them. Instead, one fence may have two strides before it, while another may have four or five.

The rider has to determine how many strides the horse needs to take and at what speed to successfully negotiate the jumps. The rider then has to communicate the decision to the horse by asking the horse to shorten or lengthen her strides accordingly. Successful estimates come with repeated practice and guidance from your instructor. Figure 16-6 shows a rider navigating a line pattern.

Being on course

When the novice jumper is ready, the riding instructor introduces a course. A *course* consists of seven to nine fences of different types. The instructor may set the course to have a couple of single fences, a couple of lines, a diagonal line, and perhaps a line of fences toward the outside of the course. Some of these jumps may include walls or oxers (which I discuss earlier in this chapter). The challenge of riding a course is to keep a rhythm to the jumping. Figure 16-7 shows an arena course.

Figure 16-6:
A line
consists
of two or
more fences
set at an
unmeasured
distance
apart.

Figure 16-7:
When riders
have
mastered
the grid and
line, they're
ready for
more
variation in
a course.

Riders must be skilled at judging distances to a fence so they can control the number of strides the horse takes in between. The distance between fences and the length of the particular horse's strides determine what this number will be. Tall, long-legged horses tend to have longer strides than shorter, more compact horses.

Horse-and-rider teams negotiate courses in both hunter and show jumper competitions. The type of course and the height of the jumps depend on the level of competition and whether hunters or jumpers are being judged. See Chapter 22 for more info on shows.

Overcoming Jumping Problems

Although jumping is natural for horses, jumping strange objects that a horse can easily go around, with a rider on her back, is not. Consequently, jumping problems do arise from time to time. Most of these problems are "manmade," meaning that horses develop these issues because of bad experiences due to poor riding.

As a novice jumper, you hopefully won't have to deal with any of the problems in the following sections. Most of the *school masters* (lesson horses) who help teach beginners how to jump are push-button; they'll jump pretty much anything, no matter what. But should you ever find yourself dealing with a horse who has jumping issues such as refusing, running out, or rushing, you want to know what's causing the problem and how to fix it.

Refusing to jump

When a horse refuses a jump, she's, well, refusing to jump. This problem usually crops up when the horse puts on the brakes at the moment she's supposed to take off over the obstacle (see Figure 16-8).

The consequences to the rider are often unpleasant. The rider, anticipating the horse's forward motion, is thrown off balance. In the best case scenario, you may fall forward onto the horse's neck and then recover. In the worst case scenario, you can fall forward over the horse's neck and end up in the dirt (aren't you glad you're wearing a helmet?).

Horses refuse fences when they lack confidence. They're afraid they can't make the jump, so they stop short. Sometimes, this fearfulness — or occasionally, disobedience — comes from a lack of confidence in the rider. The horse senses the rider's uncertainty and becomes uncertain, too.

Figure 16-8:
Refusals are
the result
of lack of
confidence
in the
horse and
sometimes
the rider.

Don't punish a horse who refuses jumps; instead, lower the jump to a height that's more comfortable for the horse and try again. You may have to lower the jump to the point where the horse can just step over it from a walk. The goal is to rebuild the horse's confidence.

Running out

Running out occurs when a horse veers around a jump instead of going over it (see Figure 16-9). A form of refusal, this habit stems from a lack of confidence on the part of the horse and/or rider. Running out can be scary because it can throw you off balance when you least expect it.

To help a horse learn to take a jump instead of running out, create a "funnel" by placing two poles on either side of the jump standard, with one end resting on the top bar of the jump and the other end on the ground. These poles create a visual guide to encourage the horse to go straight over the jump rather than around it. When guiding the horse toward the funnel, keep the reins a little bit shorter than usual while applying an even amount of leg pressure to help give the horse confidence.

Figure 16-9: Horses run out on fences when they lack confidence to jump them.

Rushing

When a horse *rushes* a jump, she approaches it too quickly and takes off from the ground at the wrong place, failing to take the correct number of strides between fences (see Figure 16-10). As the horse tries to take the jump, she strikes the fence with her hooves and knocks it down.

The causes of rushing can be multiple. Sometimes, the rider is unwittingly *gunning* the horse, or pushing the horse too quickly with too much leg pressure. The horse gets excited and overanticipates the jump. Horses also rush jumps because they're anxious about jumping, are worried they won't make the jump unless they approach it with a lot of speed, or simply aren't listening to the rider.

To reschool a horse who rushes, keep gentle pressure on the reins without making them too taut when approaching the jump. Trot to the fence, jump over it, and then stop after it. Do this step repeatedly until the horse understands that jumping doesn't mean a mad dash around the arena. The grid obstacle, which I describe earlier in this chapter, can be helpful in teaching the horse patience. This setup works because the jumps come quickly one after another, forcing the horse to slow down and think before leaping.

Figure 16-10:
A horse who over-anticipates the jump or is pushed too fast by the rider may rush the fence.

Part IV
Riding into Advanced Pastures

The 5th Wave   By Rich Tennant

Still having trouble controlling that horse of yours, huh Colburn?

In this part . . .

*P*art IV takes you to the next level of horsemanship by showing you what's involved in horse ownership. You also find out whether you need to find a new instructor — or whether you need additional conditioning — to help you reach your maximum potential.

Chapter 17

Graduating to the Next Level of Riding

In This Chapter

▶ Sleuthing out a more advanced instructor

▶ Exploring the possibility of switching disciplines

▶ Improving your riding skills by cross-training

*L*earning to ride is hard work, and just as with anything in life, hard work pays off. If you've taken lessons and practiced your riding to the point where you're now an intermediate rider, congratulations! Of course, this new prowess comes with some responsibilities and benefits.

In this chapter, I help you take advantage of your newfound skills. You discover how to find a new instructor and/or explore other disciplines. You also find out how to get your mind and body ready for greater challenges in the saddle.

Finding a New Instructor or Trainer

Some horse trainers and riding instructors teach students at all levels of horsemanship in their chosen discipline. Others teach only beginners or just beginners and intermediate students. If you've moved to the next level of riding and feel your instructor or trainer can no longer give you valuable learning opportunities, consider switching to a teacher who focuses on more-advanced riders.

Saying goodbye as you graduate

If you decide to switch instructors, you can either let your old teacher know why you're leaving or take the coward's way out and just change your phone number. Of course, letting your original instructor know that you've moved on to the next level and feel you can develop your skills more with someone else is the nobler way to handle the situation. Soften the blow by giving your instructor a nice gift or card to show your appreciation for all you've learned.

When searching for a new instructor, follow a procedure similar to the one you used to find your original instructor (see Chapter 3 for details). This time, keep in mind that your skills are much more honed. Here are some steps you can take when searching for someone to help you at your new level of riding:

- **Contact an organization that certifies riding instructors:** Certification organizations may be able to provide you with the contact information of instructors in your area (for a list of some of these organizations, see the Appendix). Some of these organizations include information on each instructor and can give you a sense of whether the instructor takes on intermediate or advanced students.

- **Attend horse shows in your area:** As you watch the classes, you should notice trainers and riding instructors working with their students on the sidelines. Take note of the instructors and trainers who work with the students who do most of the winning or whose riding you most admire. When the show is over or during the lunch break, approach the trainer or instructor and find a good time for you two to talk. The person should be happy to discuss his or her program with you over the phone or in person at a later date. (Chapter 22 has general information on horse shows.)

- **Ask other riders for a referral:** Talk to riders at your boarding stable or horse club and find out whom they ride with. You can learn a lot about instructors and trainers and their reputations by talking to fellow horse people.

After you meet an expert or two whom you're interested in working with, take a few private riding lessons with that person. Gauge whether the trainer seems comfortable teaching someone at your riding level, and make sure you like the person's teaching style. Then discuss your riding goals and see whether the trainer feels he or she can take you to the next level.

Switching Disciplines

Perhaps you ride Western and look with envy at the hunt seat riders sailing over fences. Or maybe you found out that dressage just doesn't offer you all the calf-roping opportunities you're looking for. If so, now may be a good time to look into other disciplines.

If you think you want to try another riding style, explore that discipline thoroughly before you make the switch. If your instructor also teaches that other discipline, take a lesson from him or her to make sure you like riding in that style before you completely switch over. Or find another instructor who teaches that discipline and take a lesson or two to see whether you like it (see Chapter 3 for information on choosing a stable and instructor).

You can always try a new discipline for a while and switch back to your original style of riding if you decide you don't like the change. That's the great thing about taking lessons as opposed to owning your own horse and tack — you aren't committed to a particular style if you discover you don't like it. In fact, you can take a lesson in all the disciplines out there if you want to, just for the fun of it.

Of course, if you're just looking for some new challenges, you may simply want to try some alternative riding styles or activities that fit within your discipline. Part V of this book runs through some of your options.

Growing Stronger with Advanced Conditioning

As you advance in your riding, you may want to condition your body for harder work. If you haven't already been *cross-training* (participating in physical activities besides riding; see Chapter 4 for details), consider working it into your routine. Although you don't have to cross-train in order to ride, doing one or more additional exercises can help. Here are some possible activities (*Note:* Make sure you check with your doctor before you begin any exercise program):

✔ **Jogging:** Jogging is helpful because first and foremost, it builds endurance. Endurance is most important for English riders because as you advance, you'll have to spend more time posting at the trot (see Chapter 14) and riding the canter (see Chapter 15), two activities that require strong wind so you don't get out of breath. Jogging also builds muscle strength in your legs and can help keep your weight down.

- ✓ **Aerobics:** Formal aerobics classes are an excellent way to build the kind of stamina you need for more-advanced riding. If you're an English rider, consider doing aerobics for 30- to 45-minute sessions so you don't have trouble keeping up in your riding lessons when posting the trot or cantering.

- ✓ **Weight training:** Lifting weights is a good way to build strength in both the arms and the legs.

  Whether working with free weights or a weight machine, keep the weights light and the repetitions many. You want to build strong, sinewy muscles rather than bulk — bulk makes you heavier and less flexible.

- ✓ **Swimming:** Swimming is great for building stamina and strength. The resistance that water provides challenges your muscles and makes them stronger without stressing the joints like high-impact exercises can. Your lung capacity can develop, too, if you start a swimming regimen, because swimming calls for a considerable amount of exertion.

- ✓ **Hiking:** If you aren't the type to join a gym or jog around the neighborhood waving at people you know, consider hiking instead. If you hike in hilly areas, you can quickly build both your wind and the muscles in your legs. Personally, I find hiking the most enjoyable of all cross-training activities. It's a day out in the country enjoying nature while building your body for riding at the same time.

- ✓ **Jumping rope:** A great way to develop stamina is to jump rope. Children tend to jump rope just for fun, but jumping rope as an adult is a lot more challenging. Not only do adults need to relearn the timing of it, but they also get winded a lot faster. You should find that if you jump rope on a regular basis (several times a week), your stamina will be surprisingly good when you ride.

As you cross-train in one or more of these additional sports and exercises, remember that no substitute exists for regular riding. Although these activities can help you build your endurance and muscle strength, actual riding hones your muscles and wind more appropriately for your number one sport. Ride as often as you can!

Improving Your Balance and Timing

The time you spend in the saddle can develop the balance and coordination you need for more-advanced work, but you can certainly help the process along. Cross-training in one or more activities that encourage balance and the development of motor skills and hand-eye coordination can make you a better rider. Here are some ideal activities:

- **Yoga:** Yoga's a great tool to make your body flexible, and it helps with balance and muscle strength. Yoga also helps you figure out how to truly relax, something that can come in handy when dealing with an easily spooked horse who takes his cue from the tension in your body.

- **Pilates:** Pilates is a type of strengthening exercise that has caught on with many people, especially riders. It improves flexibility and builds strength without adding bulk. The mental conditioning that's a part of Pilates training can also be helpful. You can take a Pilates class or buy a Pilates DVD to watch at home.

- **Dance:** In a sense, riding is like dancing with your horse. If you can master dancing with a human partner or even by yourself, you'll be more in tune when it comes time to "dance" with your horse (the best dance partner with two left feet you'll ever have!).

  For cross-training, try just about any kind of dance you like to do, whether it's ballroom dancing, square dancing, line dancing, or club dancing. Ballet in particular takes real dedication, but a class or two can really help. So get your groove on! Dancing helps improve both your balance and your timing, so if you do it regularly, you'll become a more coordinated rider.

- **Tennis:** Although tennis is much more aerobic than the other activities I list here, it works in this category because it requires considerable coordination. If you can develop the kind of timing it takes to precisely hit a ball that's coming at you with considerable speed, you should be better able to coordinate the parts of your body in a fraction of a second when you're riding.

Just about any sport can improve your work in the saddle. And just think: If you take on one of these hobbies in addition to your riding, no one can accuse you of being completely horse crazy!

Chapter 18

Taking the Plunge by Buying a Horse

In This Chapter

▶ Exploring the idea of horse ownership

▶ Considering various factors when you choose a horse

▶ Getting some helps as you shop

*I*f you're like many people who take up horseback riding, it isn't long before you start wanting a horse of your own. Horses are addictive, and after they get into your blood, it's impossible to get them out.

Horse ownership is serious business, and not just because horses can be expensive; they require a huge amount of time and energy. Horse ownership calls for a serious commitment, so make sure you're ready before you take the plunge.

In this chapter, I give you an overview of the horse-buying process and what you need to consider when you're involved in this exciting task. Chapter 19 explains general horse care, but for even more details on the issues I cover in this chapter and the next, check out my other book, *Horses For Dummies*, 2nd Edition (Wiley).

Deciding Whether to Get a Horse of Your Own

Owning a horse is wonderful. You can ride whenever you want and are in complete control of your horse's well-being. But horse ownership also requires a significant investment of both time and money. In the following sections, I outline the realities of horse ownership to help you decide whether you're ready for such a major commitment.

Understanding ownership realities

Taking care of Fido and Fluffy when you were a kid probably taught you a lot about responsibility, but horse care tends to be a little more involved. Consider the following realities about horse ownership before you make a purchase:

- ✔ **Hard work:** Horse ownership involves more than just riding and having fun. If your horse lives with you, you'll be the one to feed her, groom her, and clean her stall. This latter task means mucking manure off the ground. It's not the greatest job, but it's absolutely necessary to keep your horse — and your neighbors — happy and healthy.

- ✔ **A lot of responsibility:** Your horse depends on you for everything: food, water, companionship, and exercise. It's only right, then, that you make your horse a priority in your life. You may have to skip some social engagements to take care of your horse after work or brave cold, nasty weather to get out to the barn. Going away on vacation involves finding and paying a horse-sitter, too. And if you board on your own property, you're responsible for upkeep of any structures. Horses can live to be 30 years old or more, so you may be doing these jobs for quite a while.

- ✔ **Financial obligations:** Owning a horse is expensive, and the purchase price is just your first outlay of costs. Also on your tab will be food, a farrier to shoe or trim your horse's hooves, the vet, and necessary equipment. And that's not even all of it. If you're keeping your horse at a boarding stable, you'll be paying monthly board, too. See the following section for financial details.

Before you say yes to horse ownership, think long and hard about whether you really want to take all this on. Remember that a horse is a large animal with very specific needs. Horses are truly special animals who deserve to be cared for by people who really want them. For info on some of the daily realities of horse ownership, flip to Chapter 19.

Totaling costs

Make sure you know how much money you have to spend on the horse hobby before deciding to buy a horse. Horses are expensive animals to care for, not just to buy. The following sections give a rundown of what costs you can expect to incur.

Research the costs of these products and services in your area and make sure the total amount fits in your budget. Costs of horse ownership vary from region to region. In general, boarding, hay, and vet care are more expensive in highly populated areas than in rural, less populated communities.

Saying "I do": Are you ready to make the commitment?

When you own a horse, you have to be there for her day in and day out, whatever the weather or your time constraints. To help determine whether you're really ready to make this commitment, ask yourself whether you're willing to

✔ Give up some of your other activities to spend time caring for your horse

✔ Drop everything and run to your horse's side should she get sick

✔ Spend time giving your horse medicine or treatment if she becomes ill

✔ Take time out of your busy day, each and every day, to groom and exercise your horse

✔ Work with your horse to solve any problems the two of you may encounter

✔ Perform the sometimes hard physical labor that horse care calls for

✔ Think of your horse as a partner, one who deserves the best care and treatment, regardless of the inconvenience you may experience

If you answered *yes* to all these statements, then you're ready to take on the responsibilities of horse ownership.

Initial purchases

The amount of money you spend on a horse depends on several factors, including the horse's age and training and whether you want to show the horse. Cost also depends on your region of the country. No matter where you are, however, you can expect to spend at least $1,500 for a pleasure horse and much more for an animal you want to show.

Equipment and supplies are another expense you need to consider. The short list includes a saddle, saddle pad, bridle, halter, and grooming tools. You also need stuff for yourself, such as riding clothes. As you can imagine, all this gear can add up. Chapters 8 through 10 describe some of this equipment.

If you want to house the horse on your property and you don't already have horse facilities, you need to put them in. This cost of this can be substantial, depending on the amount of work you have to do and the type of housing you want to provide. See Chapter 19 for details on housing a horse.

Ongoing expenses

Most people think the initial outlay for a horse and equipment is the largest expense they'll have after they enter the realm of horse ownership. The reality is that maintenance will cost you more.

Horses for rent

Many people believe the only way they can ride whenever they want is to commit to horse ownership. In reality, horses can also be leased, both full time and part time. A good option for a person just getting into horseback riding, leasing provides a great opportunity to find out what horse ownership is all about before you get up to your neck in horses. As a lessee, you function as the horse's owner without suffering the same financial and long-term commitment.

Finding a horse to lease isn't difficult. After all, trainers often lease horses to make money. Individual horse owners usually do it because they don't have time to ride the horse every day, don't have the money to care for the horse, or no longer have the desire or ability to ride.

Rather than sell the horse, these owners prefer to lease because it allows them to stay in control of what happens to the horse.

Leasing a horse can cost you anywhere from $100 a month to $500 a month or more, depending on the horse you're leasing, how often you'll have access to the horse (full or part time), and other variables. Leases are usually negotiable, especially with individual horse owners.

Leasing is a great way to find out whether you really want to own a horse, but there is a downfall: You may fall in love with the horse you're leasing, and if you want to buy, the owner may not want to sell the horse to you — or the owner may charge more than you can afford.

Expect to incur regular expenses when owning a horse. The cost of each item or service in the following list varies depending on where you live, so do some research. Call local veterinarians, *farriers* (the people who trim and put shoes on hooves), and tack and feed stores to determine how much each item will cost you; you may want to estimate high, just to be safe:

- **Boarding:** If you don't have your own horse property, you need to keep your horse somewhere else. Your most likely option is a commercial boarding facility. The stable where you take lessons may offer this service. When boarding, you have to pay monthly for a stall, pasture, or paddock (a fenced enclosure). This fee usually includes food and stall maintenance; it may or may not include bedding.

- **Bedding:** If your horse is boarded somewhere that doesn't provide bedding, or if you keep her at home, you have to provide shavings or another type of bedding, which you need to clean and freshen daily.

- **Feed:** If your horse lives at home with you, you need to provide feed, which includes hay and/or pasture maintenance. Don't forget to include extras, such as pellets and food for special diets.

- **Dietary supplements:** Feed supplements, which you can add to help your horse's joints, attitude, or other issues, are plentiful at tack and feed stores. If you plan to give one or more of these supplements to your horse, add this cost to your monthly expenses.

✔ **Preventive veterinary care:** Adult horses need regular preventive care in the form of vaccinations and deworming several times a year. Teeth *floating* (filing down of overgrown teeth) must also take place once or twice a year.

✔ **Veterinary treatment:** Horses get sick, and when they do, you have to call out the vet. The problem may be minor and need minimal treatment, or it may be major and require surgery. Vet bills can be very costly, and they can rise quickly if a horse has a serious or chronic illness.

✔ **Shoes and hoof trimming:** Horses who wear shoes require new ones every six to eight weeks, and a farrier still needs to trim the hooves of horses who go shoeless. (Whether your horse should wear shoes depends on how much work she's doing and whether you prescribe to the "barefoot" method. For details on this method, see Chapter 19.)

✔ **Insurance:** If you insure your horse for major medical, mortality, loss of use, and/or liability, add the premiums to your list of expenses.

✔ **Training/lessons:** As a beginning rider, you should continue your education (and your horse's) by riding with an instructor or trainer. Training is also a must if you intend to show your horse. You need to add weekly training or lessons for you and your horse to your budget.

✔ **Show expenses:** If you plan to show your horse, you have to spend money on show clothes and tack, entry fees, and transportation. (See Chapter 22 for details on showing.)

Find your total costs and figure out whether horse ownership fits into your monthly budget.

Figuring Out What Kind of Horse to Buy

Choosing the right horse for purchase can be a challenge, and even the most experienced horse people struggle with it. That's because finding the right horse is often like finding the right mate: It's not easy, but when it happens, you know it's right.

Your riding experience, what you plan to do with the horse, and costs are several factors to consider, and your preferences for breed, age, and gender also come into play. And of course, whether a particular horse suits your personality is of utmost importance. I explain the factors that go into choosing a horse in the following sections.

Recognizing the ideal equine personality type

As a beginning horse owner, you need a first horse who has a gentle, quiet demeanor, one who'll be forgiving when you make mistakes and patient when you don't know what to do. She shouldn't be apt to overreacting to her environment. Your first horse also shouldn't take advantage of the fact that you're a beginner by trying to get away with as much as possible. You need a horse who's experienced in life and will help you learn — not one you have to teach.

Just like humans, horses are individuals, and each one has a unique personality; therefore, horses who fit the ideal come in every age, breed, and gender. The only way to get to know whether a horse truly has a compatible personality is to spend some time with her and have an equine professional assist you with your evaluation (see the later section "Finding help upfront").

Taking age into account

When looking for a horse to buy, you need to consider age. Although buying a young horse who you'll have for a very long time may seem like a neat idea, getting a young horse as your first mount is rarely wise. Young horses are typically inexperienced and lack training. They don't have much confidence or knowledge, either, though exceptions do exist.

If you're a fairly inexperienced rider, the last thing you need is an inexperienced horse. Some people think that maybe a young, untrained horse and an inexperienced rider make a good team because they can "learn together." In reality, the horse usually ends up becoming unmanageable, the rider becomes miserable, and the relationship dissolves.

When you're learning to ride and care for a horse, it's best to pair up with an older, experienced horse who already knows the ropes. Horses over 6 years old are considered adults and are capable of the equine maturity you need in a first horse. However, the horse's level of training and experience under saddle are the most important factors; some horses who should be mature at 6 still have some growing up to do.

A great age for horses is in their teens and into their early 20s. I got my first horse when I was 13. I'd been riding for a couple of years but was definitely a neophyte when it came to horse ownership and serious riding. The horse my parents chose for me was a quiet, affectionate, older mare named Peggy, who was about 15 years old. Peggy had seen it all — including little kids who didn't really know how to ride — and she patiently taught me much of what I know today about horses.

How old is too old? Well-cared for horses are often rideable well into their 20s. Horses in their 30s are often plagued with lameness problems and aren't the best choice, although you may find exceptions.

Considering your riding discipline

As a beginning rider, you want a horse who's been well-trained in your discipline of choice. Taller, leaner horses are often trained for hunt seat and dressage. Western horses, on the other hand, tend be smaller and stockier.

Of course, as with everything else in life, you can find exceptions to the rule. You may see English-trained horses who are small and stocky and Western-trained horses who are tall and lanky. This situation is not the norm, however. Most horses end up trained in whatever discipline they're most physically suited to.

Determining your interest in competition

Many people enjoy riding their horses just for fun, taking strolls on the trail, or just working in an arena on their own or with an instructor. But a lot of people also enjoy competing with their horses in the one or more exciting events open to horse owners. (See Chapter 22 for details on equine competitions.)

Before you make your purchase, decide whether you want to compete with the horse you buy. A horse you want just for casual trail riding (see Chapter 21) is going to be a lot different from a horse you want to win ribbons with. In order to be truly competitive, the horse you use for showing or other events needs to have talents and training geared toward the horse's sport.

If you want to show or compete with the horse you buy, have a professional help you with your purchase. This professional should be your instructor, or better yet, a trainer who is very experienced with the type of competition you plan to do. See the later section "Finding help upfront" for more information on finding someone to help you with your horse shopping.

Checking out breeds

Hundreds of horse breeds exist throughout the world, and each breed has a distinct appearance and history. Some of them are incredibly rare, while others number in the millions.

In Chapter 2, I list breeds that are considered the most popular riding horses in the United States. Based on the number of individual horses registered with their respective breed associations each year, these breeds are the ones you'll see most often when you're shopping. (You may also see *grade* horses, which are horses of mixed breeding. They can make great riding horses as well.) Use this primer to get an idea of breed history, appearance, and height, as well as general info on a breed's common uses, skills, and demeanor.

Thinking about gender

Essentially, as a beginning rider and novice horse owner, you're limited to the following two gender choices:

- ✓ **Geldings:** Geldings are castrated males. Many horse people think geldings make the best mounts because riders don't have to deal with the horse's sex hormones. Hormones can affect a horse's behavior, just as they can with cats, dogs, and other animals.

- ✓ **Mares:** Mares are female horses age 4 and over. I think mares make wonderful companions, although many people find some mares difficult to handle whenever the horses come in season (heat). (Mares can be spayed, although it's a difficult and expensive procedure.)

You may have noticed that *stallions,* uncastrated males, aren't one of the choices here. That's because stallions are rarely suitable for a beginning riders and first-time horse owners. Stallions are full of testosterone and usually require an experienced handler. They also come with logistical problems: Most boarding stables won't allow stallions to be kept on the premises. Also, stallion owners are legally liable if their horse breaks out of his stall and impregnates a neighbor's mare.

The question of whether to get a mare or a gelding is a big one to some horse people, and it isn't something everyone agrees on. Many people own only geldings; others swear by mares. Some people don't have a preference one way or another. The decision on whether to get a mare or a gelding ultimately rests on you. You can spend time with both genders to see whether you develop a preference. If you don't have a favorite — and most people don't — then just look for the best horse regardless of gender.

Walking through the Horse-Buying Process

The task of horse buying can be daunting — so many horses are available, and so many people are trying to sell them to you. And buying from the wrong place and without qualified help can land you with the wrong horse. Luckily for you, the following sections explain where to look and where to get help before you embark on this task. I also discuss having a vet look over your potential purchase for health problems.

Finding help upfront

The biggest piece of advice I can give you about horse shopping is to do your homework. Find out as much as you can about the process of horse buying before you write out that check.

Getting experienced people to help you find and choose your horse is vital. They can come in the form of

- Your riding instructor or trainer
- Your veterinarian
- Your farrier
- Other equine experts

These people can guide you and help you choose your new horse — for a fee — so make sure you select your horse authority carefully. Get to know each individual in your future horse's life. (See Chapter 3 for details on finding a riding instructor; Chapter 19 has information about finding a vet and a farrier.)

Looking in all the right places

Buying a horse can be a bit complicated, in large part because you can find horses for sale in a lot of different places. The process would be easier if you could just pick one out of a catalog, but things don't work that way!

Horses are sold by individual sellers, horse dealers, and breeding and training operations. Also, if you prefer to adopt a horse rather than buy one, rescue groups usually have horses available, as do occasional private individuals. You'll acquire your horse from one of these places, but you should look into more than one type of seller when you're shopping. Check out each of the following sources, and then settle on the one that feels right to you.

Individual sellers

Buying a horse from an individual seller rather than from a trainer, breeder, or horse dealer can be a good way to find a horse. Individual sellers may advertise in the classifieds section of your daily newspaper, in regional horse publications, or on the bulletin board at your local tack and feed store.

Horse dealers

Horse dealers are people who make a living buying and selling horses, and you can find them in most areas that have an active horse industry. Dealers typically purchase horses at auctions or from individuals and then sell those horses to others at a higher price. In essence, they're the middlemen of the horse-buying world.

You can buy a good horse from a reputable horse dealer. Most horse dealers are experienced horse people who know how to judge a horse's disposition, quality of training, and athletic ability.

If an instructor, trainer, or other horse expert is helping you with your search (as I suggest earlier in this chapter), ask whether he or she can recommend an honest horse dealer. Don't go to a horse dealer without the recommendation of someone you know well and trust. Horse dealers are much like used car dealers: Some are ethical; others aren't.

Breeders and trainers

Horse breeders and trainers routinely sell horses to individual buyers. In fact, doing so is usually a large part of their business. Here's how the two horse sources compare:

- ✔ Breeders typically deal in purebred horses and sell very young stock. The weanlings and yearlings most often available from breeders aren't suitable for a first-time horse owner because they're so young. However, a breeder does occasionally offer an older horse for sale, possibly a retired show horse or a *broodmare* (a mare used exclusively for breeding) who's been trained for riding. The earlier section titled "Taking age into account" talks about the importance of buying a mature horse

- ✔ Trainers are often a good source of older, trained horses — the kind you should be looking for. The horse for sale may be one who the trainer purchased with only basic training and then schooled to a higher level. Or the horse may belong to a trainer's client; perhaps the client outgrew the horse, so the trainer took on the task of selling her. Sometimes, a trainer is looking to sell off a lesson horse to a private owner — maybe even the lesson horse you learned to ride on! When healthy and *sound* (free from lameness), former lesson horses can make good mounts for beginning riders, so consider them when you shop.

If you've been taking lessons from a trainer and intend to keep working with this person after you have your own horse, consider buying a horse directly from that person. The trainer you've been working with knows your skill level and personality and may be selling a horse who's perfectly suited to you.

As with anything else you buy, the seller's reputation is very important — especially when dealing with breeders and trainers. If you don't know the breeder or trainer, ask for referrals or inquire about him or her from other horse people in the area. Make sure the business or the individual has a good reputation before you get involved in any business dealings.

Rescue groups

If you like the idea of giving a home to a horse in need, consider adopting a rescued horse. Rescue organizations, such as Horse Lovers United (`www.horseloversunited.com`) and the Horse Protection League (`www.cohpl.org`), may let you adopt a horse for nothing or for a minimal fee.

Although horse adoption is a noble cause, it's not always the right road to take for a beginning rider and first-time horse owner. Some horses who are available for adoption make great riding horses for beginners, but others aren't suited to inexperienced riders or can't be ridden at all. If you'd like to pursue this option, do so with your horse-shopping expert in tow. Remember to be rational and critical, just as you would if you were buying.

Don't take home a horse who isn't right for you just because she's free or because you feel sorry for her. If the relationship doesn't work out (and chances are that it won't), the results can be disastrous for both you and the horse you're trying to help. If the rescue group you're working with is reputable, it should match you only with a horse who's appropriate for your experience level.

Having a horse undergo a pre-purchase exam

After you find a horse that both you and your trainer or expert agree on, it's time to get a vet in on the decision. Most equine veterinarians offer a service known as a pre-purchase exam, or a *vet check*. If you hire a vet to perform such an exam, the doctor comes out to where the horse resides and thoroughly examines the animal. I walk you through the pre-purchase exam process in the following sections.

Preparing for the exam

After you find a horse you're interested in, you need to choose a veterinarian, decide whether you want an extensive exam or just the basics, and schedule the actual appointment.

Some aspects of the pre-purchase exam are included in the basic price, although other services will cost you extra. The more tests you have the vet perform, the more you'll learn about your prospective horse — and the more you'll pay for the exam. Pre-purchase exams can run anywhere from a few hundred dollars to $1,000 or more, depending on where you live and whether you have the horse's legs X-rayed. The following section explains some of these checks.

Make sure you select an independent veterinarian to perform the pre-purchase exam — not one the seller suggests or who considers the seller a client. If you're unable to locate an independent veterinarian on your own, contact the American Association of Equine Practitioners for a referral (www.aaep.org or 859-233-0147). Chapter 19 has more information on finding an equine vet.

If you're working with a reputable trainer to find a horse, your veterinarian may recommend that you take the horse you're considering for a one-week or longer trial period before conducting the pre-purchase exam. That way, you have a chance to spend time with the horse, and you can ensure that the horse is drug-free before the exam.

Taking note of what the vet checks

Following are just some of the things the vet looks at in a pre-purchase exam:

- **Vital signs:** The vet checks the horse for normal temperature, respiration, and pulse while the horse is at rest. After the horse gets some light exercise, the vet checks these vital signs again. Abnormal readings are sometimes a way to detect illness.

- **Heart and lungs:** The vet listens to the horse's heart and lungs with a stethoscope to determine whether any problems are present.

- **Gut sounds:** Using a stethoscope, the vet listens to the sounds coming from the horse's gastrointestinal system. Normal gut sounds indicate a healthy digestive system.

- **Teeth:** The vet examines the horse's mouth for problems with missing teeth, overgrown molars, poor alignment, and the wear from *cribbing* (an obsessive habit of biting on a fence, feeder, or other object and sucking air in at the same time).

- **Eyes:** Using a light source, the vet checks the health of the horse's eyes, looking for corneal scarring, cataracts, inflammation, and other signs of disease.

✔ **Lameness:** The veterinarian evaluates the horse's *conformation* (the way the horse is put together) for any faults that may affect the animal's ability to perform in the role you intend for her. The horse then undergoes something called a *flexion test,* in which she's gaited in front of the veterinarian on hard and soft ground and in circles so the doctor can determine any problems in movement. Also during the lameness part of the examination, the vet palpates the lower limbs in search of abnormalities and examines the hooves visually and with a device called a *hoof tester,* which checks sensitivity on the underside of the hoof.

✔ **X-rays** At your request, the veterinarian takes X-rays of the horse's legs to further evaluate soundness and health.

✔ **Blood:** At your request, the vet draws blood from the horse and has it tested for equine infectious anemia (EIA), problems with thyroid function, and other issues.

Ask your veterinarian to do a blood or urine test for drug detection. I've heard stories of sellers who tranquilize or otherwise drug horses before selling them, leaving the unfortunate buyer to discover the truth after the drug wears off and the horse's true personality comes out.

The veterinarian who's conducting the pre-purchase exam should ask the seller about the horse's medical history and current use. The vet should also question you about what you intend to do with the horse if you buy her so the vet can determine whether the horse is physically capable of performing the job you want her to do.

Following up after the exam

The veterinarian won't give the horse a pass or fail on the exam; he or she simply alerts you to the horse's condition at the time of the exam. The vet may tell you whether the horse seems suitable for certain disciplines or sports depending on the correctness of her conformation, although many veterinarians aren't willing to give an opinion on this subject for liability reasons. If the horse is suffering from a serious illness, the vet will indicate the abnormal finding on the horse's report.

The results of the examination can give you a good idea about any health problems the horse may have. Keep in mind, however, that the pre-purchase exam isn't foolproof. A disease or medical condition can evade discovery during a vet check.

You can discuss the results of the pre-purchase exam with your instructor, trainer, or other expert to get his or her input as well, but the decision on whether to purchase the animal is ultimately yours.

Chapter 19

Exploring Horse Care

So you're thinking of adding a horse to your family, an equine companion to care for and ride. Before you bring your new horse home, you need to how to take care of him. In this chapter, I give you the rundown on how to house, feed, and groom your horse. I also fill you in on the basics of equine health, including how to prevent illness and when to call the vet.

For even greater detail on the topics covered in this chapter, see my other book, *Horses For Dummies,* 2nd Edition (Wiley).

Gimme Shelter: Proper Horse Housing

You're probably not surprised to hear that housing a horse is a lot more complicated than housing a cat or a dog. Horses are big animals that have very specific needs. And they live outside, so keeping them in the bedroom is out of the question.

If you're lucky enough to have your own horse property, your horse can live where you do. If not, you need to keep him at a boarding facility. Both of these options require some careful thought.

Getting on board with commercial boarding facilities

A *boarding stable* is a commercial establishment that provides housing and limited care (such as feeding and stall cleaning) for horses for a monthly fee.

Some boarding stables also offer horse owners additional horse care, such as exercising or blanketing their horses. In the following sections, I explain the benefits of boarding and what to look for when touring boarding stables.

Advantages of boarding for new horse owners

Boarding offers many benefits, particularly to first-time horse owners. Even if your dream is to keep your horse in your backyard, explore the possibility of boarding for at least the first year you own your horse. The advantages of boarding include the following:

- **Trainers and instructors:** Boarding stables have resident trainers and/or riding instructors who work there. If you need help with your horse or with your riding, you have experts you can call on for assistance.

- **Other knowledgeable horse owners:** You find out so much more about horses and riding if you're around other horse owners. You can ask other people for help or advice, as well as get referrals for vets or farriers.

- **A social life:** When you become a horse owner, you instantly become a member of a very special community. Boarding stables are great places to make friends. Plus, you always have someone to ride with if you keep your horse at a boarding stable.

Traits to look for in a boarding stable

Chapter 3 has tips for finding riding stables in your area, and some of the same ideas apply when you're looking for a place to board. Before you commit to keeping your horse at any commercial facility, check the place out thoroughly. Go down to the stable and spend some time walking around and talking to other boarders. Here are the things you're looking for:

- **Safe, sturdy accommodations:** Keep an eye out for dangers such as barbed wire and broken boards on pasture fences. When examining stalls, make sure the fencing is secure and in good repair.

- **Clean, safe surroundings:** Look for a well-maintained property that's free of junk and debris.

- **Reliable water supply:** The horses at the stable should all have water in their stalls. Ask how water is supplied and find out how it's kept from freezing in the winter.

- **Quality feed:** Make sure feed isn't moldy. Hay should be relatively dust free. Grain and pellets should be secured from rodents and other wildlife.

- **Good care:** Find out what goes into the horses' daily care. Look for daily stall cleanings, at least twice daily feedings, and fly and rodent control.

- **Written health requirements:** Ask what kinds of inoculations are required of boarders. You want to see influenza/rhinopneumonitis and equine encephalitis requirements at the very least.

- **Round-the-clock security:** Not all stables have this luxury, but it's a definite bonus. A security guard or live-in caretaker helps protect your horse from thieves.

- **Good riding facilities:** Look for a well-kept riding arena (or two), a *round-pen* for training (a round 40- to 60-foot-diameter arena), and trail access.

- **Tack storage:** Unless you want to lug your saddle and bridle back and forth every time you come to ride your horse, make sure the stable offers tack storage for boarders.

- **A professional demeanor:** Expect to sign liability waivers and a boarding agreement. The stable management should also ask for your emergency contact info so they can reach you if your horse is ill or injured.

Be aware that the nicer the stable, the more you have to pay for board. Don't opt for a stable that isn't up to par just because the fees are low. With boarding stables, you really do get what you pay for. Boarding stables charge anywhere from $100 to $700 or more a month, depending on where you live and the care and facilities offered.

No place like home: Keeping your horse on your own property

If you've always dreamed of having a horse in your backyard, a home stable may be the right housing option for you, provided you live on property that's been zoned for horses. If you live in a suburban or even rural neighborhood that forbids the keeping of livestock, you have to board elsewhere — horses, after all, are a little hard to hide.

In the following sections, I describe your responsibilities as a home-stable owner and the types of homes you can build for your horse.

The responsibilities of having a home stable

Although having a horse in your backyard is a great experience, don't overly romanticize the notion. Keeping a horse on your property requires an investment of time, money, and hard work. If you decide to keep your horse at home, you must uphold a number of responsibilities:

- **Cleanliness:** You have an obligation to your horse and to your neighbors to keep your property clean and well maintained. You do so by mucking out your horse's stall daily, using a manure fork.

- **Continuing education:** Because you and your horse are pretty much on your own, you need to learn as much as possible about horses and horse-keeping. If you don't continue to learn, you'll end up shortchanging both yourself and your horse. You can continue your education by joining local horse clubs, subscribing to horse magazines, and reading books about horses and horse care. See the Appendix for some possible resources.

✔ **A good image:** Whereas horse property was commonplace at one time, finding communities that are accepting of horses is becoming harder and harder. You can do your part by being friendly and considerate toward your neighbors.

Types of enclosures you can create

You can find three basic types of enclosures in the horse world: the pasture, paddock, and box stall. Look for designs in books on barn building, buy these enclosures prefabricated from manufacturers, or have an architect and contractor design and build them for you. Here are your options:

✔ **Pasture:** I define pasture as a substantial portion of fenced land where high-quality grass grows for equine consumption. If you have the land, motivation, and ability to create and manage a pasture for your horse, this is the best way to go. Horses who live on pastures suffer the least from colic, leg problems, breathing disorders, stable vices (bad habits resulting from boredom), and other maladies that tend to afflict horses confined in stalls. They also don't need as much exercise from you because they get it on their own, romping around the pasture — so if you have time to ride only once a week, your horse won't feel pent up.

✔ **Paddock:** A paddock is a small outdoor enclosure that's void of pasture grass that's rich in nutrition. In certain parts of the Eastern United States, a paddock is typically a large pen with board fencing. In the more urban areas of the Western U.S., most horses live in small, 12-x-12- or 12-x-24-foot paddocks made of a pipe enclosure called *pipe corrals*. Horses who live in paddocks need daily exercise because they don't get much of a workout in this small space. If you can't ride every day, you need to turn your horse loose in an arena or take him for a walk to provide him with a way to stretch his legs.

A paddock is the next best thing to pasture because it gives the horse some room to move around. Because paddocks are outdoors, they also provide good ventilation and more opportunities for mental stimulation for your horse than a box stall does.

✔ **Box stall:** Some horse owners prefer to keep their horses indoors, in a box stall. A box stall is just what it sounds like: a stall in the shape of a box. Box stalls are compartments within a barn.

Keeping a horse in a box stall provides a couple of advantages. Stall-kept horses stay cleaner and neater. Horses don't end up muddy when it rains or dusty when it's dry. They also avoid bites and other injuries delivered by other horses.

The downside of keeping a horse in a box stall is that living there is less healthy for the horse than living outdoors. A horse who stands in nearly the same place for hours on end is more prone to colic, leg problems, and boredom, which often results in stable vices. Also, because ventilation isn't as good in a stall as it is outdoors, stall-kept horses are more prone to respiratory disease.

Like horses in paddocks, horses in box stalls need daily exercise because they don't have much room to move around. You need to ride your horse daily, walk him around the barn, or turn him loose in an arena.

Chow Time: Dealing with Your Horse's Hunger and Thirst

A steady supply of food is very important to a horse, probably even more important than it is to humans. Nature designed the horse to spend the majority of his time chewing, swallowing, and digesting. The equine digestive system is meant to be constantly on the go and to process vast quantities of fibrous foods.

What you feed your horse and how often you feed him plays a big part in determining your horse's physical and psychological health. In the following sections, I cover the basics of feeding and watering your horse.

Feeding your horse

In the horse world, many people debate about the best feed to give a horse. The reason for the confusion probably lies in the fact that individual horses have different nutritional requirements. Where and how the horse lives, the age of the horse, what kind of work the horse does, and the horse's own physiological makeup can affect the best diet for a horse. Generally speaking, horses that are ridden hard in demanding disciplines, such as endurance or cattle work, need more calories than horses used for casual trail riding. The following sections give general information on horse feeds to get you started.

The best person to guide you on your horse's diet is your veterinarian. Your vet is familiar with your individual horse and therefore with his nutritional needs. Furthermore, your vet should also be up on the local availability of different kinds of hay. For example, alfalfa hay, popular and readily available in California, is often hard to come by in the Northeast. (I give you guidelines on finding a vet later in this chapter.)

Hay

Hay is basically a feedstuff composed of plants that have been cut, dried, and baled. Two types of hays exist: legumes and grasses. Alfalfa, which is rich in protein, calcium, and other nutrients, is the legume horses most commonly eat (although many horse people think it's too rich for horses and is best fed only to cattle). Timothy, orchard, and Bermuda are the most common grass hays.

Hay is a good feed because it provides roughage in addition to proper nutrition. The roughage keeps the horse's digestive system working properly and also satisfies the horse's natural urge to chew.

Hay cubes

You can feed your horse concentrated blocks of hay called hay cubes. Hay cubes tend to be cheaper than hay and are good for older horses with worn-down teeth (because cubes break apart quickly when chewed) or respiratory problems (because cubes are less dusty than hay). They're also ideal for horses who have trouble keeping on weight. Still, most horses prefer baled hay to cubes because baled hay gives them plenty to chew on.

Pasture grass

Horses do best when they can graze in a pasture; however, providing your horse with a lush pasture requires work and knowledge. If you happen to live on property where pasture has already been cultivated, your task is to carefully maintain it. On the other hand, if you want to start a pasture from scratch, you'll need considerable help. Contact your local agricultural agency for assistance in starting and maintaining a quality horse pasture.

If your pasture doesn't yield a substantial amount of good-quality, nutritious grass, you need to supplement your horse's diet with a daily ration of hay. If you don't, the horse may suffer from malnutrition. To verify that your pasture is of good quality, call your local agricultural office and ask an expert to inspect your pasture and help analyze its nutritional content.

Watering your horse

I can't overemphasize the importance of providing plenty of clean, fresh water as part your horse's daily care. Your horse needs water — lots of it — to stay alive and to ensure a healthy digestive system. You can water your horse with an automatic waterer set up in the horse's stall, a large bucket that you refill several times a day, or a trough that holds enough water for a day or two at a time.

If you live in a climate where temperatures fall below freezing, you need to keep your horse's water supply from turning to ice. Consider using a heating element made especially for horse waterers or manually break the ice whenever it forms. I recommend the heating element because it requires less work on your part and also keeps the water at a warmer temperature, encouraging your horse to drink.

Hey, Good Lookin': Grooming Your Horse

Not only does grooming make your horse look good so you're proud to ride him, but it also helps you bond with him and keep him healthy. You and your horse have time to get to know each other before you get on to ride, and grooming lets you give his body a thorough going-over as you keep an eye out for lumps, bumps, and anything else that shouldn't be there.

If you like grooming, you're in luck. Horses are dirty critters by nature and need daily grooming. Although cleaning up a half-ton animal who's been milling around in the dirt for days may not sound like a picnic, grooming can be one of the most enjoyable parts of horse ownership. And besides, most horses absolutely love the attention! In the following sections, I describe the grooming equipment you need and walk you through the steps of brushing and bathing your horse.

Getting into gear

Before you start grooming, assemble all your tools in a tack box or organizer. Make sure everything's clean and in good working order. At the very minimum, your tools should include the following items (see Figure 19-1):

- ✔ Stiff brush
- ✔ Soft brush
- ✔ Mane and tail brush
- ✔ Cloth, sponge, or small towel
- ✔ Sweat scraper
- ✔ Hoof pick
- ✔ Rubber curry comb
- ✔ Shedding blade

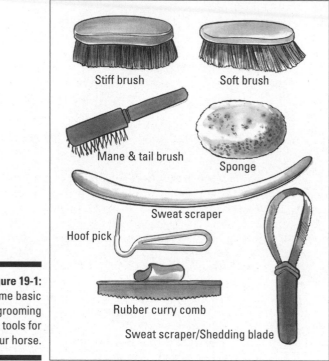

Stiff brush

Soft brush

Mane & tail brush

Sponge

Sweat scraper

Hoof pick

Figure 19-1:
Some basic
grooming
tools for
your horse.

Rubber curry comb

Sweat scraper/Shedding blade

Brushing your horse

Horses are messy, and dirt absolutely clings to their coats. You need to use elbow grease to get your horse's coat clean and shiny. If your horse is stabled indoors all the time, he won't get too dirty. Horses who live in pastures or paddocks, however, usually require more work to clean. (For more on equine housing, see the earlier section called "Types of enclosures you can create.")

To clean the body of your horse (which includes the head, neck, legs, rump, and everything in between), you use a hoof pick, a rubber curry comb, a stiff brush, a soft brush, a mane and tail brush, and a cloth. With these tools at your disposal and your horse safely tied, follow these steps (see Chapter 5 for safety info on working with a horse in close quarters; Chapter 11 explains handling a horse from the ground):

1. **Clean out all the horse's hooves with the hoof pick to remove packed-in dirt, manure, and rocks.**

   Take the pick in your right hand, with the handle in your fist and the point of the pick facing away from you. Stand at the horse's left shoulder, facing the back of the horse. You're in the right position if your left shoulder is next to your horse's left shoulder. Ask the horse for his hoof, and then support this uplifted foot in your left hand as you start scraping out the dirt from the inside of the hoof with the tip of the hoof pick. Be sure to clean out the areas around the *frog* (the triangular area on the underside of the hoof), but don't scrape the frog itself. Look for rocks, nails, or other items that may be lodged in the hoof.

When you're finished, gently release the hoof. Clean the hooves on the left hind leg, the right hind leg, and then the right front leg. On the horse's right side, lift a hoof with your right hand and hold the pick in your left.

2. **Use the curry comb to bring the dirt to the surface of the coat by rubbing in a circular motion (if your horse has a very thin coat, proceed gently or skip this step altogether).**

   Start on your horse's left side with the curry comb in your right hand. Begin rubbing where your horse's neck joins the head and work down toward the horse's body. Groom the neck, chest, shoulders, back, belly, rump, and haunches, in that order. After finishing the left side, move over to the right, switch the curry comb to your left hand, and repeat the process. If your horse is the least bit dirty — and I'm sure he is — the dust should come to the surface of his coat.

   Be very gentle when working around the horse's flanks and underbelly. Some horses are very sensitive in this area and may kick out at you. Rub gently when you get to any areas where you can feel the horse's bones under the skin. These areas are particularly sensitive.

   If mud is caked on the horse's legs, use a very gentle circular motion to shake it loose from the coat. Do so only with dry mud, because wet mud is impossible to remove. Also, use a rubber curry comb, not a metal one, because a metal comb can damage the skin on your horse's legs. And don't kneel or sit — you want to be able to move away quickly should the horse become frightened.

3. **Use the stiff brush to dissipate the dirt into the air by brushing in short strokes in the direction that the hair grows (see Figure 19-2).**

   Go on the horse's left side with the stiff brush in your right hand and start at the top of the neck, moving down the horse's neck to his chest, shoulder, back, barrel, belly, rump, and haunches. You can also use the stiff brush to loosen the dirt from your horse's legs, but be sure to be gentle. After you finish the left side of the horse, move over to the right side and repeat the process with the stiff brush in your left hand.

   As you brush your horse with the stiff brush and soft brush, continuously clean the brushes by rubbing them against the rubber curry comb. Doing so helps get rid of the dust that accumulates in the brushes and keeps the dirt from going back on the horse.

Figure 19-2:
Brush along
the grain of
your horse's
hair.

4. **Use the soft brush to remove the remaining dust from the coat, brushing along the lay of the coat by using short strokes.**

   Start on the horse's left with the brush in your right hand and move from the horse's neck to his chest, shoulder, back, barrel, belly, rump, and haunches. Move to the right side of the horse with the brush in your left hand and repeat the brushing process. You should begin to see a shine on your horse's coat.

5. **Complete the body-grooming process by wiping down the horse's body with the cloth, giving the coat even more shine.**

6. **Use the cloth to clean the insides of your horse's nostrils, where dirt and mucus tend to accumulate.**

   Make sure your horse isn't afraid of the cloth before you wipe his face with it. Let him look at it and sniff it, and then very slowly raise it to his face. Take note of his reaction, and don't force the issue if the horse continues to act afraid. Try again the next day using the same approach until the horse gradually gets used to the cloth.

7. **Use the soft brush to gently groom your horse's head with long, soft strokes.**

   Stand at the side toward the front of your horse to do this step.

.

.

.

.

.

.

.

.

.

.

.

Most horses enjoy having their heads groomed, but some don't. Be sure to calmly approach your horse's head with the brush, showing him the brush and letting him smell it before you use it on his head. Be careful when brushing his ears, because some horses are funny about having their ears touched.

8. **Use the mane and tail brush or a soft brush to groom the mane and tail.**

Pick out any burrs or shavings caught in the horse's mane and tail and separate the tangles. Use a horse hair detangler if the tangles are really bad. Brush the forelock, mane, and tail in the direction the hair grows.

The horse wash: Scrubbing down

Bathing a horse isn't that much different from washing a car. Both are large and require a lot of soap, water, and work. Horses get dirty often, but you should bathe your horse only when it's really necessary and not more than twice a month. Too much bathing can strip the horse's coat of its natural oils.

You can choose any number of ways to bathe your horse, but here's my favorite way of doing it: The weather outside is not cold, and the sun is out. Your horse is securely tied in a wash area, which has a hitching post or cross-rails, access to a garden hose, and a non-dirt, non-slip surface. And your shampoo, conditioner, bucket, sponge, and sweat scraper are ready to go. Follow these steps to give your horse a bath:

1. **Starting on the left side of your horse — you wash and rinse one side of the horse at a time — run lukewarm water from a garden hose on the horse's legs.**

Hosing down the horse's legs allows him to get used to the water and the idea that he's about to be bathed. If you don't have easy access to a garden horse and a heated water supply, use warm water in a bucket for this step.

2. **After the horse has had a bit of time to adjust to the water, slowly move the hose up to where the neck joins the head and wet the body all the way to the rear end of the horse.**

Be careful not to get water in the horse's ears.

3. **Apply shampoo to your sponge and begin lathering your horse's coat, starting where the neck joins the head and working your way down across the body.**

Be sure to scrub underneath your horse, where the girth lies, as well as along the back where the saddle sits, because sweat and dirt tend to accumulate in these areas. Wash your horse's legs too, as well as the outsides of his hooves.

4. **After you're confident that you've loosened the dirt and sweat from your horse's coat, take the hose or a bucket of water and begin rinsing the shampoo from your horse's coat.**

   Rinse very thoroughly; you don't want to leave behind any soap residue that may irritate your horse's skin.

5. **Shampoo, condition, and rinse the horse's mane.**

   If the mane is on the right side of the horse, move over to that side.

6. **Repeat Steps 1 through 4 for the right side of the horse.**

7. **Wash the horse's tail.**

   Stand at the side of your horse near the hind legs and grasp the tail gently. Pull it around the horse's hip toward you. Wet the tail with water and apply shampoo. Be sure to work the lather into the tail so you get all the hair. Rinse, condition, and rinse again. Be sure to get all the soap residue out of the base of the tail — if soap residue irritates the horse's skin, he'll probably rub his tail on whatever he can find.

8. **Wash the horse's head.**

   Wet the horse's face with a sponge and warm water. Don't forget to wet the *forelock* (the hair that hangs down on the forehead between the horse's ears), because you wash this hair when you do the head.

   Rinse the face with a clean sponge and water and avoid using shampoo there. Shampoo is difficult to rinse off thoroughly, and it can get in the horse's eyes. Also, avoid the temptation to wash your horse's face by squirting his face with the garden hose. Some horses tolerate it, but all clearly hate it.

   Be gentle and considerate when washing your horse's face, and stand back and be cautious. Most horses are very cooperative when having their faces cleaned, but others have had bad experiences or simply are wary of the process. Some horses swing their heads to avoid the water and can accidentally hit you in the face.

9. **Dry off.**

   To help your horse dry off more quickly after his bath, squeegee the water from his coat with a sweat scraper (go in the direction that the hair lies) and then hand walk him in the sun. Don't put him back in his pasture or paddock until he's almost completely dry, because he may roll in the dirt.

A Little TLC: Maintaining Your Horse's Health

Despite their size and physical strength, horses are actually rather delicate creatures in terms of health. They need regular preventive care to keep them healthy and able to perform the tasks asked of them. In the following sections, I discuss a few important preventive care tasks and describe some signs of illness and common health conditions.

Providing preventive care

Making sure your horse is, well, healthy as a horse can make riding a much better experience for both you and your equine friend. Particularly for horses, preventing a problem is always better than trying to fix it after it occurs. As an owner, your job is to take care of the following tasks in prevention.

Finding a horse vet

Choose a veterinarian *before* your find yourself in an emergency situation. A veterinarian already familiar with your horse can be a huge plus during an emergency. Also, if you're a regular client, your request for an emergency barn call will receive priority treatment over a similar request from a non-regular client. (You may have found a vet you liked when you had your horse checked in a pre-purchase exam; see Chapter 18 for details.)

Locating a good equine veterinarian usually takes a bit of research. You shouldn't settle on the first name you see in the telephone book or use the vet your next-door neighbor is using without investigating first. Ask a few other horse owners whom they prefer and why. Also, ask your trainer or instructor for a referral to a good equine vet.

The best choice for your horse's health care provider (preventive, regular, and emergency care) is a veterinarian who specializes in horses. Equine veterinarians are specially trained to diagnose and treat equine illnesses, and they have more knowledge of horse issues than their small-animal counterparts. If you can't find a veterinarian in your area who deals exclusively with horses, make sure the vet you choose has at least moderate experience in equine medicine.

Going barefoot

Horses in the wild don't wear shoes, and neither do horses belonging to advocates of the barefoot method. Farriers who practice the *barefoot method* believe that horses don't need shoes, just the proper trim and care of their feet to keep them healthy. In fact, barefoot advocates believe that shoeing a horse is harmful to the health of his feet.

Critics of this method disagree vehemently with barefoot advocates, stating that not every horse in every situation can go sans shoes. To find out more about the barefoot method as you make your own decision, visit www. thehorseshoof.com.

Finding a farrier

Nearly as important as choosing a veterinarian for your horse is finding a skilled and qualified *farrier*, a specialist in trimming and shoeing your horse's hooves. Choose your farrier wisely; the health of your horse's hooves and legs depends on it.

The best way to locate a good farrier is through a referral, and the first person you should ask for a referral is your veterinarian. Most equine veterinarians are well acquainted with the farriers in their area and can recommend one or two good ones.

You can ask other horse owners for farrier referrals as well. If you go this route, be sure to take a consensus and see which farriers get the most thumbs up. Don't base your decision on the comments of only one owner — you want to get a feeling for which farriers are able to successfully handle horses with different shoeing needs.

Most horses get shoes and/or trimming every six to eight weeks. After you choose a farrier, monitor his or her work closely. You want a shoer who comes when he or she is supposed to so your horse's feet don't go weeks overdue, but the farrier also shouldn't trim or shoe your horse too frequently just to pad his or her pockets. If your shoer wants to work on your horse more often than usual, ask for a detailed explanation as to why.

If you horse is having trouble with his hooves or legs, consider the job your shoer is doing and talk to your vet about the possible causes. A shoer can make or break a horse's soundness.

Vaccinating

A number of dangerous infectious diseases plague the horse world, but the good news is that vaccines exist for many of these. To keep your horse in his optimal state of health, you need to commit to a regular vaccination program, developed with your veterinarian, to protect your horse from serious illness.

Although a host of other vaccines exist, the following four represent the absolute minimum your horse should receive. Your vet may add other vaccines to the list as well, depending on where you live:

- Influenza/rhinopneumonitis
- Equine encephalomyelitis
- Tetanus
- West Nile virus

Reputable boarding stables require that all horses on the property be kept up-to-date on inoculations against contagious disease. If your horse is boarded, maintaining a consistent schedule of inoculations is imperative. (I discuss boarding your horse earlier in this chapter.)

Deworming

Roundworms, strongyles, pinworms, bots, lungworms, stomach worms, and hairworms — the list of baddies that can affect your equine friends can be enough to make your skin crawl! Horses, like most other animals, are quite susceptible to a number of internal parasites. These parasites, collectively known as *worms,* can cause serious damage to your horse's internal organs. Uncontrolled, they lead to chronic colic (abdominal pain) and even death.

Although keeping worms from infecting your horse is nearly impossible, controlling their numbers is very doable. Regular deworming with a chemical agent kills parasites in their various stages of growth and is a necessary part of your horse's preventive care.

Several over-the-counter dewormers are available to horse owners, and you can use them on a regular basis under the supervision of your veterinarian. You can also ask your vet to deworm your horse for you.

Deworm your horse on a regular basis; the frequency depends on the climate and environment where you reside. Discuss your horse's deworming needs with your vet so the two of you can come up with an effective program.

Taking care of teeth

Because the food horses eat is so difficult to chew and digest, good dental health is vital.

To combat the normal wear that occurs from chewing such tough, fibrous foods, nature has equipped the horse with teeth that grow constantly; they slowly erupt from the gum as the top layer of the teeth wears down. However, the horse's upper jaw is wider than his lower jaw, so the upper outside teeth and lower inside teeth have nothing to wear against as they erupt, and ridges and sharp points result. These ridges and points restrict the horse's normal side-to-side rotary chewing motion, resulting in poor and painful chewing and the dropping of food. Horses with this condition tend to chew up and down rather than side to side, making horses with neglected teeth prone to problems such as choking and colic. These sharp points also hurt the horse when the noseband on the bridle is tightened and when the bit hits the horse's teeth.

To keep sharp points from interfering with your horse's ability to chew and subsequently digest his food, have your veterinarian file down those pointy teeth as often as once or twice a year, depending on how fast they grow. Called *floating,* this procedure is an absolute must in preventive care. During these exams, the vet can also spot any other dental problems that may be developing, such as infected teeth or abnormal wear patterns.

Recognizing signs of illness

You don't have to call the vet every time your horse sneezes; you can deal with some problems at home, or at least monitor them *before* making that call. Pay attention to your horse's health before you climb on his back.

Here are signs to look for when your horse seems under the weather. If your horse has one or more of these symptoms, the condition is an emergency that warrants a call to and a visit from the vet:

- Bleeding
- Blood in urine
- Choking
- Colic (see "Colic," later in this chapter)
- Diarrhea
- Fever (temperature above 101°F)
- Inability to stand
- Injury
- Labored breathing
- Painful eye
- Refusal to eat
- Severe pain
- Straining
- Swelling

Checking out common ailments

Although horses are susceptible to a wide variety of ailments, the same handful of problems routinely crop up. Some of these illnesses have the potential to become serious, while others are simply annoyances to both human and horse. In each situation, prompt treatment from a veterinarian can keep the problem from getting out of hand.

The following sections outline the most common equine health problems, along with their symptoms. Your veterinarian can give you even more information — specific to your individual horse — on any one of these conditions.

Arthritis

People aren't the only ones who get arthritis. Horses get it, too — and often. Simply put, *arthritis* is the inflammation of a joint, and it's the most common form of lameness in horses. Several different forms of arthritis exist, ranging from an infection to a severe, crippling fusion of joints.

The key symptom of arthritis is lameness. Horses with arthritis limp — some very mildly, others dramatically. Your vet can treat arthritis with anti-inflammatory drugs.

Colic

Colic, a rather common problem among horses, is actually a symptom, not a disease. The term *colic* refers to abdominal pain, which can have any number of sources. Because horses are designed to be grazers, they're meant to ingest plant material at a slow and constant rate. The equine digestive system is often upset when humans confine horses and give them concentrated feeds.

Colic can be serious or mild, but it's always a cause for concern and *always* warrants a call to the vet. Take away the horse's food and walk him while you wait for the vet to arrive. Walking can help ease the pain and prevent him from rolling and thrashing in pain, which can injure him further.

Horses suffering from colic are usually in a great deal of pain. They express their discomfort by doing some or all of the following:

- Biting at the flanks or abdomen
- Kicking at the belly
- Lying down
- Pacing
- Pawing
- Rolling

- ✔ Standing with legs stretched out
- ✔ Straining
- ✔ Sweating profusely
- ✔ Swishing the tail violently

These bouts of pain often come in waves, so the horse may seem all right one minute but frantic the next. The pain can also start out mild and get progressively worse or simply remain mild.

Equine influenza/rhinopneumonitis

People and birds aren't the only ones who get the flu. Horses have their own versions of the virus, known as *equine influenza* and *rhinopneumonitis* (the latter is caused by the equine herpes virus). The infection attacks both the upper and lower respiratory tracts. Like the human versions of the flu, these viruses spread across the U.S. every fall and winter, and they're just as contagious (not to humans, however!).

Although equine influenza and rhinopneumonitis are two different viruses, they both cause the same symptoms, and veterinarians handle the two infections the same way. If your horse has a mild case, he may just have a runny nose and seem a bit lethargic for a few days. If his case is moderate to serious, he may run a high fever, have a runny nose and eyes, cough, and appear stiff. He may also lose his appetite.

Vaccines are available to prevent the equine flu, but if your horse does come down with the disease, the usual treatment involves supportive care such as drugs to reduce the fever and antibiotics to treat any secondary bacterial infections.

Thrush

Thrush, a bacterial infection of the foot, is one of the most common problems afflicting horses today. Horses who don't undergo regular feet cleaning are prone to this disease. The bacteria can take hold only if the foot is routinely packed with mud, soiled bedding, and manure for long periods of time.

Horses with thrush have a foul-smelling black discharge on the bottom of the hoof surrounding the *frog* (the triangular part of the underside of the horse's hoof). When you scrape the bottom of the hoof with a hoof pick, a clay-like material comes off, leaving deep grooves in the hoof. Left untreated, it can result in a more severe foot infection. The bacteria can also damage the horse's tendons. In serious cases, thrush can cause lameness.

If you suspect that your horse has a mild case of thrush (odor and some discharge but no lameness), you can try treating the condition yourself with an over-the-counter thrush medication available at tack and feed stores. If this treatment isn't effective or if thrush seems to cause your horse pain when he stands or walks, call your veterinarian.

Part V

Having Fun with Other Styles and Activities

The 5th Wave   By Rich Tennant

"Okay, very nice. Denise, you're still letting the horse drag you through the turns. Just take command and keep his head bent to the left."

In this part . . .

Part V is all about enjoying your horse in a lot of different ways. You discover gaited horses, equines who move differently than most other horses do. You also get the details on horse shows and how to get involved in them (so you can show everyone that your horse is no one-trick pony!). I also cover activities such as competing on the trail and riding in parades. The horse world is wide open to you.

Chapter 20

Step Up: Riding Gaited Horses

ost horses perform the traditional three gaits — walk, trot or jog, and canter or lope. However, a select group of horses have one or more gaits that they use in addition to or as a substitute for the trot or jog. In the horse world, these skilled steppers are called *gaited horses*.

In this chapter, I explain what a gaited horse does and why so many people love these types of horses. I also cover some of the breeds of gaited horses and tell you the basics of how to ride one of these special animals.

Defining the Four-Beat Gait

Gaited horses come in different breeds, and each gaited breed has a distinct way of moving that sets it apart (see the next section for info on breeds). But no matter what the breed, this special way of stepping is known as a four-beat gait. A *four-beat gait* means that each leg hits the ground at a different time.

Four-beat gaits usually replace the trot or jog. With trotting or jogging, which are two-beat gaits, two of the horse's legs hit the ground at the same time (see Chapter 14). If you count beats when you're riding a horse who's trotting or jogging, you count "one-two, one-two." When riding a gaited horse, however, you find yourself counting, "One-two-three-four, one-two-three-four."

The horse in Figure 20-1 shows the footfalls associated with the four-beat gait:

✔ Figure 20-1a shows the horse with two legs on one side on the ground at the same time.

✔ Figure 20-1b shows a subsequent footfall, with the left foreleg on the ground and other legs in the air.

✔ Figure 20-1c depicts the horse with a footfall that follows, with the right hind leg on the ground.

✔ Then the right foreleg and right hind leg strike the ground (not shown).

Figure 20-1:
Each of a gaited horse's legs hits the ground at a different time.

a   b   c

The four-beat gait is incredibly comfortable to ride. Instead of the jarring bounce of the trot or jog, the four-beat gait is often as smooth as silk. More and more adult riders, after learning to ride on a non-gaited horse, are choosing gaited horses over "trotting horses" because gaited horses are easier on the human body. People can ride gaited horses for hours on end with little effect on the bones and joints of the rider, which is a huge bonus for those of us who are starting to feel our age.

If you want to discover how to ride a gaited horse, seek out an instructor or trainer who specializes in this type of riding. Most gaited-horse trainers focus on a particular breed, which also determines the riding discipline. Check out Chapter 3 for more information on finding a riding instructor or trainer.

Picking up the pace, a two-beat gait

Most gaited horses perform a four-beat gait, which means their legs each hit the ground independently, but some gaited breeds, such as the Icelandic Horse and the rare Tiger Horse, also have a two-beat gait called the *pace*. Some Standardbred racehorses who pull *sulkies* (two-wheeled carts) on the racetrack also perform the pace.

If you watch a horse pace, you see that the legs on both sides of the horse move in unison. When a horse is pacing, she can go very fast. In fact, pacers on the racetrack can get up to speeds of nearly 40 mph. However, pacing isn't as comfortable as a four-beat gait, so in most gaited breeds, it's not preferred.

Checking Out Breeds Who Display Fancy Footwork

Gaited breeds come in a variety of shapes, sizes, and colors. Equine historians agree, however, that most of these breeds come from a now-extinct horse called the Spanish Jennet, which Spanish Conquistadors brought to the New World in the 1500s. The Spanish Jennet passed along its genes to a variety of gaited breeds. Some gaited horses are born knowing how to perform the gaits almost perfectly; others need training to hone their special gaits.

Each breed of gaited horse has a distinct style of four-beat gait. The primary differences lie in the exact timing of the footfalls and the speed of each gait. Here are some of the gaited breeds most known in the United States:

- **American Saddlebred:** This breed found popularity in the Southern United States during the 1700s and 1800s. American Saddlebreds perform the *slow gait* and the *rack*. Western and saddle seat are the two most popular disciplines for this horse.

- **Colonial Spanish Horse (some individuals):** The horse from which all North and South American breeds descended, the rare Colonial Spanish Horse (also known as the Spanish Mustang) was brought to the New World by the Spaniards. Because of its close relation to the Spanish Jennet, a good number of Colonial Spanish Horses possess gaits found in other gaited breeds. These include the *running walk, single foot, amble, pace,* and *paso* gaits. You can ride these horses in any discipline.

- **Icelandic Horse:** Developed in Iceland and believed to go back to the horses of the Vikings, the Icelandic horse is small in stature but big in gait. Icelandics perform the *flying pace* and the *tolt,* both four-beat gaits. Icelandics can be ridden any style, although many Iceland aficionados prefer to use genuine Iceland saddles, which are similar to endurance saddles (Chapter 23 discusses endurance riding).

- **Missouri Fox Trotter:** As the name suggests, this breed was developed in Missouri during the 1800s. Traditionally a Western breed, the Missouri Fox Trotter performs the *flat walk* and *fox trot* (though this horse isn't nearly as good at the tango or waltz). Western is the most popular discipline for this breed.

- **Paso Fino:** Hailing from the country of Columbia, the Paso Fino has also found considerable popularity in the U.S. over recent decades. The Paso Fino is known for its *paso fino, paso corto,* and *paso largo* four-beat gaits.

- **Peruvian Paso:** Created by Peruvian plantation owners over several centuries, this breed has gained increasing popularity in North America over the years. The Peruvian Paso's four-beat gaits are the *paso llano, sobreandando,* and *huachano.* In the show ring, the Peruvian Paso wears a Peruvian saddle (similar to an endurance saddle). On the trail, Western and endurance saddles are popular choices for this breed.

- **Rocky Mountain Horse:** Descended from a single stallion brought to Kentucky from parts unknown sometime in the 1800s, the Rocky Mountain Horse was officially recognized in 1986. Members of this breed perform a *single-foot* gait or a *rack.* They're most often ridden in Western saddles.

- **Tennessee Walking Horse:** Developed in the Deep South during the 1700s, this popular gaited horse performs the *flat walk* and the faster *running walk.* Both are very smooth. Tennessee Walking Horses are often ridden Western and saddle seat.

Tack it up: Gear for the gaited horse

Gaited horses are distinct from non-gaited horses, so what kind of tack do you ride them in? The answer depends mostly on the breed. Each breed of gaited horse has tradition behind it that typically dictates the style of saddle and bridle you should use. For example, the Peruvian Paso is ridden in a traditional Peruvian saddle that's unique among saddles. The Saddlebred is often ridden in a saddle seat saddle, its traditional tack for centuries. (See Chapter 23 for more about saddle seat riding.)

That said, you can ride any of the gaited breeds in Western or English saddles, although saddles that allow you to sit deep — Western, dressage, and endurance — are the most comfortable on a gaited horse.

In most cases, gaited horses are ridden with *leverage bits*; these bits have shanks, whether long or short, that help keep the horse's nose tipped down as she gaits. Saddlebreds are often ridden with a double-bridle, which features both a leverage curb bit and a snaffle bit. (See Chapter 9 for illustrations of both curb and snaffle bits.) The horse has both of these bits in her mouth at the same time, and each bit performs a different function in maintaining the horse's head carriage.

The type of tack you use on a gaited horse depends on her breed and the type of riding you want to do, whether it be show or casual trail riding. An experienced gaited-horse trainer or instructor can help you decide on the best tack for your particular gaited horse.

Riding a Gaited Horse

Because gaited horses move so differently from other horses, you have to ride them in a different way. Many people believe these horses are easier to ride than trotting horses simply because they have a smoother way of going. However, you still need to know how to sit and control the horse to get the wonderful gait your horse is capable of performing; I explain what to do in the following sections.

Figure 20-2 shows the overall position for riding a gaited horse. Most of these breeds were developed for riding over long distances, so the gaits are most comfortable if you sit back and relax.

Positioning your body

When riding a gaited horse of any breed, you have to relax. You want a soft, relaxed back and should sit very deep in the saddle. Unlike in Western and English riding, your rib cage should be high for gaited riding, and you should have no hollow in your back at all (refer to Figure 20-2).

Although this position would be uncomfortable, if not difficult, to ride at the trot, this position is easy to maintain because gaited horses are so smooth when performing their gaits.

Figure 20-2:
Riding a gaited horse, such as this Tennessee Walking Horse, calls for a deep seat, a lifted rib cage, and relaxed muscles.

Holding the reins

In order for a gaited horse to maintain her gait, she must be *collected* (carefully controlled). Therefore, you need to have constant contact with the horse's mouth through the reins. If you "throw away the reins" by making them too loose, your gaited horse won't be able to maintain her gait.

To keep your horse in gait, hold the reins taut without pulling too hard on the horse. Maintaining the proper tension takes practice, so try holding your hands higher than your elbow, making a slight V-angle. You don't want a straight elbow.

Your wrists should be relaxed as you ride, and your hands should be held over the horse's withers (refer to Figure 20-2). If you're riding in a Western saddle, you can use the horn as a guide as to where the withers are located.

As you advance in your riding, your instructor or trainer may show you how to influence the horse's head carriage using the reins.

Putting your legs in position

Part of keeping a gaited horse in control is maintaining contact with the horse's sides with your legs. On the other hand, you don't want to squeeze the horse like a tube of toothpaste. Keep your legs relaxed but touching the horse.

Your stirrups should be set long, similar to their position in Western riding, regardless of the type of saddle you're using (see Chapter 11 for details on Western stirrup length). Keep the balls of your feet in the stirrups, with your heels down (refer to Figure 20-2). Your legs should lie just behind the cinch, although this position may vary, depending on which gait you're asking for (which in turn depends on the breed you're riding — see the earlier section "Checking Out Breeds Who Display Fancy Footwork"). Your instructor can help you determine the correct stirrup length.

Moving with the gaited horse

Moving with the horse is the best part of riding a gaited horse. All you need to do is sit deep and relax, allowing your body to move with the gentle rhythm of the horse's motion. Whatever you do, don't tense up, which can cause you to resist the movement and bounce in the saddle. Riding a gaited horse is all about smoothness, so relax and let the horse make you feel like you're floating on air.

To help yourself stay relaxed, breathe deeply and be conscious of your muscles. Pretend you're floating in a swimming pool. Let all tension slip away.

Chapter 21

Don't Fence Me In: Trail Riding

In This Chapter

▶ Getting set to go on a trail ride

▶ Staying safe in the great outdoors

▶ Exploring etiquette on the trail

*T*he number one activity among horse owners throughout North America is trail riding, a hobby that takes both horse and rider into the wide open spaces just for the sheer joy of it. Whether you live in the urban wilds of New York City or the untamed wilderness of Western forests, trail riding is something you and your horse can enjoy together.

Hitting the trail is a very old activity. Before the days of automobiles (you know — those horseless carriages), riding a horse on the trail was usually the only way to get from point A to point B. Today, people trail ride just for fun. Few activities are as relaxing and therapeutic as riding a horse out in the open. Horses have a way of helping humans feel connected to nature, and never is this truer than when you're riding on a shady, wooded trail or through a sweet-smelling meadow.

In this chapter, I tell you all about trail riding and how to prepare for it. You discover how to choose the best horse for trail riding as well as the gear and knowledge of safety and etiquette you need to enjoy this relaxing pastime. (For info on endurance and competitive trail riding, flip to Chapter 23.)

Preparing for a Trail Ride

Before you hit the trail, you need to get ready. This prep work includes getting the right horse, knowing where you're going, and sporting the proper gear. In the following sections, I describe how to prepare for an enjoyable trail ride.

Using the right horse

Just because a horse is easy to ride in the arena doesn't mean he'll be a good mount for the trail. From the horse's perspective, trail riding is completely different from arena riding. Because it involves being out in the open, sometimes in unfamiliar territory, beginning trail riding requires a horse who's calm, confident, and easygoing.

Good *ground manners* — or the way the horse behaves as you handle him when you're not on his back — are an important quality in a trail horse (Chapter 11 has details on working with a horse from the ground). A horse with good ground manners stands quietly while he's being groomed, doesn't fuss or move around when you're saddling and bridling him, and walks quietly alongside as you lead him.

Trail horses need to have good ground manners for a number of reasons, including the following:

- ✔ With a trail horse, you never know what kind of situation you may find yourself in. Trail riding by its very nature requires that you be away from home base. The last thing you need is a horse you can't control if you're far from the stable.

- ✔ Emergencies happen on trail rides, too. Horses become lame, get rocks embedded in their feet — just about anything can happen out there. If your horse has good ground manners, he's more likely to cooperate in an emergency situation if you have to dismount.

- ✔ You may find yourself in a situation where you need or want to get off your horse and walk beside him. If this happens, you'll be happy to have a horse who behaves himself while you're leading him.

- ✔ Stopping along the trail for a bite to eat, a bathroom break, or just to stretch your legs means you need to get off your horse. A horse with good ground manners stands quietly when tied and is easy to mount.

The horse you ride on the trail should be obedient and sensitive to your commands. A good trail horse has a good work ethic, which means he knows he has a job to do in this world and is willing to do it. The best trail horses are also virtually unflappable. Not much scares them, and when they do become frightened, they don't lose their minds but assess the situation before deciding to take off in mad flight.

If you're a novice rider, you may want to choose an older, more mature mount for a beginning trail horse. Older horses tend to be quieter than younger horses. The horse needs to have extensive experience on the trail, too. Otherwise, he's unlikely to be calm out there, no matter how old he is.

Turning your arena horse into a trail mount

Most horses can become decent trail horses with the right training and exposure, so if your arena horse is easily startled on trail, it's probably because he hasn't had much exposure to it. Your horse needs time and practice on the trail, and you may need a professional to help your horse get it if he's not safe or if you feel like you just don't know how to deal with him out in the open.

Remember that horse is an individual. Although some horses need just a few jaunts on the trail

to get the hang of it, others need six months or more of consistent exposure to be able to relax.

If you want to make your arena horse into a trail horse and you're a beginning rider, getting help from an expert is a good idea. A horse trainer or a very experienced friend should take your horse out on the trail to evaluate whether he needs a lot of work before you get on and start trying to conquer your local trail system.

Deciding where to ride

In the old days, riders had only one kind of trail to explore: the wilderness trail. Horses either traveled through town on a dirt road or carried their riders through the deserts, through the woods, and over the mountains.

Things have obviously changed, and trails are quite different from what they were even 50 years ago. Nowadays, equestrians are faced with a variety of trail choices. They include the following:

- **Urban trails:** A great many urban and suburban dwellers are limited to riding on urban trails. These types of trails are in city areas and suburban neighborhoods. Urban trails usually share all or part of their boundaries with a city street, which means traffic and pedestrians — and everything that comes with those two elements — are part of the mix.

  Although most riders would rather be out in the wilderness, for many people, these trails are their only option. Urban trails can be a good substitute for a more rugged and untamed trail experience, and they often offer opportunities to see wildlife and breathe relatively fresh air.

- **Local parks:** Many urban and suburban dwellers, as well as some rural residents, take advantage of trails in local parks. Although small city parks aren't conducive to trail riding, many regional parks have extensive trails that can provide an enjoyable wilderness experience. These types of parks are accessible from areas where horses are kept or can be easily reached by horse trailer. Because local parks get a lot of use and are managed by local municipalities, they're often well marked and well maintained. Some even permit horse camping, and some connect to wilderness trails, which you can ride on all day without seeing anything that reminds you of civilization. See Chapter 23 for details on trailering and camping.

✔ **State parks:** Managed by state government parks departments, state parks are often wonderful places for trail riders. Beautiful and often pristine wilderness areas make up the state parks system throughout the U.S. Many state park trail systems are open to equestrians, and they generally feature well maintained and well marked trails.

✔ **National Forests:** The National Forest system provides the greatest number of trails open to equestrians in the U.S. You can find National Forests throughout the country, and they encompass all kinds of terrain, from shoreline to deserts to mountains. Because National Forests are open to a wide variety of uses, equestrians are often welcome in these protected areas. National Forests are managed by the U.S. Department of Agriculture Forest Service (www.fs.fed.us). Horse camping is usually permitted in the National Forests.

✔ **National Parks:** The most beautiful and well-kept trails in the country are part of the National Parks system. Areas such as Yosemite National Park, Bryce Canyon National Park, and the Great Smoky Mountains National Park are all examples of National Parks that allow equestrian use. Although not all National Parks allow horses, the ones that do can provide you with some spectacular trail riding. The U.S. government's National Park Service manages the National Park system (www.nps.gov).

✔ **Designated wilderness areas:** Several other types of designated wilderness areas are open to equestrians, including some national monuments and conservation areas. Many designated wilderness areas have wonderful trails that are little used.

Stop off at a visitor center to pick up a trail map, talk to other riders for suggestions, and do a bit of research. Trail difficulty and length can vary, but you can find easy trails for beginners at all these places.

Check out Figure 21-1 to see some riders on a beautiful nature trail.

Know the rules before you go. Before you can ride, some parks require proof of a negative Coggins test, which confirms that the horse is free from a contagious disease called equine infectious anemia (swamp fever). Also, if you plan to go horse camping (see Chapter 23), you may need to make reservations or get an overnight permit from the Forest Service.

Gathering important gear

In order to make the most of your trail riding experience, you want to have certain gear along on your ride, as I explain in the following sections.

Figure 21-1:
Trail riding is a great way to bond with your horse and fellow riders.

Helmets

In many Western riding circles, helmets are considered a nonentity. The original cowboys didn't wear them, and in keeping with tradition, most Western riders don't, either. Most English riders, on the other hand, always wear helmets. Helmets are also a staple for those who ride competitively on the trail. So should you wear a helmet when you trail ride? The decision of whether to wear a riding helmet is a personal one.

The benefit of wearing a helmet is a powerful one: In the event of a fall from your horse, a helmet can save your life. According to the Centers for Disease Control and Prevention (CDC), the rate of serious injury for horseback riders is greater than that for motorcyclists and automobile racers. State medical examiner records from 27 states over an 11-year period identified head injuries as the cause of 60 percent of horseback riding-related deaths. Given the potential for serious head injury, the CDC suggests that all riders wear helmets approved by the Safety Equipment Institute (SEI) and American Society for Testing and Materials (ASTM) for equestrian use.

The downside of helmets is that they can be mildly uncomfortable if you aren't used to wearing one (although newer models are very lightweight and well ventilated), and they can really mess up your hair. If you care about fitting in with the crowd and you're a Western rider, you'll probably stick out among your Western buddies if you decide to protect your skull.

Although you may have an image of yourself on horseback with your hair blowing in the wind, stop and think about what could happen to you if you fall from your horse and hit your head. The possibilities are horrific and hardly worth the risk. Do yourself and those who love you a favor and wear an ASTM/SEI-approved helmet when you trail ride. Chapter 5 has additional information on safety.

Appropriate clothing

Check the weather before you head out and make sure you're wearing the right apparel. If you'll be out all day, you may need to wear layers so you can take them off as the day warms up. If rain or snow is a possibility, be sure to bring appropriate outerwear so you don't get wet. Nothing is more miserable than trying to ride back home when you're cold and soaked to the bone!

You should also wear proper, safe riding apparel when you trail ride. See Chapters 5 (on safe clothing) and 10 (on riding apparel) for details on what to wear.

Additional handy gear

In addition to a comfortable saddle that fits your horse well (see Chapter 8), a bridle that provides you with plenty of control (see Chapter 9), and important items necessary for your safety (which I discuss later in the section "Following some important guidelines"), you can also opt to add some of the following items to your trail-riding ensemble:

- **Saddle packs:** If you plan to be out on the trail for many hours, you want to have a saddle pack attached to your saddle. Most saddle packs fit on the back of the saddle, although some packs are designed to sit on the front. Saddle packs come in a wide variety of shapes and sizes. Almost all feature holders for sports bottles, and all have at least one large pouch where you can put your lunch, sunscreen, horse treats, or anything else you want to carry along.

- **Seat covers:** Long hours on the trail can be tough on your hind end. Trail riders often equip their saddles with seat covers made from sheepskin (or fake sheepskin) or gel. Seat covers are designed for Western, English, and endurance saddles (see Chapter 23 for more about endurance riding), and they come in a wide range of prices.

- **Water bottle holders:** For shorter rides where a saddle pack isn't necessary, trail riders can opt for a water bottle holder designed to clip onto one of the D-rings located on the front or back of most saddles.

- **Miscellaneous goodies:** All kinds of other items designed to make the trail rider's life easier are available. Foldaway water buckets for horses, portable corrals, straps to hang and attach to saddle packs, combination sponges and bags, folding hoof picks, portable water tanks — you name it, it's out there.

The best sources for unique trail gear are catalogs and online retailers specializing in equine products. You can find a list of some retailers in the Appendix.

Getting ready for a ride of any length

Trail riding is a pretty simple activity. You just locate a trail (I discuss different types of trails earlier in this chapter), saddle up your horse, mount up, and start riding. Trail rides can be as short as an hour or as long as an entire day. Some trail rides even stretch out over a week or more. You just have to decide how much trail riding you want to do and prepare accordingly. The following sections explain how ride lengths compare.

Warming up for short trips

Short rides don't call for much preparation. Your tacked-up horse and an idea of where you're going are all you really need. Assuming that trails are available in proximity to where you keep your horse, you can probably ride to the *trail head* (the place where the trail starts). Otherwise, you need to trailer your horse to get there. See Chapter 23 for info on trailering.

After you reach the trail head, begin your ride at a walk and slowly increase the speed to a jog or trot and eventually to a lope or canter (if you're ready to go that fast) as your horse warms up. This warm-up is especially important if you haven't ridden your horse for a few days.

Conditioning for longer journeys

If you plan to take longer rides, be sure both you and your horse are conditioned for this kind of riding. The worst thing to do to a horse is let him stand in his stall all week and then get on him on a Saturday and ride him for four hours on the trail. He'll be sore and miserable the next day and will be less than enthusiastic the next time you come to take him out.

To condition your horse for an upcoming long ride, ride your horse at least several days a week, for an hour at a time or more, gradually building up the time over a period of a few weeks.

Staying Safe on the Trail

The trail is a wonderful place where you can commune with nature and bond deeply with your horse. It's also a place where and your horse can get into trouble if you aren't careful. In the following sections, I provide some basic safety rules and guidance on handling a spooked horse. Chapter 5 has general information on safety, too. Also, the upcoming section "Happy Trails: Minding Your Manners" explains rules of etiquette that can help protect you.

Following some important guidelines

Because you're out in the open and away from civilization, safety is an especially important issue when riding on the trail. Follow these safety rules while enjoying the wide open spaces, especially if you're riding alone:

✔ **Choose an appropriate trail.** Pick a trail that matches your ability level and the desired length of your ride. You can chat with the visitor center staff or other riders or look for a map or another source that indicates trail difficulty. If your trail closes during certain seasons or after periods of heavy rainfall, make sure it's open.

✔ **Know where you're going.** If you're heading out on a trail that you've never ridden before, map out your route carefully. You need an idea of how long the ride will take from start to finish. If the trail is long, bring a trail map with you. Make sure you'll be able to give emergency personnel general information about where you are if necessary.

✔ **Tell someone about your plans.** Just as if you were going on a solo hike, tell someone where you're going and when you expect to be back. That way, if you fail to return within a reasonable amount of time, someone will know you're missing and have an idea of where to look.

✔ **Identify yourself and your horse.** Carry ID on your person and put a tag on your horse's halter or bridle with your name, phone number, and address. If you fall and are knocked unconscious, ID can help your rescuers, and if you become separated from your horse, his ID tag can eventually get him back to you.

✔ **Carry a cellphone.** In the event of an emergency, a cellphone can be your lifeline. For instance, if your horse gets injured, you may need to call for help if he's too hurt for you to get off and lead him out.

Bring a charged cellphone with you whenever you ride, and make sure you keep the phone on your person and not in your saddle bag. If you fall from your horse and need help, you want the phone to be in reach. Note that your cell phone may not work if you're riding in a wilderness area, and remember that you can't recharge the batteries out there. Turn off the phone when you don't need it if you plan on a long ride.

✔ **Bring appropriate food and water.** If you plan to be gone all day, bring enough food and water to keep yourself hydrated and nourished while you're gone. Water is especially important if you're riding in hot weather.

✔ **Protect your horse from bugs.** Unless you're riding in extreme cold or desert heat, horse-eating insects will likely be a problem. Spray your horse with equine insect repellent before you go on your ride, and bring some fly wipes along so you can reapply if needed. If gnats are a problem in your area, you may even want to invest in a simple knitted or mesh bonnet that protects your horse's ears from these biting insects (these bonnets are available from tack stores and catalogs — see the Appendix for some possible retailers).

- **Bring sunscreen and a first-aid kit.** Protect yourself from the sun and carry a small first-aid kit in your saddlebag if you're going on a longer ride. The kit should include items for both you and your horse, such as bee-string treatment, adhesive bandages, antibiotic ointment, blood-stop powder, a roll of elastic bandaging, and a hoof pick.

- **Stay on the trail.** Although blazing new trails can be fun, stay on the beaten path if you're riding alone in unfamiliar territory. Most riders and hikers get lost when they stray from well-marked trails. Also, many parks and wilderness areas forbid riding off the trail.

Handling spooks

The trail is the place you're most likely to encounter spooking, which is the horse's reaction to something that frightens him (such as a scary bridge or stream). The type of behavior your horse exhibits when he's afraid depends largely on his personality. Each horse has his own way of responding, but here are some ways a horse may react when he's afraid of something:

- Back up in an effort to avoid going toward whatever scares him

- Spin away from the object

- Dance around the scary thing in an effort to avoid approaching it

- Plant his feet and refuse to move (this maneuver is often followed by a spin if the rider keeps insisting that the horse go forward)

- Agree to pass the object but prance by it, his head pointing slightly toward it and the ear closest to the object cocked; the horse's idea is to keep a close watch on the object should it decide to come to life and try to eat him

The goal when dealing with spookiness is to keep your horse controllable, even though he's afraid of something. In other words, he's allowed to be scared, but he isn't allowed to become uncontrollable at the same time. Try to remain calm and confident as you ask for obedience.

Finding your way home

If you get lost, your horse may be able to find his way back. Horses have a strong sense of direction and are often motivated to get back home. If you're completely disoriented and don't know how to get back, give your horse his head — he may know the way. This technique works at night, too, because horses can see very well in the dark (although note that using a flashlight can make their night vision less effective).

The work you do in the arena to enhance your horse's basic training can do a lot to help you keep your horse controllable out on the trail. Listening and responding to your cues should be second nature to your horse. You can practice giving direction in the arena by asking your horse to perform certain tasks, such as stopping, backing, turning, and circling (see Chapters 13 through 15 for details). After you've achieved this level of obedience, repeated exposure to trail riding and positive experiences on the trail should help your horse stay reasonably calm when you ride him outside the arena.

Some horses can become downright dangerous when they're afraid of something. If you have a horse who tends try to run away with you, rear up, buck you off, or do anything that you can't handle, don't hesitate to get professional help from a qualified horse trainer.

Happy Trails: Minding Your Manners

Riders who practice good trail etiquette are a pleasure to ride with and encounter along the trail. Whether you're going on a short ride or a long one, alone or with a group, trail etiquette is something you should know and follow. In trail riding, good etiquette is not just for the sake of courtesy; it's a question of safety as well (see the earlier "Staying Safe on the Trail" section for more safety issues).

In the following sections, I give you some etiquette guidelines for riding in a group, riding by yourself, and sharing the road with folks who aren't riders.

Following etiquette when riding in a group

If you're riding with one or more other people, you need to follow some basic rules to make your excursion fun and safe for everyone involved. Follow these fundamental rules of trail etiquette:

- **Tie a red ribbon.** If you're riding in a group and have a horse who's a kicker, tie a red ribbon at the base of his tail. This universal signal tells other riders that your horse kicks and that they need to stay back.

- **Keep a safe distance.** Staying back can be difficult to do at times, because many horses prefer to travel with their noses just behind the tail of the horse in front of them. If the horse in front of you stops suddenly, your mount may then find himself plunging into the other horse's rear end. Also, the horse in front of you may become annoyed at your horse's crowding and kick out, which can injure you or your horse. Try to keep your horse at least one horse's length from the animal in front of you.

Tip: If you find you're having trouble keeping a safe distance between you and the horse in front of you, make your horse turn in a circle to create some space between you and the front horse. If you don't have room on the trail to circle, stop your horse for a few seconds to let the horse in front get a safe distance ahead.

✔ **Go slowly.** Keep your horse at a walk unless you have a consensus from other riders to pick up the pace. Keep in mind that horses tend to get excited when the speed picks up in a group situation. The quiet lope you have in mind may turn into an out-of-control gallop if a number of horses are involved. Not all riders are equal in their skill levels, and although you may be able to control your horse at a trot or lope, a less-skilled rider in the group may lose control of his or her mount when you start going fast.

✔ **Don't pass without permission.** If your horse wants to be at the front of the line, ask those in front of you for permission to pass and lead the group. Don't let your horse barge ahead of everyone. Not only is this act rude, but it's also unsafe, especially on a narrow trail.

✔ **Use good manners as your horse stops to drink.** If you come across a water source along the trail and the horses want to drink, be courteous and wait your turn, especially if the source is a small trough. Keep your horse quiet and passive during the watering session. Avoid the following actions, which could discourage a fellow rider's horse from drinking:

- Allowing your horse to aggressively barge in and threaten another horse while he's partaking of the water

- Letting your horse to pin his ears at other horses while they're drinking

- Pulling your horse away from the water source too fast when the other horses still have their muzzles in the water

- Riding off before all the horses are finished drinking, causing other horses to feel they're being left behind

If you're having trouble getting your horse to behave, pull him aside and wait till the other horses are finished before you let him have his share.

✔ **Help calm spooked horses.** If you see another rider in trouble ahead of you on the trail, stop and wait until that person has his or her horse under control before you proceed.

Another option is to ask the other rider whether he or she would like you to pass so your horse can help calm the frightened one. Obviously, this technique works only if you're sure your horse won't be spooked by whatever is scaring the other rider's horse. Horses tend to take cues from one another, so your horse may object to passing the object as well. In that case, hang back and wait for everyone to calm down before you proceed. I discuss handling spooks earlier in this chapter.

✔ **Be courteous to dismounted riders.** Horses tend to follow each other, so if one of the riders in your group has to dismount, keep your horse still while he or she gets off. Continue to keep your horse quiet while the other rider mounts, and don't head down the trail until the other rider gives you a verbal signal that he or she is ready to move on.

✔ **Communicate with your fellow riders.** Remember that people have different skills and confidence levels when riding. Trail riding can be the most challenging type of riding for timid or less-skilled riders. Check in with your fellow riders to make sure everyone is feeling okay and secure, and try to solve problems calmly as they come up.

Be sure to communicate with your fellow riders when you're riding on a tree-dense trail and are encountering low-hanging branches. After you push a branch out of your way, it can snap back and hit the rider behind you. Warn the rider behind you that you're approaching low-hanging branches and be sure he or she is prepared for them.

Encountering other riders when you're out alone

Although riding with another person is much safer, some people prefer to ride alone. When riding by yourself, you have much more autonomy, and you can pick your own pace and route. Of course, even though you're out in the great outdoors, you may still see other people. You have to honor the rules of trail etiquette should you encounter other riders.

When you meet other riders on the trail, keep the following rules in mind:

✔ **Pass slowly and quietly.** When passing another rider on the trail from behind, pass on the left at the walk. Many horses can become out of control when they hear or see a horse trotting or loping up behind them. Make sure the rider ahead of you knows you're there and is okay with your passing, especially on narrow trails. Avoid yelling or doing anything that may spook the other horse.

✔ **Make a slow approach when another rider is coming from the opposite direction.** When approaching another rider, slow to a walk if you're trotting or loping and maintain your slow pace until you're well past the other horse. If the trail is narrow, pay attention to your horse's body language to make sure he doesn't kick or try to bite the other horse as he goes by.

✔ **Be patient with dismounted riders.** Don't try to ride past someone who's attempting to mount a horse. Stop and wait until the rider is safely back in the saddle before you proceed.

✔ **Resist the urge to hot rod.** A good canter on the trail can be a lot of fun, but you need to pick the right moment to let your horse go for it. Choose a trail that

  • Is flat

  • Has good, even footing

  • Allows you plenty of visibility up ahead

  Walking the trail first is a good idea.

✔ **Take your time around blind curves.** Narrow single-track trails in areas of high brush can harbor a lot of blind curves. Always negotiate blind curves at a walk. You never know when another horse (or another trail user) is coming in the opposite direction.

✔ **React calmly when you see spooked horses.** If you see another rider in trouble ahead of you on the trail, either offer to help or stop and wait until that person has his or her horse under control before you proceed (see the earlier section "Handling spooks")

Sharing the trail with non-riders

Most trails accessible to equestrians these days are multiuse trails, meaning people use other modes of transportation on them. Hikers and mountain bikers are the most common users of trails located near urban and suburban areas. Wilderness backcountry trails are often used by backpackers as well.

Representing equestrian trail users

Because hikers and mountain bikers are more populous than equestrians, they often have more political clout concerning trail use. Equestrian groups around the U.S. are continuously fighting to keep the rights of trail riders intact. More than one trail has been made off-limits to equestrians while other special interest groups are permitted to continue their use.

Keep in mind that when you encounter a hiker or mountain biker on the trail, you represent all equestrian users to that person. Be particularly courteous and considerate — it's your responsibility help create goodwill.

A horse has significant potential to seriously injure a trail user on foot, leaving riders with a great amount of responsibility in keeping trails safe. The following guidelines can help keep trails safe for various users and create good feelings toward equestrians:

✔ **Use your right of way.** Technically, equestrians have the right of way on narrow trails, and some parks and recreational areas are quick to point that out to all trail users. If you encounter a hiker or mountain biker and he or she stops to give you the right of way, politely accept it. However, if the other user doesn't give you the right of way, take it in stride and pull your horse over so he's safely out of the way.

✔ **Take care around blind curves.** You should always go through blind curves slowly to avoid crashing into another rider, but caution is even more important when you're riding on multiuse trails. A mountain biker can come around a turn very quickly, and the more slowly you go on your horse, the more time the biker has to stop or swerve to avoid hitting you. You can also avoid running down a hiker on your horse if you're walking around a blind corner instead of trotting or cantering through it.

✔ **Remove manure.** Although horse people know that manure is innocuous and quickly degrades in the environment, many urban hikers and mountain bikers consider horse manure to be as noxious as dog poop. If your horse relieves himself on a well-traveled trail, dismount and kick the manure off into the bushes. Although this cleanup may sound like a needless and silly task, horses have been banned from a number of trails because of manure complaints.

✔ **Be understanding with people who aren't comfortable with horses.** Although the idea is hard for most horse people to fathom, some folks are terrified of horses. If you encounter a non-equestrian trail user who seems afraid of your horse, go out of your way to avoid getting too close to him or her.

✔ **Be polite.** Whenever you pass a hiker or mountain biker, offer a smile and say hello. Thank the other trail user for giving you the right of way, and avoid getting angry and losing your temper if the other user doesn't seem to know proper etiquette.

Chapter 22

Show Off: Riding in Competition

*I*f you love horseback riding and have a competitive streak, you'll soon start to gravitate toward horse shows. These fun events test both the horse and rider and reward those who display the most talent and evidence of hard work.

Horse shows are judged exhibitions of riders and/or horses and ponies. Participants compete in different classes, each with specifications for the type of riding, age of the horse, age of the rider, and so on. Depending on the class, the competitors may be judged against each other or against written rules. Each horse-and-rider team faces evaluation alone in the arena or, more commonly, within a group. The type of show determines the classes, the rules applied to exhibitors, and even the types of awards.

People love horse shows for a number of reasons:

✔ The beautiful horses, all groomed to their very best, are a big reason for the popularity of horse shows. Even people who don't know much about horses love to watch a group of exquisite equines displaying their talent in the show ring.

✔ For competitors, not only is the show day itself full of excitement, but all the preparation for the event is great, too. Many riders enjoy having a goal to work toward with their horses, and an upcoming horse show provides plenty to shoot for.

✔ Everyone wants to win, and the thrill that comes along with taking top honors in your class at a horse show is hard to beat.

These shows come in many forms and have different rules, depending on which organization is sanctioning the competition. In this chapter, I tell you about some of the kinds of horse shows out there. You discover how judges award prizes and how to prepare both you and your horse for these exciting events.

Understanding How Horse Shows Work

Although horse shows may seem a bit chaotic to the untrained eye — with horses and people wandering everywhere — events are very well organized. A lot goes into putting on a horse show, from securing the venue and sending out the show *premiums* (the list of classes and the entry form) to finding the judges.

As you watch a horse show, you'll be very aware of the judges and the awards they give out. After all, most competitors are there to win. In the following sections, I explain the judging, placings, and awards that are part of every horse show. Knowing how horse shows work can help you get the most out of them, whether as a participant or a spectator.

Looking at the judging system

Horse show judging, in most classes, is subjective. In other words, the judge of a particular class determines the first place winner and other placings based on his or her opinion. Although judges try to adhere to a standard when making their decisions, the choice is ultimately a personal one. Still, make sure you remain respectful of the results. Many judges volunteer their time and don't get paid for the work they do; others receive just a moderate stipend from the sponsoring club.

The exception to this lack of objectivity comes with timed events such as gymkhana or show jumping, in which the horse either accomplishes the goal or doesn't. The results in these classes are fairly cut-and-dried.

So who are these judges who often wield so much power? Most are very experienced equestrians who have themselves competed in the events they're judging, and many are trainers in these disciplines. Some have to take tests to show that they're knowledgeable enough to judge, and all have proven themselves qualified to evaluate other riders.

An eye on the prize: Placings and awards

As you hear the judge's decision in each class, placings come into play. At most shows, the announcer names the horse and/or rider with the last placing first. The announcer then works up the list until finally giving the name of the first place winner.

Most shows place horses from first to sixth place, although some bigger shows go as far as tenth place. In a large class, even a tenth place award is an honor.

The types of awards at horse shows depend on the particular show. Just about all horse shows give ribbons to the winners. Each placing has a different color, though color standards can vary from country to country. In U.S. shows, ribbon colors usually follow these guidelines:

Place	*Ribbon Color*
First	Blue
Second	Red
Third	Yellow
Fourth	White
Fifth	Pink
Sixth	Green
Seventh	Purple
Eighth	Brown
Ninth	Gray
Tenth	Light blue

For higher awards, such as Champion or Reserve Champion (at bigger national shows, these awards go to the first and second place winners, respectively), winners take home trophies and/or large, fancy ribbons. In some shows, cash awards are even part of the deal. Cash prizes depend in large part on the particular discipline. For instance, they can come into play at certain Western events, such as reining. And at large jumping shows, horse-and-rider teams can earn thousands of dollars for taking a top prize.

Surveying Different Types of Shows

When you start exploring the world of horse shows, you may discover that the types of shows out there are as numerous as the breeds of horses — more so, in fact. And those shows offer a variety of *classes,* or categories of competition — pleasure classes so you can show off your horse's body structure and movement, dressage classes so you can flaunt your horse's training, and equitation classes to demonstrate that your riding technique is just right. Test your jumping skills in hunter hack and hunters over fences; evade obstacles in trail and gymkhana classes; let the cow classes show you how you'd fare as a ranch hand out West; and through vaulting classes, do gymnastics on a moving horse. You and your horse can even get all decked out for heritage classes and compete with an authentic costuming look. If nothing else, shows certainly give you plenty of options.

The type of show or shows you choose to participate in depends on your level or riding, your chosen discipline, your breed of horse, and how much commitment you want to make to riding and showing. Your instructor or trainer can help you determine which shows you should enter, depending on your riding level.

Ultimately, the sky's the limit for horse shows. If you had unlimited amounts of time and money, you could do them all. But because that's pretty unlikely, focus on the particular type of show that's best for you at a given time. I provide some guidance on different horse shows in the following sections.

Learning the ropes at schooling shows

When you're a beginning rider and a novice exhibitor, the first type of show you want to enter is a schooling show. These shows are just as they sound: they're for *schooling,* or training. Under very little pressure, both you and your horse gain experience showing at a schooling show. Your competition is other beginners like yourself, so the playing field is fairly level.

You can find schooling shows by checking in a local horse publication, looking for signs in your local tack and feed store, or checking your newspaper for upcoming events. Schooling shows are usually put on by local riding clubs or commercial stables. The classes vary depending on the discipline of the show, and the shows usually last only one day. The entry fees are very affordable, usually around $10 to $15 per class.

I describe the three types of schooling shows in the following sections: Western only, English only, and shows with both disciplines.

Western only

Some schooling shows feature only Western riding classes. Among others, these classes usually include

- **Western pleasure:** Horses in Western pleasure are judged in how well they carry themselves and move with a Western rider. The horses are judged at the walk, jog, and lope.

- **Trail obstacle:** In trail obstacle classes, judges evaluate horses one at a time and observe them as they encounter obstacles such as a mailbox, a wooden bridge, and a tarp laid out on the ground.

- **Equitation:** Riders, not horses, are judged in equitation classes. Judges look for proper body position at the different gaits of walk, jog, and lope.

Western schooling shows sometimes have timed *gymkhana events,* in which horses run one at a time around barrels or poles. On occasion, the shows also have *showmanship classes* (which require a handler, who's being judged, to present a horse for evaluation) and *halter classes* (which are performed with the horses "in hand" instead of under saddle). However, halter classes are more typically part of a breed show, which I discuss later on.

Riders are expected to dress in Western apparel, although they don't need fancy clothes or expensive tack on their horses. See Chapter 10 for details on Western apparel.

English only

A great many schooling shows are for English riders, specifically those who ride hunt seat. Classes usually include

- **Hunters over fences:** Horses are judged one at a time as they negotiate a series of fences. Judges look for good form as the horse approaches and jumps over each obstacle.

- **Hunter hack:** One at a time, horses are judged as they're asked to negotiate two small fences. Judges look for good form as the horse approaches and goes over the jumps.

- **Equitation:** Only riders face judging in this class. They're evaluated for proper body position at the walk, trot, and canter.

Jumping is the primary focus of these shows, which are great for helping novices in the show world get their feet wet in the ring (check out Chapter 16 for details on jumping). Riders in these classes enter the arena by themselves and perform the course as prescribed by the show steward. Before the class begins, riders memorize the course and walk it on foot to become familiar with the pattern and distance between jumps.

Figure 22-1 shows riders in an English schooling show.

Western and English

Some schooling shows feature classes in both disciplines, usually on different days. Because multidisciplinary shows have a large number of classes, they usually take two days to complete.

Finding a one-day schooling show with both disciplines is fairly rare, but some do exist. They give riders a chance to find out about the other discipline and see how different Western and English horses really are.

Figure 22-1:
A class at a hunt seat show lines up for the judge's decision.

Raising the bar at rated shows

Beyond the world of schooling shows lie the rated shows. These events are recognized by the United States Equestrian Federation (USEF), formally known as the American Horse Shows Association and the United States Equestrian Association. The USEF represents the United States in the Fédération Equestre Internationale (FEI), the international group that recognizes high-level competitive equine events around the world.

The USEF, which is a national body, rates horse shows *A, B,* or *C,* with *A* shows offering the greatest competition and prestige. *C*-rated shows are the events most attended by novices to the show world. *B* shows are for those who are beyond *C* shows but aren't quite ready for the *A* level. The shows are often part of a *circuit,* which means that several shows are held during a given show season in a particular region.

Local horse show associations usually hold rated shows over two days or more, and the shows can be discipline specific or open to all breeds and disciplines. These shows follow USEF rules. Points are frequently awarded in certain disciplines, and in these situations, competitors may receive year-end awards. (For details about rules, points, entry fees, and more, contact the USEF; see the Appendix for contact information.)

Welcoming competition in open shows

Shows that allow all breeds of horses are called *open shows.* An open show can be a schooling show or a rated show (see the preceding sections). The term distinguishes a particular show from a breed-specific show, where only one breed is allowed to compete (see "Focusing on breed shows").

Open shows can be Western or English or both. These shows can be a lot of fun to watch because you can see horses of every size, shape, and color competing against one another.

Focusing on breed shows

Nearly every breed of horse has a national association that represents it. Associations for the more popular breeds often have enough active members to sponsor breed-specific shows. Regional member clubs that belong to the national association usually put these shows on, although the national association may directly hold large national shows each year. The larger associations have one of these events annually, usually at the same venue each year. (The Appendix has contact information for a variety of breed associations.)

Breed shows typically offer classes in both Western and English. Many classes are the same as those you see in schooling shows (see the earlier section on schooling shows), although some shows also include *driving classes* (in which horses are judged in harness while pulling a cart) and other events specific to the breed. Paso Fino shows, for example, include a class in which the horses display their special gait on a wooden board so the judge can hear the quality of that gait (Chapter 20 can give you details on Paso Finos and other gaited horses). At Appaloosa shows, a Native heritage class allows exhibitors to dress themselves and their horses up in period attire.

Most breed shows have a *halter class,* in which horses are not ridden but are rather presented to the judge wearing only a show halter. The judge evaluates the horses for their *conformation* (the way they're built) and places them according to how closely each horse matches its breed's blueprint, or *standard.* Figure 22-2 depicts an Appaloosa halter class.

If you're interested in a particular breed, check out a local breed show. You can discover a lot about how these horses are shown and meet many other people with a passion for the same kind of horse. If you decide you'd like to compete in one of these shows, start working with a trainer who specializes in your breed of choice.

Exploring specialty shows

Some shows focus exclusively on one event within a discipline. Before you can compete at a specialty show, you need to advance quite a bit in your riding, and you have to be mounting a horse who's specifically trained for one of these events. These shows may highlight one of the following:

- **Reining:** In this Western activity, horses go through a pattern at the lope and are judged on their responsiveness as well as their abilities.

- **Cutting:** A Western activity, cutting requires that the rider ask his or her horse to separate a cow from a herd and keep that cow from joining the group for a specified amount of time.

- **Dressage:** Called the ballet of the horse world, horse-and-rider teams are judged on their ability to execute a series of complex moves. See Chapter 7 for details on dressage.

- **Jumping:** Events strictly for show jumping feature classes designed to challenge a horse and rider's courage and ability to negotiate high fences. For more information on show jumping, see Chapter 16.

- **Gymkhana:** This Western activity involves timed events in which horse-and-rider teams individually negotiate either barrels or poles with speed and precision.

✔ **Vaulting:** A form of gymnastics on horseback, vaulting features riders who perform various maneuvers on a cantering horse who's moving in a circle while attached to a lunge line.

At these shows, all breeds are usually welcome.

Gearing Up for a Horse Show

Before you hit the show circuit, you need to do a lot of work to get ready. Although showing may look easy when you're watching exhibitors strut their stuff at a show, getting to the point where you can hold your own — even at a schooling show — takes many hours of practice and hard work.

The better prepared you are, the more comfortable you'll feel on show day, and the same goes for your horse as well. You can both be more relaxed and have more fun if you know what you're doing. I give you some preparation tips in the following sections.

Preparing yourself

Showing at a breed show or rated show is exciting stuff, and you may be tempted to just jump right in and give it a try. However, attempting such shows too soon can scare you and your horse and leave you humiliated and overwhelmed.

Start small with schooling shows. Your instructor may even insist on this, because schooling shows are the best way to figure out the ropes of the show game in a nonthreatening environment. Schooling shows are much more laid back than rated or breed shows and are meant for novices. You're surrounded by people just like you, who are there to learn.

You can expect your trainer to accompany you to shows (he or she may be the one to trailer your horse to the event), although clarifying this arrangement in advance is a good idea. Remember to pay your trainer extra for his or her services.

In the following sections, I explain several tasks that you need to tend to before you compete in a show: paperwork, training, and grooming.

Handling paperwork

Before you can compete at a horse show, you need to fill out a premium. A *premium* is basically an entry form, and it asks your name, address, phone number, and information about your horse. You also have to indicate which classes you intend to enter.

Next, you write a check for the total cost of the classes you'll be competing in. Fees range anywhere from $10 to $50 or more per class, depending on the show; most schooling shows are fairly inexpensive. Mail the whole thing to the show secretary, whose address is listed on the premium. The premium indicates the date by which you need to mail the form.

If you're participating in your first show, your trainer will likely provide you with the premium and help you fill it out. You can get the hang of filling out premiums pretty quickly — it's fairly easy stuff.

Training

Before you start showing, even at the schooling level, make sure you and your horse are in full training. In full training, you or your trainer is riding your horse five days a week. Or if you don't have a horse and plan to show one of your trainer's horses, you should be taking lessons at least twice a week, preferably more often. How early you begin full training depends on the individual horse and rider. Attend shows and watch the types of classes you'll be competing in to get a sense of what's expected and who your competition will be.

Don't enter a show until your instructor says you're ready. You need his or her help anyway to get you to the show and coach you while you're there. After you have a few schooling shows under your belt and are doing well at them, you can talk to your trainer about moving to the next level, whether it be a breed show or rated show.

Looking good

An important part of being prepared for the show ring is looking the part — so go to horse shows, see how the riders are dressed, and then find yourself similar apparel. Horse show attire is very traditional, and you need to dress appropriately to fit in and be competitive. Chapter 10 can give you general information on show apparel for different disciplines.

However you're dressed, make sure your appearance is neat. If you have long hair, tie it back. Women should wear a little makeup if they can, and men should be clean-shaven (unless you normally sport a beard or mustache). Going into the ring looking sloppy is considered disrespectful to the judge, so looking neat is a must.

You can find all the show apparel you need at your local tack store, or you can order from catalogs or online. See the Appendix for the contact info of some possible retailers.

Preparing your horse

As you find out in the following sections, horses need preparation to show, just as riders do.

Training

Before you take your horse to a show, she needs to be in proper condition and have the right training, and you need to be able to control her completely. Here are a couple of training guidelines:

- ✔ If you have your own horse and plan to show her, put her in full training. She should be ridden by you or your trainer at least five days a week, and the horse should be obedient and competent in whatever discipline or sport you intend to show her in.

- ✔ If you have your own horse and she's new to showing, she's likely to be excited and maybe even a bit unruly the first time you take her to one of these events. Try taking her to her first show without entering her in anything. Just let her stand tied to the trailer and take in her surroundings. Then, when you come back next time to compete, the situation won't be as strange to her.

Grooming

Your horse needs to look her absolute best when you enter her in a show. In fact, she has to be immaculate.

Turning your normally dusty equine into a picture-perfect example of a horse starts a day or so before the show. Getting your horse ready for a show includes bathing, clipping, and sometimes braiding:

- ✔ Bathe her thoroughly with horse shampoo. If she's white or has white on her, consider washing her with a whitening shampoo made for horses. Keep her wrapped up like a mummy until show day to make sure she stays clean. Horse clothing designed to keep horses clean is available through tack and feed stores.

- ✔ Clip your horse the day before a show. Get rid of the whiskers on her muzzle and the hairs sticking out of her ears. Don't forget her feet; be sure to trim her fetlocks so her legs look long and clean. You may want to clip her legs about a week before the show to eliminate clipper tracks.

   Note: Before you clip your horse for the first time, have an experienced horse person walk you through this process.

- ✔ Depending on the show you attend, you may need to braid your horse's mane and tail if you're showing English or *band* the horse's mane (make a series of little ponytails) if you're showing in Western pleasure. Figure 22-3 shows a rider braiding a horse's mane. Check the premium list to find out the requirements of the particular show.

Chapter 19 can give you more details on grooming a horse.

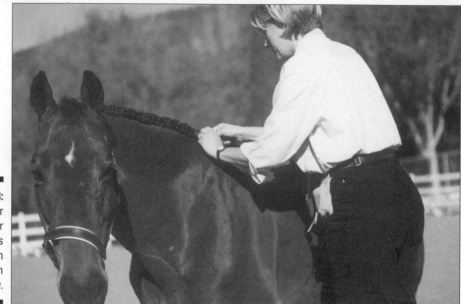

Figure 22-3: An exhibitor braids her horse's mane for an English show.

Displaying Good Manners at Horse Shows

As in any social setting, horse show attendees are expected to maintain a certain standard of behavior for the safety and enjoyment of everyone involved. In the case of horse shows, both you and your horse need to follow established horse show etiquette. I tell you what you need to know in the following sections.

Behaving yourself

Behaving well at a horse show comes naturally for some people. These folks are always looking out for others. Most people, however, need to take a look at some guidelines for good manners.

Here's a list of ways you can show good etiquette at a horse show:

✔ **Be aware of your surroundings.** Know your horse and her behavior, and be aware of anything in your surroundings that may frighten or excite her. The safety of everyone around you depends on your being able to control your horse in all situations.

✔ **Give the right of way.** If you're walking your horse through a show, keep an eye out for spectators and always give them the right of way. Remember that your horse could potentially injure someone if she's not under control when spectators — who are not always horse savvy — are around.

✔ **Warm up right.** When riding in the warm-up arena at a show, ride left-shoulder-to-left-shoulder to avoid crashing into riders who are going the opposite way (stay in the right lane of horse traffic). If other riders are schooling over jumps, be conscious of staying out of their way. Anticipate where they'll land and make sure you and your horse aren't in the landing zone at the wrong time.

✔ **Look out for other riders.** When riding in a class with others, be aware of where other horses are and avoid getting in their way. Be sure to keep a safe distance from other horses as well.

✔ **Keep the in-gate clear.** Don't congregate or starting mounting or grooming your horse at the entrance of the arena, the *in-gate*. Leave this area free and clear for other riders to enter and exit.

✔ **Be a good sport.** Horse shows are about having fun. If you don't win, don't be a spoilsport. Throwing ribbons on the ground and saying angry comments out loud are considered rude, and losing your temper only makes you look bad.

Handling your horse appropriately

Your horse doesn't know much about human social customs, so you're responsible for making sure she behaves. Keep the following in mind when handling your horse at a show:

✔ **Tie a red ribbon on kickers.** If your horse has a tendency to kick at other horses when they get too close, tie a red ribbon at the base of her tail to warn others to keep back. Likewise, if you see a horse wearing a red ribbon, keep your horse far away from the horse's back end.

✔ **Give your mischievous horse some space.** If you have a horse who likes to pin her ears at other horses and nip at them, keep her far away from others. This idea also applies when she's tied at the trailer or just lounging around in between classes.

✔ **Unload and load properly.** Don't take your horse to a show unless she willingly and easily gets in and out of a horse trailer. Having a horse who flies out of a trailer backwards when she unloads is a hazard to all around her. And fighting to get your horse back into the trailer at the end of the day only makes things difficult for those around you as they struggle to avoid the chaos going on at your trailer. See Chapter 23 for information on trailering.

Chapter 23

Even More Riding Styles and Activities

. . . .

In This Chapter

▶ Discovering alternative disciplines

▶ Competing outside the show ring or just having fun

▶ Taking a horse on trips

. . . .

*I*n previous chapters, I cover three of the most common ways to ride a horse: Western, hunt seat, and dressage. I also describe the most popular equine activities available to riders, such as trail riding (Chapter 21) and horse shows (Chapter 22). But the horse world is a diverse one, and people who enjoy riding have options besides the standard fare.

In this chapter, I tell you about other ways to ride and other interesting activities you can pursue on horseback. I also give you advice on how to get your horse where you need to go when you become more involved in these wonderful events — or when you just want to take a trip with your horse.

The Road Less Ridden: Trying Other Disciplines

If you like riding Western, hunt seat, or dressage but think you may want to try something a bit different, consider experimenting with another, more unique discipline, such as those in the following sections. You don't have to give up your main discipline — just add one or two riding styles to your repertoire. Of course, if you try an alternative discipline and like it better, you can give up the tried and true and just be different!

If you decide to try a new way of riding, make sure you do so with a qualified instructor. If your current instructor isn't familiar with the discipline you want to learn, seek out someone who is. (See Chapter 3 for details on finding a good riding teacher.)

Holding on with bareback

Before stirrups were invented in Central Asia back in ancient times, everyone rode bareback. Feet dangling and upper thighs gripping the horse for security, soldiers went into battle on horseback with nothing to hold them onto their horses other than talent and sheer will.

Centuries later, I grew up riding bareback on my little bay mare, Peggy. She roamed all over the hills of Southern California with me clinging to her back like a monkey. Although my bareback riding was borne out of not being able to afford to buy a saddle, the experience ended up being a blessing in disguise. I figured out how to stay on a horse using balance. When the time came to ride with a saddle, I was ahead of the game.

I don't recommend that you initially try to learn to ride without a saddle; however, riding your horse on occasion with just a *bareback pad,* which is a cloth pad held onto the horse's back by a cinch, can help your seat and balance — after all, you don't have a saddle to support you. (You can see a rider using a bareback pad in Figure 23-1.) Bareback pads are available at tack and feed stores, in catalogs, and on the Internet — see the Appendix for some resources to get you started.

Figure 23-1: An equestrian uses a bareback pad when riding without a saddle.

Bareback riding is enjoyable for a couple of reasons:

✔ Getting your horse ready for a ride is easier when you're going bareback. No saddle to haul out of the tack room — just put on the bareback pad and you're set for a ride. You can also ride without a pad, but be aware that your horse will sweat where your legs touch him. This sweat can leave you with big, embarrassing, horsehair-covered sweat marks on your seat and the back of your legs!

✔ Riding bareback makes you feel at one with your horse. No leather comes between you and your mount. You experience the movement of the muscles in your horse's back and sides as you ride. You also feel a bit wild sitting up there without a saddle to hold you or stirrups for your feet.

You can ride bareback in any discipline. If you normally ride English, you can use the same bridle and cues on the horse even though you're riding without a saddle, and the same goes for Western. If you're a Western rider and are so inclined, you can even compete with your horse in bareback classes at horse shows (see Chapter 22 for info on showing).

When riding bareback, make sure your pad is tightly cinched and doesn't slip as you ride. And be sure to wear a helmet in case you and your horse should happen to part company.

Your instructor should give you the go-ahead to ride bareback before you try it. You have less to support you when riding bareback, so you need to be skilled enough to stay on the horse on your own. Your instructor can tell you when you're ready.

Getting your kicks in saddle seat

The English discipline of saddle seat is the youngest of the three styles of English riding. Developed in the Southern U.S. during the 1700s, this type of riding was created to give plantation owners a comfortable way to ride when supervising their large tracts of land.

Saddle seat riders sit deep in the saddle, and they sit farther back on the horse to help elevate the animal's front end. This setup is in part the purpose of saddle seat riding: to allow the horse to lift his front legs high, producing a showy action.

In saddle seat, you can ride a horse with a single rein bridle or a double bridle (see Chapter 9 for more on bridles). The double bridle is unusual in that it has two bits, whereas most bridles have one. Riders using a double bridle have to figure out how to use each bit by manipulating the reins on each side individually.

Saddle seat riders may ride for pleasure, but most are into showing. They compete on gaited horses such as the Saddlebred and Tennessee Walking Horse and on other breeds with showy action, including the Arabian and the Morgan. (Chapter 2 has details on all these breeds, and Chapter 20 discusses gaited horses.) Check out Figure 23-2 to see a saddle seat rider in action.

Sidesaddle: A feminine tradition

One of the most interesting styles of riding is sidesaddle, a discipline that started during medieval times during an era when gallant knights rode forth into tournaments and battle to impress their ladies. In order for these women to truly appreciate the heroics of their knights, they needed to follow them on horseback. Sitting astride a horse was considered unladylike — and impractical given the elaborate dress women wore back then — so someone conceived the notion of riding with both legs to one side instead of straddling the horse.

It wasn't long before women throughout Europe were riding sidesaddle. It became a popular pastime among the well-to-do women of Europe over the next several centuries. These women brought the discipline to the United States, and the tradition became a part of American culture as well.

Figure 23-2:
Saddle seat riding, which features high stepping, was developed in the Deep South during the 18th century.

Today, sidesaddles are made in all the same styles as traditional astride saddles, including Western, hunt seat, and dressage. Each of these saddles is used in its respective discipline, just as if it were an astride saddle. Sidesaddle riders can even compete in most of the same events as astride riders — and not always in special sidesaddle classes. Sidesaddle riders sometimes show up in regular classes at shows, although they are rare.

Not too many riders use a sidesaddle, which is designed very differently than a traditional saddle is. The saddle has only one stirrup, on the left side of the horse, and it has two pommels instead of one. The top pommel is curved, allowing the rider to hook her right leg on it.

Riding sidesaddle uses very different muscles than traditional riding does because riders need to balance in the center of the saddle with both legs on the left side of the horse. This balancing act can be challenging at first because your body wants to list to the left. You need muscle strength to keep your pelvis pointing directly forward. Figure 23-3 shows a sidesaddle rider.

People who ride sidesaddle love this discipline. I tried it and really liked it. It's a whole different way of riding! The good news is that you don't need a specially trained horse for this discipline. All you need to know is how to sit in a saddle with both your legs on one side.

For more information on sidesaddle, contact the International Sidesaddle Organization, listed in the Appendix.

Figure 23-3:
A rider keeps both legs on the left side of the horse in sidesaddle.

Horseplay: Surveying Sports, Exhibitions, and Other Equine Activities

If you're the kind of person who loves to get involved with activities and wants a horse to be part of your experience, you're in luck. A whole slew of equine activities are out there for horse owners (and even non-horse owners) who want to spend quality time with horses.

If you're the competitive type, you'll find plenty to do outside the show ring to keep you busy. If you just like to do horse stuff for the sheer fun of it, you'll find no shortage of events to choose from. Whatever your style or preference, chances are there's a horse activity out there for you, as you can see in the sections that follow.

Most of these events are geared toward people who own their own horses, with the exception of vaulting. If you don't own a horse, consider leasing one you can use for your activity of choice. Just be sure the horse's owner is okay with what you intend to do. See Chapter 18 for more information on leasing a horse.

Taking part in trail events

In days of old, most horseback riding took place out in the wilderness, on trails that had been forged by mounted travelers or migrating game. Riding on these trails was both exciting and challenging, and only the toughest horses and riders survived the harshest journeys.

Decades later, horse people who appreciate this legacy developed two events that celebrate trail riding while also adding a competitive factor: endurance riding and competitive trail riding. The following sections look at both of these sports. (And Chapter 21 can tell you about riding on trails just for the fun of it.)

Endurance riding

The sport of endurance riding has grown in popularity over the past 20 years. Its most noteworthy event, the annual Tevis Cup, takes place in Northern California and receives international coverage. Hundreds of smaller, local events are also conducted around North America every year.

The object of *endurance riding* is to cover a given number of miles on horseback in the shortest amount of time. Endurance competitions often consist of 25- to 100-mile-per-day rides or multiday rides that usually cover 50 miles per day over a period of four to six days. The horse-and-rider team that gets to the finish line first is the winner. (Horses receive mandatory veterinary checks throughout the competition, and only horses who are considered physically fit are allowed to finish the event.)

Endurance riding calls for a horse-and-rider team that's extremely fit and athletic. The team has to undergo serious training in the form of conditioning over a period of months before it can compete in an endurance ride. This rigorous type of riding calls for a horse who's extremely well-conditioned and comfortable on the trail. Riders must be very fit, too. Imagine sitting in the saddle for 100 miles with only a few short breaks in between. Achieving that kind of muscle strength and stamina takes considerable work.

All lighter-weight horse breeds can participate in endurance competitions, although Arabians dominate the sport because of their great capacity to travel long distances (see Chapter 2 for information on Arabians). Horses in endurance rides wear any type of tack that the rider prefers, although most people use specially made endurance saddles and halter/bridle combinations. Figure 23-4 shows an endurance rider in competition.

The American Endurance Ride Conference (AERC) can provide you with more info on endurance riding; see the Appendix for contact information.

Figure 23-4: Endurance rides cover anywhere from 25 to 100 miles in one day.

Competitive trail riding

Competitive trail riding is for those riders who enjoy conditioning their horses for trail riding and want to hone it to a fine art. Competitive trail events consist of approximately 25- to 50-mile-per day rides through various terrains. Unlike endurance riding, *competitive trail events* are not races; instead of using time as a determining factor, judges evaluate horses primarily on their physical condition, with their obedience to the rider along the trail also a factor in many events. Speed is not important, as long as the horse and rider complete the ride within the minimum and maximum time limits. A veterinarian and a lay judge periodically examine the horses throughout the ride to determine their fitness as the day progresses.

In order to compete successfully in competitive trail rides, horses must be comfortable being ridden on the trail, in excellent physical condition, and well trained and obedient. Riders need to be in good shape, too, because even a 25-mile ride can mean a minimum of five straight hours in the saddle.

The rider determines the type of tack, although most riders use endurance saddles and halter/bridle combinations. Just about any breed can participate in competitive trail riding.

The North American Trail Ride Conference (NATRC) has more details on competitive trail riding; head to the Appendix for contact information.

Playing polo, the sport of kings

Although the fast-paced sport of polo is thought of as a contemporary activity, this game is actually thousands of years old. Historians believe that polo originated in the Middle East around 500 BC — amazing that this sport is still played today!

Nearly everyone has heard of polo, but few people know how it's played. Like soccer on horseback, *polo* is a team sport with the objective of scoring goals against the opposing team. Riders use a long-handled mallet to drive a ball into a goal. Four riders make up a polo team, although many riders have more than one horse so they can trade off mounts throughout a game — hence the notion that wealthy people play polo with a "string of polo ponies."

Although the mounts used in polo are called ponies, they're not actually ponies at all. (*Ponies* are a type of small equine that measures 14 hands or less.) Just about any breed of horse can be used for polo, but the faster and more athletic the mount, the better.

You don't need to own a string of polo ponies to play polo. In fact, you don't need to own a horse or even know how to ride at all. Polo schools are available throughout the country, and they provide riding and polo lessons to adults at costs that run about the same as skiing or scuba diving lessons. Contact the United States Polo Association for help in finding a polo school in your area. You can find their contact information in the Appendix.

Vaulting into gymnastics

I love watching the gymnastics competition at the Olympics every four years, which is probably why I get such a big kick out of vaulting, too. *Vaulting* is basically gymnastics on horseback.

In vaulting, participants perform a number of actions on the back of a moving horse who has been fitted with a special *surcingle,* a leather strap with handles that goes around the horse's barrel (see Figure 23-5) and gives the vaulter something to hold onto. Rider movements include

- **Basic seat:** The vaulter sits on the horse with arms held out to the sides.
- **Flag:** The vaulter jumps to his or her knees on the horse's back and extends one leg out straight behind with arms extended.
- **Mill:** This move is equivalent to the work done on the pommel horse in gymnastics. The vaulter swings his or legs and body into different positions while holding onto handles on the surcingle.
- **Scissors:** The scissors requires swinging into a handstand on the horse's back as the legs scissor out to either side.
- **Stand:** The vaulter stands on the horse's back with arms held out to the side.
- **Flank:** In this complicated series of movements, the rider holds onto the vaulting saddle and swings his or her legs up and through the air. Eventually, the vaulter lands next to the horse in the finale of the movement.

Vaulting is done competitively and also for exhibition. In vaulting competition, you can participate as an individual or as part of a pair or team. You start off competing at the trot and work your way up to the canter. Some therapeutic riding programs also use vaulting maneuvers to help the physically and mentally impaired gain balance and muscle strength. Vaulters learn their craft a on a *barrel horse* (a fake horse) first before graduating to using a real horse.

To get involved in vaulting, join a local vaulting club. You can find a club by contacting the American Vaulting Association, listed in the Appendix.

Figure 23-5:
A rider performs in vaulting, a form of gymnastics on horseback.

Drilling on horseback

If your favorite scenes in Hollywood Westerns feature dramatic footage of the cavalry coming to the rescue, drill team riding may for you. *Drilling* is having a group of riders perform maneuvers together as a rider who sits alone calls out directions. Drilling on horseback is tons of fun, and it gives riders an opportunity to meet and socialize with others who enjoy the same activity.

Drilling on horseback is a very old activity, one that goes back all the way to the Roman legions and possibly before. In the olden days, when horses were the primary vehicles of war, drilling was used to train mounted soldiers to follow commands with precision and obedience. Today, drill team work is for fun. Riders who enjoy drilling get together and form clubs that practice at least once a week. They perform their precision drill work in parades, at county fairs, and during horse shows.

Most drill teams consist of ten to twelve horse-and-rider duos, sometimes more. A drill caller gives commands that horse-and-rider teams follow. Each command requires a specific movement, and when several horse-and-rider teams perform these moves in conjunction, the group ends up moving as a unit. Figure 23-6 shows a drill team working together.

Because of its military foundation, drill-team work calls for discipline on the part of the rider and obedience on the part of the horse. You need to memorize each maneuver and have your horse execute it at the moment you hear the command. In drilling, you rehearse exhibition drills, and after a few practices with your group, you know exactly what's coming from the drill caller. The choreographed drills you perform at exhibitions, horse shows, and drill team competitions are the same drills that you and your team have practiced at home (or in the arena) many times over.

Most drill teams use Western tack and apparel, although English saddles and breed-specific tack (such as traditional saddles made especially for the breed being ridden) may also make an appearance.

You can locate a drill team in your area by asking at your local tack and feed store for a referral. Or try looking in your daily newspaper or regional horse publication for notices of exhibitions or drill teams seeking new members.

Figure 23-6: Drilling is based on military movements from the mounted cavalry.

Riding in parades

If you've always wanted to participate in a parade but you can't walk and play the sousaphone at the same time, then a horse may be just the answer. Maybe you can ride and play the sousaphone, instead! Then again, maybe not, but have you ever seen a parade without horses in it? Horses and parades go hand in hand. And as an equestrian, you automatically qualify to move from parade watcher to parade participant.

Riding in a parade can be tremendous fun. You and your horse are in the spotlight (along with your mounted comrades), and all you have to do is look good and wave!

The equestrian units you see in big parades are part of organized riding groups. The riders may be members of a youth riding club, representatives of a breed organization or local riding club, or part of a horseback drill team group (see the preceding section). The group's theme in the parade usually represents whatever the club is all about. For example, if the club is a military-style riding group for youngsters, the kids wear their uniforms and most likely carry flags. If the riders represent a local palomino horse club, all the horses are palominos tacked up in their finest garb.

To participate in a big parade, you have to be a member of an organized riding group (unless you're a local celebrity and can justify participating on your individual merits). In many smaller towns and cities, however, the parades are small and informal enough that individual riders can also sign up.

If riding in big parades is for you, your first step is to join a local riding group. Of all the different kinds of riding groups, pick the one that best suits your age group and riding interests. Your parks and recreation department should be able to provide you with some names and numbers of riding groups in your area.

Reenacting history

If you like to watch period films, particularly those set during the Civil War or Native American wars, you've no doubt seen reenactors in action. Although the vast budgets of today's motion pictures may lead you to believe all those soldiers and cowboys you see on the silver screen are professional actors, in reality, these characters are usually mounted reenactors who dress up in period garb and ride their own horses in mock battles on a regular basis, whether cameras are present or not.

Reenacting famous battles has been the hobby of thousands of horsemen for decades, as well as of non-horsemen who play the part of foot soldiers in this mock warfare. These people live in all parts of the country and recreate battles from a variety of wars and periods. Civil War reenactments are the most well-known, although reenactments of Native American and U.S. cavalry fights, Revolutionary and British battles, and scuffles from the Mexican-American War are among the many other events that are commemorated year-round in the U.S. by riders who seem to be possessed by the spirits of those who've gone before us.

 Getting involved with reenacting first means joining a reenactment group. These groups aren't hard to find if you have Internet access. Putting "reenactment" and "horse" and your state in any of the popular search engines should give you a list of groups near you.

After you find the reenactment groups in your area, you can decide what type of person from the past you want to portray. If the Civil War intrigues you, you need to decide whether you want to be on the Union side or the Confederate side. If you like the idea of reenacting U.S. cavalry battles, you have to decide which role you'd like to play. After you join a group, you find out all about how reenactments work and how you can incorporate your horse.

Traveling with a Horse

You may have been riding long enough to have bought a horse of your own, or you may be leasing one (see Chapter 18 for more about purchasing or leasing a horse). If you think having a horse at home is fun, wait till you try traveling with your equine companion! With the help of a horse trailer, you can get your horse to just about any destination you choose, whether it be an equine vacation spot or just a special trail an hour's drive away.

Explore the possibility of traveling with your horse with the information I provide in the following sections. Not only can you get more from your horse hobby, but your horse may also appreciate the change of scenery.

 Before you head out, make sure you know the rules of the place you'll be visiting. You may need reservations and/or health papers for your horse, including proof of a negative *Coggins test,* which shows that the horse doesn't have equine infectious anemia (swamp fever). If you know you'll be traveling with your horse within the next month, consider contacting your vet about getting these documents.

Field trips: Exploring faraway trails

If you're an avid trail rider, you may like the idea of loading up your horse and going off into the great wide open to find new and exciting trails to ride. You can find equestrian-use trails all around the U.S. in a variety of terrains and environs. You obviously want to seek out trails that are easy to get to, although if you aren't averse to traveling for a day or two, you can head for more exotic locales. (You may find overnight stabling at a horse motel — an Internet search can help you locate places that can put your horse up for the night.)

Here are some places to consider when looking for a trail riding adventure (see Chapter 21 for more information):

- State parks
- National Forests
- National Parks
- Designated national wilderness areas

Vacationing with your mount

If the idea of going on vacation doesn't involve getting away from your horse, consider taking him with you! The practice of taking a horse along on vacation is becoming more and more popular every year. People are discovering that having their horse along on a trip — when they can do more than weekend riding — is just plain fun.

You can take your horse on vacation with you in one of two ways:

- You can go camping with your horse in specially designated horse-camping campgrounds or in the backcountry (where the paved roads don't go).
- You can trailer your critter to a horseback vacation resort that allows you to bring your own horse.

Horse camping

If you love regular camping, then you'll really love horse camping. Few things are as wonderful as waking up on a dewy morning in your tent and hearing your horse munching his hay just outside.

Horse camping is not a new activity. Before the days of cars, plenty of people on long journeys were forced to horse camp. Today, horse camping is a recreational activity and an enjoyable one.

Horse camping has all the same elements as regular camping, except your horse comes with you and you get to ride him on your camping trip. You can do horse camping the same way as car camping, in which you drive up to your campsite, or the same way as backpacking, in which you hike (or in this case, ride) to your campsite.

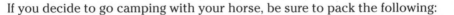

Some people bring RVs along when horse camping so they can have a bit of luxury in the great outdoors; however, many people think that the best horse camping comes when you sleep in a tent, with your horse tied or corralled outside. When you tent camp, you stand a better chance of hearing your horse moving around through the night. Not only are you able to keep watch on your horse, but you also get neat, regular reminders that he's out there. Sure, if you're a light sleeper, you won't get a really good night's rest this way, but knowing your horse is okay is better than sleeping like a rock.

The biggest reason people take their horses camping is so they can go trail riding. (Chapter 21 can tell you more about trail riding.) Although most campers hike on camping trips, horse campers *ride*. Coming out of your tent in the morning, feeding the horses, cooking up your breakfast, and then heading out on the trail is a great feeling.

To find places to camp with your horse, check with regional and state parks and National Forests in your area. Many such places allow horse camping. The cost varies from place to place, although fees are usually minimal.

If you decide to go camping with your horse, be sure to pack the following:

- ✔ Enough feed for the time you'll be gone
- ✔ A blanket for your horse if you're traveling to a climate that's colder than where you live
- ✔ Your horse's grooming equipment (see Chapter 19 for details)
- ✔ A bucket for water for your horse
- ✔ A manure fork for cleaning up after your horse
- ✔ Any health papers for your horse that the park requires

If you're new to horse camping, make sure you go with a seasoned horse camper and take horses who are used to this activity.

Horse resorts

Horse resorts are places of rest and relaxation with facilities and activities that are horse friendly. They're usually located in wilderness areas, and they feature homey, country-, or Western-style themes. Many offer organized trail rides, riding lessons, and other horse activities. Many also offer a number of wonderful luxuries for non-horsy human guests. Prices range from a few hundred dollars a night to a few thousand for a week to ten days.

Before you pick a horse resort for your vacation, do some research. First, figure out how far you want to drive to get there (remember, your horse will be in tow). Then start scoping out the horse resorts that are within driving distance by looking on the Internet or perusing the ads in horse publications.

Ask a lot of questions about each vacation spot and get referrals from other guests to make sure the vacation destination lives up to its hype. Then pack your boots and your helmet and go have some fun!

You can also consider shipping your horse ahead of you by using a horse transportation company and then flying to the resort yourself. This method costs you a bit of dough, though, so be prepared.

Moving your horse with a trailer

You can't just toss your horse in the back seat of the Buick when you need to take him somewhere. If you want to move him, you need to put him in a horse trailer.

 If you plan to compete with your horse or take him to parades, trail rides, vacations, and other activities away from home, consider investing in a trailer. But before you do, find out how to hitch up a trailer, change a tire, load a horse, and drive with all that weight behind you. A horse person who has done plenty of trailering can be a terrific help in teaching you the ropes. In the meantime, the following sections have the basics.

You can buy a trailer from a horse trailer dealer (similar to a car dealer), rent a trailer from a dealer, or pay someone (such as your instructor) to trailer the horse for you. Remember that if you buy or rent a horse trailer, you need an adequate towing vehicle to pull it. A pickup truck or SUV with a minimum of 5,000 pounds towing capability is required to pull a two-horse trailer.

Just visiting: Spending vacation with other people's horses

If you can't take your horse with you or would rather not go through the hassle of transporting your equine buddy (or if you don't own a horse yet), you can still have a horsy vacation. In fact, if you want to combine horses with your holiday, you have a plethora of options to choose from:

✔ Some horseback vacations take place at resorts, where riding is only one of several activities you and your family can participate in.

✔ Others are intensive adventures where you ride for days on end while you see the countryside. Spending time on a horseback vacation is a great way to learn to ride, provided you choose the right kind of vacation. A weeklong, training-intensive vacation at a horse resort that specializes in providing this service can provide an incredible opportunity to learn while you get away from it all.

✔ If you just want to enjoy some new scenery on horseback, you can go to a dude ranch or other riding vacation facility where daily trail rides are the main activity.

Examining types of trailers

Horse trailers come in two basic exterior styles — bumper-pull and gooseneck:

- ✔ **Bumper-pulls:** The most common type of small horse trailer, bumper pulls are so named because they attach to the bumper of a tow vehicle with a hitch. Bumper-pulls are sometimes called *standards* or *bumper hitches*. These trailers tend to be smaller and less expensive than gooseneck trailers.

- ✔ **Gooseneck trailers:** These trailers get their name from their shape. Unlike a bumper-pull, which is essentially a box-shaped container hauled behind a vehicle, goosenecks have a front section that fits over a truck bed, where the trailer is hitched. Some people prefer gooseneck trailers because they're easier to handle when turning.

The other significant design difference in trailers concerns the interior. Horse trailers essentially come in three loading styles: slant, straight, and stock:

- ✔ **Slant-load:** Slant-load trailers feature partitions that position the equine occupants at an angle to the front of the trailer. Instead of facing the back of the towing vehicle, the horses stand at a nearly 45-degree angle to the front of the trailer. Slant-load trailers can hold anywhere from two to four horses, sometimes more, depending on the design. Some people prefer slant-load trailers because they believe balancing in them is easier for the horses.

- ✔ **Straight-load:** The most common trailer type, the straight-load trailer has partitions that separate the horses and make them face the direction they're traveling. These structures are the most popular horse trailers around, and they usually come in two-horse trailer designs. Straight-loads are usually less expensive than slant-load trailers, and according to some people, they're easier on the traveling horse.

- ✔ **Stock:** These trailers are essentially open boxes without partitions that allow the horse to stand in just about any position. Most people tie their horses in a stock trailer and position them so they're at a 90-degree angle to the front of the trailer. Others allow the horses to stand loose, which permits the horses to choose their own positions while traveling. Stock trailers are the least expensive of all trailer types.

Loading your horse

It's a fact of life that a horse won't load into a trailer unless he chooses to. You simply can't force 1,000 pounds of horse flesh to climb into a small metal box. The horse has to want to do it.

Most horses are cooperative at trailer loading. Assuming your horse is accommodating — and that's something you want to be sure of before you attempt to take him to an event on a Saturday morning — you should be able to just lead him into the trailer and tie him to the hitching ring.

Loading a horse into a trailer can be tricky, so do it with the help of an experienced horse person before you attempt it on your own. If the horse you're loading is an "easy loader" (he goes into the trailer without objection), here are the steps you need to take to get him inside:

1. **Lower the ramp (if the trailer has one) or open the trailer doors.**

2. **Lead the horse, who's wearing a halter and lead rope, up to the open trailer door.**

   Let him look at it and sniff the floor if he wants to. (See Chapter 11 for details on haltering and leading a horse.)

3. **When the horse is standing quietly, lead him into the trailer by stepping in first yourself and asking him to follow by putting gentle pressure on the lead rope.**

   Be sure you don't stand directly in front of him in case he decides to rush quickly into the trailer. The horse may need some coaxing to get in, so you may have to cluck to him with your tongue. If the horse doesn't move forward, ask someone to stand behind but off to the side to likewise encourage the horse by clucking at him.

4. **Immediately secure the "butt bar" or chain that hooks across the back of the horse so the horse can't try to back out.**

If the horse refuses to go in after several attempts or becomes unruly, get a horse trainer to work with the animal to get him into the trailer. Don't attempt to deal with the problem yourself — you may get hurt!

To help make things easier and safer for your horse while on the road, follow these guidelines after loading:

- Put some hay in the manger of the trailer stall.

- Tie your horse to the inside of the trailer, using a safety knot (see Chapter 11 for steps on tying this type of knot). Be sure the lead rope is long enough to let your horse lower his head but not step on the rope.

- Open the windows of your trailer to allow your horse the optimum amount of ventilation.

   Don't open the windows so wide that your horse can stick his head out, which is dangerous for horses.

Driving safely

Driving a trailer takes special skill for several reasons. Here are some ways hauling a trailer can (or should) affect your driving:

- ✔ **Maneuverability:** Simple driving maneuvers such as backing up and parking are a whole new experience when you have a trailer hooked to your vehicle. The trailer doesn't move in the same direction as the back of your vehicle when you turn and back up. Spend some time behind the wheel with an experienced trailer hauler in the passenger seat so you can get advice and hopefully acquire some skills with an empty trailer before you add your precious cargo.

- ✔ **Turning, accelerating, and braking:** You need to move relatively carefully when horses are in your trailer. If you aren't clear why, think back on times when you were on a bus or train. Remember how your body lurched and you nearly lost your balance every time the vehicle stopped, started, or turned? Although horses have two extra feet, sudden moves can cause them to lose their balance — and their willingness to ride in a trailer. Turning, accelerating, and braking should all be done slowly. Braking is also harder on you because of the heavy weight behind you, so leave plenty of distance in front of your vehicle.

- ✔ **Speed:** With freeway or highway driving, travel mostly in the right lane at a slow pace, perhaps just below the speed limit. Traveling to the right when hauling horses is also safer, just in case you need to pull over quickly in the event of an emergency.

Practice driving with your trailer, sans horse, for as long as it takes for you to feel comfortable. Before you put your horse in the trailer and drive off, make sure handling the towing vehicle and trailer feels like second nature to you.

Unloading

When you're ready to unload the horse, follow these steps:

1. **Park the trailer in an area where you can safely unload the horse.**

   Make sure no obstacles will be in the horse's way when he steps out of the trailer, and be sure you're out of the way of traffic.

2. **Lower the trailer door gently, undo the "butt-bar" or chain that's behind the horse's back end, and walk inside to the left side of the horse.**

3. **Untie the horse's lead rope and give it a slight tug backward to cue the horse to back up.**

   Remember, horses can't see directly behind them, so let the horse go slowly to find his way with his feet.

4. **Back up the horse until all four feet are on the ground.**

   The horse's back feet touch the ground first. (If you're using a step-up trailer, the horse needs to take a step down before he comes into contact with the ground.) Continue backing him up until his front feet are on the ground, too. You can then turn the horse and walk away from the trailer.

If you're unloading a horse from a two-horse or slant-load trailer, don't allow the horse to turn around and exit the trailer head first — this move is dangerous because he can run you over. However, you may need to let the horse walk out head first with a stock trailer if the trailer has a very steep ramp that's dangerous to back out of. Ask an experienced person for advice on unloading with the trailer you are using.

Part VI
The Part of Tens

The 5th Wave   By Rich Tennant

@RICHTENNANT

"I told you they were very social animals."

In this part . . .

The Part of Tens is a hodgepodge of useful information regarding riding. In these chapters, I give you the basic rules of riding etiquette, as well as games you can play on horseback to help boost your riding skills.

Chapter 24

Ten Rules of Riding Etiquette

Riding is a dignified hobby, and riders are expected to behave a certain way when they're astride a horse. Nearly all the expected behaviors in this chapter are related to safety, and they can keep you in good stead with those around you. Chapters 5 and 21 have additional details on staying safe while you ride.

Tie a Red Ribbon on a Kicker's Tail

If you're riding in a group and are mounted on a horse who's a kicker, your horse is potential threat to other horses and riders. I once saw a horse kick another horse just behind him and shatter that horse's leg.

The universal signal of a kicker is a red ribbon tied at the base of the horse's tail. This ribbon tells other riders that your horse kicks and that they need to stay back. Likewise, if you see a horse with a red ribbon on his tail, keep at least one horse's length between you for 360 degrees around that horse.

Go Slowly after You Mount

When a cowboy wants to go for a ride in the movies, he leaps onto his horse and gallops off in a flurry. In the real world, equestrians don't behave this way unless they want to harm their horses and incur the wrath of everyone around them.

When you first mount your horse, walk slowly to your point of destination, whether it's a riding arena or a local trail head. Don't trot or canter through the aisles of the stable, and don't stress your horse by tearing off into a gallop from a standstill. This behavior labels you as a yahoo and puts you, your horse, and those around you in all kinds of physical danger.

Communicate with Your Fellow Riders

Always keep in mind that people have different skills and confidence levels when riding. Trail riding (which I cover in Chapter 21) can be the most challenging type of riding for timid or less skilled riders. Check in with your fellow riders to make sure everyone is feeling okay and secure, and try to solve problems calmly as they come up. Don't increase your speed without getting the consensus of other people in the group first.

In the arena, be sure to communicate with those around you, especially if you plan to jump or run barrels. Make sure the other riders are okay with your doing this, because some young, inexperienced horses may become unruly when they see another horse galloping or jumping. Let other riders know you're approaching as well so you don't have any accidental collisions.

Avoid Hollering

Yelling, hollering, and yee-hawing while on horseback is fine for actors in cowboy movies, but in real life, this kind of behavior frightens horses, annoys others, and makes you look like a dope. The only exception to this rule is when you're riding in gymkhana or some other competitive speed event where such vocalizations are considered acceptable because they encourage the horse to go faster (see Chapter 22 for details on horse competitions).

Keep a Safe Distance from Others

The rule of thumb when riding in a group is to keep your mount one horse-length from the horse in front of her. Keeping this distance can be difficult at times, because many horses prefer to travel with their noses just behind the tail of the horse in front of them, especially on the trail. One problem is that if the horse in front of you stops short, your horse will crash into her. Another problem is that the horse in front of you may not appreciate your horse's nose in her rear and may kick out.

If you practice your riding skills and teach your horse to obey your cues, you should be able to slow her down if she gets too close to the horse in front of you, thereby creating a safe distance between mounts. If you find that another rider is following too close behind you, nicely ask that rider whether he or she would like to pass. If not, suggest to the other rider that he or she circle the horse to create distance between you.

Approach Courteously from the Rear

If you're approaching a horse from behind while in the arena, do *not* run your horse up behind that rider. If you do, the rider's horse will almost certainly spook or take off, which could cause a serious accident.

Instead, if you're trotting or cantering and are going to pass a rider from the rear while that rider is at the walk, give the rider and horse a wide berth so you don't upset the horse.

This rule also applies out on the trail. When approaching another rider from the rear, slow down to a walk and let the rider know you're there. Running up behind another horse is a sure way to cause an accident.

Pass Left Shoulder to Left Shoulder

When riding in an arena, you're bound to find yourself going in one direction while one or more riders are traveling the opposite way. When passing one another in a riding arena, riders use the *left shoulder to left shoulder* rule. In other words, when riders go past one another in opposite directions, their left shoulders pass each other. This approach is the equestrian equivalent of driving on the right side of the road.

To accomplish this feat, you may need to stay close to the rail so the approaching rider passes you on your left. Or you may need to stay to the inside, away from the rail, in order to have the approaching rider pass you to the left.

A good way to remember this rule is that if you're traveling counterclockwise, you should stay along the rail if another rider is coming toward you. If you're traveling clockwise, you need to pass that rider on the inside of the arena, allowing him or her to stay on the rail.

Prepare Your Horse for Trail Riding

Before you take an inexperienced horse out on the trails with other riders, make sure she's safe. Expose her to some of the things horses regularly encounter on trails in your area, such as traffic, water crossings, train tracks, logs, bridges, and so on.

If your horse tends to be nervous and easily spooked, inform the other riders in your group of this temperament so they can determine whether they want to ride with your horse. Some horses pick up on the nervous energy of another horse and can become unruly themselves. This havoc can ruin everyone's ride and make your fellow riders not want to go out with you again. Chapter 21 has more information on preparing a horse for a trail ride.

Be Courteous during Water Breaks on the Trail

While out on the trail, you may come across a water source, whether it's a creek or a water trough set up for the use of trail riders. If you're riding with others and their horses want to drink, be courteous and wait your turn, especially if the source is too small for more than one or two horses.

Drinking along the way on the trail is important for horses, especially on long rides, and you shouldn't do anything that can discourage a fellow rider's horse from drinking. Actions that can stop another horse from drinking include

- ✔ Allowing your horse to aggressively barge in and threaten another horse while she's partaking of the water

- ✔ Allowing your horse to *pin* her ears (lay them flat against her head) at other horses while they're drinking

- ✔ Pulling your horse away from the water source too fast when the horses still have their muzzles in the water (this maneuver may make the other horses stop drinking and want to leave with you)

Keep your horse quiet and passive during the watering session. If you're having trouble getting her to behave, pull her aside and wait till the other horses are finished before you let her have her share. Also, don't ride off until all the horses are finished drinking, because many horses will forego getting a drink if they feel they're being left behind.

Help Others during Times of Trouble

Whether you're on the trail or in the arena, stay aware of other riders. If you see another rider fall off while you're riding in the arena, or if you see a horse bolt and take off with the rider, immediately stop your horse and wait until the rider's horse has been brought under control and the rider is being attended to. If you're the only other person around, dismount and call for help if needed.

Out on the trail, a rider up ahead of you in your group may start having trouble with an easily spooked horse. If so, stop your horse and wait for the rider to get the horse under control. Another option is to check with the rider to see whether he or she would like you to pass so your horse can help calm the frightened one. Obviously, this method works only if you're sure your horse won't be spooked by whatever's scaring the other rider's horse. Because horses tend to take cues from one another, your horse may object to passing the object as well. In that case, hang back and wait for everyone to calm down before you proceed.

Chapter 25

Ten Horseback Games to Improve Your Riding

Games on horseback are a great way to break up the strict regimen of riding lessons while still helping you develop good riding skills. They're fun, too, for both riders and horses!

The games in this chapter are all suitable for beginning riders and should be played under the supervision of a riding instructor. Safety's a primary concern while playing horseback games, so all participants should wear an approved equestrian safety helmet. See Chapter 5 for more information on riding helmets and general safety.

If you're taking group lessons, ask your instructor to make some of these games a part of your lesson program. If you're taking private lessons, see whether your instructor can put together a play day for his or her students. Any number of riders can play — from 2 to 20!

Simon Says

In the arena, Simon Says helps riders stretch their legs and develop their balance. This game also increases your confidence in the saddle by proving that you can do more than just sit there without falling off!

Simon Says on horseback is very much like Simon Says on the ground. Riders have their horses walk in single file along the rail. The instructor periodically calls out different gaits or asks for certain maneuvers, such as *circle, reverse direction,* or *stop.* (Part III has details on riding maneuvers and gaits, such as the walk, jog or trot, and lope or canter.) Riders have to follow all instructions that the instructor precedes with the words *Simon says*. If riders fail to perform the gait or maneuver — or if they perform a maneuver without *Simon says* in front of it — they're eliminated. The last remaining rider wins.

Ride-a-Buck

The popular horseback game Ride-a-Buck is often performed bareback (see Chapter 23 for info about this riding discipline). It teaches riders good balance at the various gaits.

Riders start at one end of the arena lined up single file. The instructor puts a dollar bill under each rider's leg, elbow, seat, or calf with half of the dollar bill sticking out. Riders then perform different gaits and maneuvers based on what the instructor calls out. The last rider with the dollar bill still in place is the winner.

Treasures on the Trail

This version of a treasure hunt conducted on horseback takes place on the trail. Riders develop their balance, mounting and dismounting skills, and proficiency in starting and stopping their horses.

The riders break up into teams (to be determined by your instructor; teams of two usually work best), and each rider receives a list of items he or she can find on trails adjacent to the stable. Items can include ordinary objects such as twigs, a certain type of flower, or a specific kind of tree bark. Sticking together for safety, team members collect the items within a given time limit. Whichever team returns to the stable first with the most items from the list wins.

Magazine Race

The Magazine Race is an arena relay to see who can best follow directions while also quickly mounting and dismounting. Teams can be as large as your instructor wants, although the number of riders should be even on both teams.

The instructor places a pile of magazines on the ground at the end of the arena. Riders line up at the other end. The instructor gives a page number to each rider, along with directions on how to hold the paper (in your teeth, between the horse and your left calf, under your seat, and so on) and which gait to use.

When the game begins, the first rider for each team rides to the end of the arena, dismounts, tears out the correct page number, climbs back in the saddle, and carries the paper back to the line as instructed. If the rider drops the paper, he or she must get off the horse and retrieve it. The first team to have all its riders finish the task is the winning team.

Ride and Tie

A fun activity for instructors and students alike is Ride and Tie. Although Ride and Tie is a recognized sport governed nationally by the Ride and Tie Association, the event is also a fun activity that trainers can organize for their students. It helps beginning riders practice mounting and dismounting quickly as well as develop skills in safely tying their horses (see Chapter 11 for more information about tying).

Traditional Ride and Tie events consist of a three-member team: two humans and a horse. All three start on a trail at the same time, with the horse and one mounted team member going on ahead. The trail should be well marked and include obstacles along the way that are suitable for tying a horse to. When the rider reaches a point where she can safely tie the horse, she stops, secures the horse to a bush or tree, and then continues on foot. The team member who began the event on foot finds the tied horse, mounts up, and continues on past the other team member. He eventually stops, ties the horse, and goes on while the horse waits for the person on foot to catch up and mount. This relay continues until all three team members cross the finish line. The winning team finishes in the shortest amount of time.

Although sanctioned Ride and Tie events run anywhere from 20 to 40 miles, a fun event organized for students can be as short or as long as the instructor or trainer wants it to be. Instructors can get rules for Ride and Tie from the Ride and Tie Association at www.rideandtie.org.

Red Light, Green Light

A version of the popular kids' game, Red Light, Green Light on horseback helps riders figure out how to stop and start their horses effectively and move them in a straight line.

A group of riders lines up at one end of the arena at the start line, and at the other end, the instructor draws a finish line in the dirt or uses cones to mark it. The instructor faces the riders and says "green light" to get them going. A few seconds later, the instructor says "red light." All riders have to stop within a three-second count of hearing this command. If the rider doesn't stop in time, he or she must go back to the starting line. The instructor continues to say "green light" and "red light" until at least one rider crosses the finish line. This game is usually played at the walk or trot, depending on the experience of the riders. Your instructor decides the gait.

Follow the Leader

Follow the Leader, which uses obstacles placed throughout an arena, enforces basic riding skills. Riders practice steering the horse and controlling the horse's speed.

The instructor picks a leader in the group, and this rider then leads the way through the obstacles, which can include barrels, poles, straw bales, cones, and logs. All the other riders have to follow the lead of the horse in front of them. Whoever follows the pattern best (according to your instructor) becomes the new leader after a period of time. Riders play this game for entertainment value; Follow the Leader doesn't have a specified winner.

Boot Bucket Race

Instructors can hold the Boot Bucket Race in an arena with just four buckets and several pairs of boots. This game is great for beginning Western riders because it teaches them to neck rein their horses (cue using rein pressure on a horse's neck), an essential skill in Western riding. It also helps riders figure out how to keep their horses at a steady gait and how to mount and dismount quickly.

A finish line cuts the arena in half crosswise. One half becomes the play area, where the boots and buckets are set up. The instructor lines up several pairs of old riding boots on the fence posts at one end of the arena. She then places two buckets on *each side* of the arena, one toward the end of the arena, by the boots, and the other near the finish line the width of a horse from the rail.

The horses and riders wait on the other half of the arena. Riders are divided up equally into two teams, and the instructor indicates where the finish line is. The riders line up single file, with each team on one side of the arena. The team on the right will use the two buckets on the right side of the arena, and the team on the left will use the two buckets on the left.

The instructor calls a gait (walk or trot), and the race begins. One at a time, a rider from each team goes to the end of the arena where the boots are located and, with the non-rein hand, picks up a boot and carries it to one of his team's buckets (switching the boot to the rein hand is allowed) and drops it in. If the rider misses, he has to dismount, pick up the boot, get back on the horse, and try it again.

As soon as the rider successfully gets the boot into the bucket, he crosses the finish line, tags the next rider, and goes back to the end of the line of his team's riders. Then another rider from the team goes through the same process. Teams receive one point for each boot that makes it into a bucket. Whichever team has the most points when the last boot gets placed into a bucket is the winner.

Egg 'n' Spoon Carry

The object of the Egg 'n' Spoon Carry, which helps reinforce a rider's balance and skill with the hands, is to perform various maneuvers on horseback while holding a hard-boiled egg on a spoon. This game is ideal for Western riders because the reins go in one hand and the spoon and egg go in the other.

Riders go around the arena performing the gaits and maneuvers that the instructor calls out. The winner is the last rider to be holding an egg.

Around the World

Around the World is challenging to beginning riders, but it's great at building confidence and trust in the horse. It works best for English riders.

With the instructor holding the reins of the horse, one at a time, each rider must drop the reins, take her feet out of the stirrups, and swing her right leg over the front of the horse so both legs are on the horse's left side. The rider then swings the left leg over the rump of the horse so she's sitting on the horse backwards. The rider then swings the right leg over the rump so both legs are on the horse's right side. Finally, the rider swings the left leg over the horse's neck so she's sitting on the horse properly again. The time ends when the rider's feet are back in the stirrups.

The instructor times each student with a stopwatch as she performs the maneuver. The student who performs it the fastest is the winner.

Resources for Riders

· ·

*H*ere's a short list of resources to check out as your appetite for horse-back riding and general equine knowledge increases.

Breed Registries

American Morgan Horse Association
122 Bostwick Rd.
Shelburne, VT 05482-4417
Phone 802-985-4944
Web site www.morganhorse.com

American Paint Horse Association
P.O. Box 961023
Fort Worth, TX 76161-0023
Phone 817-834-2742
Web site www.apha.com

American Quarter Horse Association
P.O. Box 200
Amarillo, TX 79168 0001
Phone 806-376-4811
Web site www.aqha.com

American Saddlebred Horse Association
4083 Iron Works Pkwy.
Lexington, KY 40511-8434
Phone 859-259-2742
Web site www.saddlebred.com

Appaloosa Horse Club
2720 West Pullman Rd.
Moscow, ID 83843-0903
Phone 208-882-5578
Web site www.appaloosa.com

Arabian Horse Association
10805 E. Bethany Dr.
Aurora, CO 80014
Phone 303-696-4500
Web site www.arabianhorses.org

Horse of the Americas (Colonial Spanish Horses)
202 Forest Trail Rd.
Marshall, TX 75672
Phone 918-458-0960
Web site www.horseofthe americas.com

International Colored Appaloosa Association
P.O. Box 99
Shipshewana, IN 46565
Phone 574-825-3331
Web site www.icaainc.com

The Jockey Club (Thoroughbreds)
821 Corporate Dr.
Lexington, KY 40503-2794
Phone 859-224-2700
Web site www.jockeyclub.com

**Missouri Fox Trotting Horse Breed
Association, Inc.**
P.O. Box 1027
Ava, MO 65608
Phone 417-683-2468
Web site www.mfthba.com

**North American Peruvian Horse
Association**
3095 Burleson Retta Rd.
Burleson, TX 76028
Phone 707-447-7574
Web site www.napha.net

Paso Fino Horse Association
101 N. Collins St.
Plant City, FL 33563
Phone 813-719-7777
Web site www.pfha.org

Rocky Mountain Horse Association
P.O. Box 129
Mt. Olivet, KY 41064
Phone 606-724-2354
Web site www.rmhorse.com

Spanish Mustang Registry, Inc.
P.O. Box 36
Wilcox, AZ 85643
Web site
www.spanishmustang.org

**Tennessee Walking Horse Breeders'
and Exhibitors' Association**
P.O. Box 286
Lewisburg, TN 37091-0286
Phone 931-359-1574
Web site www.twhbea.com

**United States Icelandic Horse
Congress**
6800 East 99th Ave.
Anchorage, AK 99507
Phone 907-346-2223
Web site www.icelandics.org

**United States Trotting Association
(Standardbreds)**
750 Michigan Ave.
Columbus, OH 43215-1191
Phone 614-224-2291 or 877-800-8782
Web site www.ustrotting.com

Riding Instructor Organizations

**American Riding Instructors
Association**
28801 Trenton Ct.
Bonita Springs, FL 34134-3337
Phone 239-948-3232
Web site www.riding-instructor.
com

Centered Riding, Inc.
P.O. Box 157
Perkiomenville, PA 18074
Phone 610-754-0633
Web site www.centered
riding.org

Certified Horsemanship Association
4037 Iron Works Pkwy.
Suite 180
Lexington, KY 40511
Phone 800-399-0138 or 859-259-3399
Web site www.cha-ahse.org

Equine Equipment Catalogs

Dover Saddlery
P.O. Box 1100
Littleton, MA 01460
Phone 800-406-8204
Web site www.doversaddlery.com

Jeffers Equine
P.O. Box 100
Dothan, AL 36302
Phone 800-533-3377 or 334-793-6257
Web site www.jeffersequine.com

Libertyville Saddle Shop
306 Peterson Rd., Hwy. 137
Libertyville, IL 60048
Phone 800-872-3353 or 847-362-0570
Web site www.saddleshop.com

Stateline Tack
1989 Transit Way
P.O. Box 910
Brockport, NY 14420
Phone 888-839-9640
Web site www.statelinetack.com

Competition and Activity Organizations

**American Endurance Ride Conference
(AERC)**
P.O. Box 6027
Auburn, CA 95604
Phone 530-823-2260 or 866-271-2372
Web site www.aerc.org

American Hunter and Jumper Foundation
335 Lancaster St.
P.O. Box 369
West Boylston, MA 01583-0369
Phone 508-835-8813
Web site www.ahjf.org

American Vaulting Association
8205 Santa Monica Blvd. #1-288
West Hollywood, CA 90046
Phone 323-654-0800
Web site www.americanvaulting.org

International Sidesaddle Organization
P.O. Box 161
Stevensville, MD 21666-0161
Phone 410-643-1497
Web site www.sidesaddle.com

**North American Trail Ride Conference
(NATRC)
(Competitive trail riding)**
P.O. Box 224
Sedalia, CO 80135
Phone 303-688-1677
Web site www.natrc.org

United States Dressage Federation
4051 Iron Works Pkwy.
Lexington, KY 40511
Phone 859-971-2277
Web site www.usdf.org

United States Equestrian Federation
4047 Iron Works Pkwy.
Lexington, KY 40511
Phone 859-258-2472
Web site www.usef.org

United States Polo Association
771 Corporate Dr.
Suite 505
Lexington, KY 40503
Phone 800-232-8772 or 859-219-1000
Web site www.us-polo.org

Other Equine Organizations

American Association for Horsemanship Safety
4125 Fish Creek Rd.
Estes Park, CO 80517
Phone 866-485-6800
Web site www.horsemanshipsafety.com

American Farrier's Association
4059 Iron Works Pkwy.
Suite 1
Lexington, KY 40511-8434
Phone 859-233-7411
Web site www.americanfarriers.org

American Horse Council
1616 H Street NW, 7th Floor
Washington, DC 20006
Phone 202-296-4031
Web site www.horsecouncil.org

North American Riding for the Handicapped
P.O. Box 33150
Denver, CO 80233
Phone 800-369-7433 or 303-452-1212
Web site www.narha.org

Horse Magazines

Equus
P.O. Box 420235
Palm Coast, FL 32142
Phone 800-829-5910 or 386-447-6332
Web site www.equisearch.com/equus

Horse & Rider
P.O. Box 420235
Palm Coast, FL 32142
Phone 877-717-8928 or 386-447-6306
Web site www.equisearch.com/
horseandrider

Horse Illustrated
P.O. Box 6050
Mission Viejo, CA 92690
Phone 949-855-8822
Web site
www.horsechannel.com/horse-
magazines/horse-illustrated

Horses USA
P.O. Box 6050
Mission Viejo, CA 92690
Phone 949-855-8822
www.horsechannel.com/horse-
magazines/horse-usa/horse-usa-
table-of contents.aspx

Practical Horseman
P.O. Box 420235
Palm Coast, FL 32142
Phone 877-717-8929 or 386-447-6317
Web site www.equisearch.com/
practicalhorseman

Western Horseman
P.O. Box 7980
Colorado Springs, CO 80933-7980
Phone 719-633-5524
Web site www.westernhorseman.com

Recommended Books

Centered Riding, by Sally Swift (St. Martin's Press, 1985)

Equine Law and Horse Sense, by Julie I. Fershtman (Horses & the Law Publishing, 1996)

Horse Conformation: Structure, Soundness, and Performance, by Equine Research (The Lyons Press, 2004)

Horsekeeping on Small Acreage: Designing and Managing Your Equine Facilities, by Cherry Hill (Storey Publishing, 2005)

Horses For Dummies, 2nd Edition, by Audrey Pavia (John Wiley & Sons, 2005)

Trail Riding: A Complete Guide, by Audrey Pavia (Howell Book House, 2005)

The USDF Guide to Dressage, by Jennifer O. Bryant (Storey Publishing, 2006)

Western Horsemanship: The Complete Guide to Riding the Western Horse, by Richard Shrake (Western Horseman, 2002)

Index

overo (color pattern), 33
ownership, horse
  buying a horse, 16
  commitment to, 243
  leasing, 16
  responsibilities, 16
  understanding realities of, 242
oxers, 15, 221, 222

• P •

pace (gait), 276, 277
pacers, 35
paddock, catching a horse in, 122, 258
pads, saddle, 96–97
pain, from colic, 271
Paint (breed), 33
palomino (coloration), 29
pants, riding, 64, 110
parades, riding in, 320
parasites, internal, 269
parts of a horse, 23–24
Paso Fino, 278, 301
paso gaits, 277, 278
passage (dressage movement), 85
passing
  in arena, 70, 291, 333
  on trail, 292
pasture, catching a horse in, 122–123, 258
pasture grass, 260
patience, importance of, 22
Pavia, Audrey
  Horses For Dummies, 241, 255, 347
  Trail Riding: A Complete Guide, 347
Payne, Larry, Ph.D. (*Yoga For Dummies*), 55
personality, of horse, 246
Peruvian Paso, 278
piaffe, 83
Pilates, 55, 239
Pilates For Dummies (Herman), 55
pinto (color pattern), 29
pipe corrals, 258
pirouette (dressage movement), 85
placings, horse show, 296–297
pleasure saddle, 90
polo, 316–317
pommel, 88
positive thinking, importance of, 23

posting the trot
  dressage, 186–187
  hunt seat, 183–184
  stamina required for, 49, 51
Practical Horseman (magazine), 346
premium, horse show, 296, 303
pre-purchase exam, 251–253
preventive care
  cost, 245
  deworming, 269
  finding a farrier, 268
  finding a veterinarian, 267
  tooth care, 269–270
  vaccinations, 268–269
private lessons, 43–44
psychotherapy, 60
pull-backs, 67
push-ups (exercise), 53

• Q •

quadriceps stretch, 55, 56
Quarter Horse (breed), 33–34
quirt, 118

• R •

rack (gait), 34, 277, 278
rated shows, 300
Red Light, Green Light (game), 339–340
red ribbon (warning), 70, 290, 307, 331
reenactments, 320–321
refusal to jump, 229–230
reining (competition/show), 78–79, 302
reins
  attachment to hackamore, 105
  braided, 83
  California style, 156, 157
  canter in dressage, 206
  canter in hunt seat, 204
  description, 102
  gaited horse riding, 280
  jog in Western riding, 180
  locking, 103
  lope in Western riding, 202
  neck reining, 75, 165, 189, 211
  traditional style, 156–158
  trot in dressage riding, 185